The Indian Office

Studies in
American History and Culture, No. 12

Other Titles in This Series

The Indian Office

Growth and Development of an American Institution, 1865-1900

by
Paul Stuart

umi
RESEARCH PRESS

Produced and distributed by
University Microfilms International
Ann Arbor, Michigan 48106

Library of Congress Cataloging in Publication Data

Stuart, Paul, 1943-
    The Indian Office.

    (Studies in American history and culture ; no. 12)
    Bibliography: p.
    Includes index.
    1. United States. Bureau of Indian Affairs—History.
    2. Indians of North America—Government relations—
1869-1934.   I. Title. II. Series.
E93.S94   353.008'4'84   79-25940
ISBN 0-8357-1079-3

FOR MY MOTHER
AND IN MEMORY OF MY FATHER

CONTENTS

TABLES

CHARTS

ABBREVIATIONS USED IN NOTES

CIA	Commissioner of Indian Affairs
IRA	Indian Rights Association
LB	Letterbook
LR	Letters Received
LS	Letters Sent
NARS	National Archives and Records Service, Washington, D.C.
OIA	Office of Indian Affairs
RG 48	Record Group 48, Records of the Office of the Secretary of the Interior
RG 75	Record Group 75, Records of the Bureau of Indian Affairs
RG 146	Record Group 146, Records of the U.S. Civil Service Commission
USCSC	U.S. Civil Service Commission

PREFACE

I began thinking about doing a study like this one while I was employed as a social worker in the Community Mental Health Program of the Pine Ridge Service Unit, U. S. Indian Health Service, from 1966 to 1969. In a period of considerable administrative turmoil in Indian affairs, many of us had occasion to think a great deal about government organizations, American Indians, and the frequently uneasy relations between the two. The separation of health programs from the Bureau of Indian Affairs in 1955 and the development of Community Action and other "Great Society" programs in the mid-1960s, some of us thought, would provide American Indian groups with much needed flexibility in dealing with an obtrusive, rule-bound bureaucracy.

But what was this bureaucracy which we believed needed "shaking up"? One of the oldest agencies of the federal government, the Bureau of Indian Affairs had been in existence for over a century. While the organization's broad policy had changed with changing times, many of the instruments of that changing policy had been created during the late nineteenth century, in particular boarding schools, Indian police, and the division of lands held in common into individually-held tracts, called "allotments." The late nineteenth century seemed a crucial period in the development of the Indian Bureau.

Fortunately, we know a great deal about the period. The policy studies of Loring Benson Priest, Henry E. Fritz, and Francis Paul Prucha provide details on the formation of Indian policy and provide the broad outlines of its development after the Civil War. While much work remains to be done in tribal history, such scholars as Donald Berthrong, William T. Hagan, and Robert M. Utley have enriched our understanding of how Indian policy was implemented in the field. My interest in the administration of Indian affairs led me to consider the work of social scientists who have studied the evolution of complex organizations, including Philip Selznick, Alfred D. Chandler, Jr., and Charles Perrow. Hopefully, an understanding of the organizational development of the Indian Office will make a better understanding of today's Bureau of Indian Affairs possible.

I have acquired many debts, both personal and institutional, while completing this study. They are imperfectly discharged by this brief note. The George Warren Brown School of Social Work provided tangible and intangible assistance over a period of years. I would like to thank Dean Shanti Khinduka and Associate Dean William Butterfield for their leadership of a school which encourages scholarship and supports the attempts of its faculty members to contribute to the development of knowledge.

PREFACE

The Graduate School of the University of Wisconsin and the Center for the History of the American Indian, Newberry Library, also provided financial assistance and less tangible aid.

Librarians and archivists are the people who really make a study like this possible. Robert M. Kvasnicka, Richard Crawford, and Michael Goldman, of the National Archives and Records Service, made many helpful suggestions during my visits to the National Archives in Washington, D.C. John Aubrey of the Newberry Library, the Inter-Library Loan staff of Olin Library, Washington University, and the staff of the Documents Division of the St. Louis Public Library were consistently helpful to me.

Mark Leff took time out of a busy schedule to help me understand what happened to the value of the dollar in the late nineteenth century. Duncan Lindsey helped me to understand the intricacies of the Washington University Computer Center. The typists of the Secretarial Services Center at the George Warren Brown School of Social Work were models of patience in dealing with an often-messy manuscript.

Allan G. Bogue and Raymond Munts read the entire manuscript. Their many criticisms and suggestions have improved its quality immeasurably. Robert F. Berkhofer, Jr., Myron J. Lefcowitz, W. Joseph Heffernan, J. Rogers Hollingsworth, and Francis Paul Prucha also read and commented on the manuscript. I am grateful to each of them. William T. Hagan, William A. Dobak, Clyde Milner, Richard White, and Martin Zanger made many helpful suggestions. My debt to all of these scholars is great. Since I did not always follow their advice, I am alone responsible for what follows.

Gordon Jones first suggested that I try to write history. Melanie Redler, who also prepared the index, has encouraged me to persevere. My children, Lisa and Caitlin, have reminded me that there is more to life than the Indian Office. My mother, Louise H. Stuart, has been a constant source of support. This book is dedicated to her, and to the memory of my father, Arthur W. Stuart, with gratitude and affection.

Paul Stuart
St. Louis, Missouri
June 1979

INTRODUCTION

THE INSTITUTIONALIZATION OF THE INDIAN OFFICE
1865-1900

American society was transformed during the half-century after the Civil War. Between 1867 and 1912, twelve states joined the union, leaving no territories in the contiguous United States. Commercial and industrial life changed as the result of the development of large corporations, which produced and distributed an increasing array of consumer goods to an increasingly large market.[1] This development, in turn, resulted from an expansion in the transportation system and the development of technologies which made possible the mass production of goods and the preservation of foods for relatively long periods of time. Social, cultural, and political life changed as commerical and political developments resulted in the creation of a national community to replace the isolated "island communities" of earlier times.[2] In addition, government, national, state, and local, changed as it expanded to meet the demands of a new society.

The United States Office of Indian Affairs, known as the "Indian Office," matured during this period. The organization grew in size, whether size is measured by the funds budgeted and expended, by the number of employees, or by the number of operating units. More significantly, the organization developed, by the 1890s, a program which would guide its work for much of the next half-century. The development of the Indian Office in the late nineteenth century was closely related to the social and economic developments of the period.

Nearly a century later, the Bureau of Indian Affairs, as the Indian Office is now known, is the subject of widespread attack. In March, 1978, a task force made up of Bureau employees concluded that a "general management crisis pervades the Bureau of Indian Affairs."[3] In October of the same year, the General Accounting Office described inadequacies in the Bureau's planning, records, and program monitoring systems. In addition, the GAO found that Bureau programs were poorly coordinated with other federal programs for American Indians.[4] These evaluations echoed the findings of a number of commissions, surveys, and evaluations of the past fifty years. Administrative incapacity, rather than a "crisis," seemed an endemic condition in Indian affairs.[5]

The origins of the fifty-year crisis in Indian administration may be traced

1

back to the late nineteenth century. The administrative and programmatic innovations of those years proved to be enduring. Civil service rules, the allotment of lands, and an educational approach to Indian work provided the parameters within which the organization would develop in the twentieth century. Between 1865 and 1900, the Indian Office became an institution.

This study examines the evolution of the Indian Office as a complex organization between the end of the Civil War and the beginning of the twentieth century. Institutionalization, the process by which organizations or social practices become valued as ends in themselves, provides the major theoretical focus. Philip Selznick, who viewed institutionalization as a consequence of decision-making which enhanced the organization's distinctive mission, its boundaries, and its integrity, emphasized the contribution of leadership to the institutionalization of complex organizations.[6] Samuel P. Huntington emphasized such factors as adaptability, complexity, and autonomy as criteria for determining the level of institutionalization of political procedures and organizations.[7] In his examination of the institutionalization of the House of Representatives, Nelson W. Polsby defined an institutionalized organization as one which was well-bounded and complex, and which used universalistic rather than particularistic criteria in decision-making.[8]

Institutionalization as a process appears to be related to the processes of political modernization and bureaucratization. The concept provides a perspective for understanding the formation of the modern political bureaucracy, a process which has been studied from a variety of viewpoints. Scholars who used political modernization as a unifying focus for their efforts have emphasized such factors as changes in the composition of political elites and the differentiation of political structures from such institutions as the family and the church.[9] Bureaucratization, as Max Weber used the term, refers to the replacement of traditional authority by legal authority, with consequent formalization, hierarchical organization, and the occupation of positions by full-time career officials.[10] The common elements among these processes include differentiation of the organization from other organizations and institutions, the primacy of written rules which provide automatic and rational decision rules for members of the organization, and an increasing internal differentiation and complexity of the organization.

In the case of the Indian Office, the organization became better-bounded in the decades following the Civil War, as the selection of organizational members and the control of their behavior became internal functions of the organization. Internalizing the selection of personnel and the organizational control of their activity resulted in a more autonomous organization. Organizational control became increasingly routinized after 1880; during the 1890s, control units became differentiated to reflect the increasing differentiation and specialization of field units. Finally, the increasing internal differentiation of units within the organization resulted from the emergence of a distinctive and dominant technology, Indian education, which provided the organization with an institutional mission.

CHAPTER I

THE PROBLEM: LARGE-SCALE ORGANIZATION, INSTITUTIONALIZATION, AND THE INDIAN OFFICE

Since the Industrial Revolution, large-scale organizations have become increasingly important in developed and developing countries. Such organizations are characterized by the attempt to coordinate the activities of many workers, holding a variety of statuses, through a hierarchical organizational structure.[1] Such organizations made possible the coordination of the activities of many employees; as a result, the emergence of the large-scale organization made possible a level of economic development and social integration which would have been impossible in the absence of such coordination.[2]

Despite the advances which large-scale organizations made possible, however, their emergence has resulted in profound ambivalence on the part of social scientists and others. Some found organizations to be "inflexible, inefficient . . . uncreative and unresponsive" to changing social conditions.[3] Thus, Robert Merton described a "bureaucratic virtuoso" who was unable to help his clients because of organizational rules which bound his actions.[4] Others found such organizations stifled "the spontaneity, freedom, and self-realization of their employees."[5] Finally, because of their efficiency, organizations were said to generate an enormous amount of power, power which insulated the organization and made it unresponsive to attempts at control or regulation from outside.[6]

The United States Bureau of Indian Affairs, created as a unit of the Department of War in 1824, provides an example of a large-scale organization. Directed by a Commissioner of Indian Affairs from 1832 to 1977, the Indian Office, as the Bureau was called during the nineteenth and early twentieth centuries, possessed primary responsibility for implementing the federal government's Indian policy.[7] Congress placed the Indian Office in the new Department of the Interior which it created in 1849.[8]

Organizationally weak and ineffective in its first half-century, the Indian Office became increasingly effective at coordinating the activities of its members during the last quarter of the nineteenth century. However, assessments of the organization published in the twentieth century described an organization which had become overly rigid, rule-bound, and unresponsive to its clientele. The Meriam Report of 1928 described an organization which was "largely ineffective" in the discharge of its responsibility for the educational and economic advancement of the Indians.[9] In 1976, a management consulting firm engaged by the American Indian Policy Review Commission found "a notable absence of

5

managerial and organizational capacity throughout'' the organization.[10] Other commentators described an organizational arteriosclerosis, an organization which had become so rule-bound and inflexible that it was unable to respond to the needs of its clients. One assessment described the organization as an example of "terminal bureaucracy."[11]

This examination of the organizational evolution of the Indian Office during the last thirty-five years of the nineteenth century addresses what Philip Selznick called "the tragedy of organizations . . . the fact of organizational frustration as a persistent characteristic of the age of relative democracy."[12] Relying on Selznick's conception of institutionalization, I attempt to describe what happened to the Indian Office—how improvements in organizational capacity resulted in the creation of an organization which failed to serve its clients. To do so, it will first be necessary to place the organization in its historical context and to describe the indicators for organizational development which I employ herein.

The decades following the Civil War were a period of massive shifts in the character of American social organization. Robert H. Wiebe characterized the years between 1879 and 1920 as a period in which isolated "island communities" were grafted together to form an integrated national community. The rise of the business corporation and professional and voluntary organizations, and an expanded role for government in economic regulation, signaled the development of a new middle class, which was oriented to national, rather than local, organizations, and which provided the political base for the progressive movement of the early twentieth century.[13] The elements of the change included the development of the railroads, which provided businesses with the capacity to move goods to new markets, scientific advance, which provided the technology on which commercial expansion depended, and the defeat of the South in the Civil War, which permitted the organization of the economy on a commercial and industrial, rather than an agrarian base.[14]

Integrated industrial enterprises, those devoted to distributing and marketing goods as well as manufacturing them, emerged in the 1880s and '90s. By a process of horizontal combination and consolidation, corporations in a variety of industries consolidated manufacturing operations and began to address questions of distribution and marketing. In doing so, they began to face problems of organizational structure, particularly those involved in coordination, appraisal, and planning.[15] Large-scale organizations, characterized by vertical and horizontal complexity, emerged as the organizing principle in American commerce.

The distinguishing characteristics of large-scale organizations included "their many statuses, the many and complex relations among the statuses, and the ordering of these complex relations and statuses into one or more hierarchies of ranked positions."[16] The many statuses and hierarchical and other orderings of the relations among the statuses functioned to coordinate the activities of the many members of such organizations.[17] In a growing, increasingly integrated society like the United States in the late nineteenth century, such organizations provided the means for creating a national society out of what had been an isolated, local society, held together by common cultural and ideological values.[18]

The growth of large-scale organizations resulted in the development of a new kind of organizing principle for business and government. Commercial and political institutions became distinguishable from other integrating institutions, in particular the family, the church, and—in the United States—the political party. Historians and political scientists interested in political development identified such differentiation as a key indicator of political modernization.[19] Differentiation from other institutions, in addition, made it possible to construct organizations on the principle of "legal" or "rational" authority, rather than on traditional forms of authority represented by the family and the church.

Writing early in the twentieth century, the German sociologist Max Weber described the consequences of the differentiation of organizational structure from other institutions. While he viewed "organization," the existence and functioning of an administrative staff, as vital to the maintenance of any form of authority, Weber argued that legal authority resulted in a particular form of organization of the administrative staff, bureaucracy.[20] The characteristics of bureaucratic organization included a hierarchical distribution of authority within the organization, the distribution of activities "in a fixed way," written regulations which circumscribed the activities, and appointment to office based on technical qualifications.[21] Such an organization was "capable of attaining the highest degree of efficiency" because it provided "the exercise of control on the basis of knowledge."[22] Its consequences included formalization, circumscribed authority, and "plutocracy," or the centralization of authority as a result of hierarchical organization.[23]

In his administrative history of the federal government between 1869 and 1900, Leonard White concluded that the period "had produced almost no interest in administration other than reform."[24] The reforms to which White referred, and which provided the framework for his review, were the increasing autonomy and leadership of the executive branch and the movement for civil service reform.[25] Both were consistent with a shift to bureaucratic administration in the federal establishment.

In an era of weak chief executives, congressional power over the executive branch was symbolized by the Tenure of Office Act of 1867, which required the consent of the Senate for the removal from office of officials appointed by the President.[26] Congress passed the act in the midst of a controversy with President Andrew Johnson regarding Johnson's management of the Reconstruction program. By limiting the President's power to remove officials, the Congress hoped to control the way in which the program was implemented. Early in the Grant administration, Congress modified the act, removing a requirement that the President state the reasons for the removal, but still requiring the President to name the removed official's successor promptly.[27] In the absence of outright repeal of the Tenure of Office Act, an ambiguous situation prevailed, which was not resolved until President Cleveland, a Democrat faced with a Republican Senate, secured a repeal of the act in 1887.[28]

While the repeal of the Tenure of Office Act reduced, to a certain extent, Congressional influence in personnel matters, the Senate's confirmation power made it a powerful force even after 1887.[29] The Pendleton Act of 1883, however, laid the foundation for a civil service system insulated from direct Congressional control.[30] The act envisioned the development of a personnel system based on merit, governed by a bi-partisan Civil Service Commission appointed by the President. By removing classified positions from the political spoils system, the Pendleton Act made possible the development of a career civil service headed by the President.[31]

In addition to major developments regarding the Presidency and civil service reform, White identified three tendencies in the administration of the Executive Branch which were consistent with the bureaucratization of governmental activity. The ideal of political administration was gradually supplanted by the ideal of a "businesslike" government, exemplified in the appointment of businessmen and members of university faculties to administrative positions. A trend toward a national civil service, mitigated by the veterans' preference provisions of the Pendleton Act, reduced the particularistic criteria for office-holding implicit in the sectional preference of the immediate post-war years. Finally, the introduction of office machines, such as the typewriter and the telephone, and the increasing complexity of government business, led to an increased emphasis on the possession of technical qualifications for office-holding.[32]

A tendency toward differentiation of the executive agencies from the political system and toward the creation of an administrative system based on legal authority and rationalistic criteria characterized the federal government during the late nineteenth century. Change was, as White pointed out, halting and incomplete. Rather than a transformation in the state of administration, the changes in the organization of executive activity laid the foundation for the "unparalled progress in developing both the theory and the practice of the art of administration" which he said characterized the first three decades of the twentieth century.[33]

The administration of the Indian Office evolved within the context of political modernization and increasing bureaucratic rationality which characterized the late nineteenth century. However, neither of these concepts captures the nature of the transformation of the organization which occurred between 1865 and 1900. Differentiation from the political system occurred as a result of a series of reforms in the selection of personnel and the means used to control the behavior of subordinates. Rational bureaucratic organization was implicit in the development of written rules and a personnel system based on civil service principles. The development of an organizational mission, based on the goal of Indian assimiliation, provided the rationale for the differentiation and bureaucratization which was achieved.

The more global concept of institutionalization comes closest to capturing the changes in administering the Indian Office which occurred between 1865 and 1900. Institutionalization refers to the process by which organizations or procedures acquire value and stability. While institutions need not be modern or bureaucratic, most writers on the institutionalization of complex organizations used indicators which overlap those of political modernization and bureaucratization. Thus, Huntington employed complexity and autonomy, in addition to adaptability and coherence, as criteria of political institutionalization.[34] In his examination of the institutionalization of the U.S. House of Representatives, Nelson W. Polsby used differentiation or "boundedness," complexity, and the use of universalistic and automatic decision rules as criteria for institutionalization.[35] Harold W. Pfautz employed size, internal differentiation, and complexity, in addition to viability, as criteria for identifying Christian Science as an "institutionalized sect."[36]

The differentiation of an organization from elements in its environment is a criterion for both political modernization and institutionalization, as these concepts have been used by analysts. Huntington's criterion of autonomy and Polsby's criterion of "boundedness" seemingly are consistent with the emphasis on differentiation of political structures from other institutions as a criterion for modernization. The criteria of internal differentiation and complexity, used by Huntington, Polsby, and Pfautz, are similar to Weber's focus on bureaucracy as a means for regulating a set of inter-related statuses. Polsby's criterion of universalistic and automatic decision rules is, of course, central to Weber's conception of bureaucracy and reflects an emphasis found in much of the sociological literature on twentieth-century institutions.[37] The institutional focus adds an emphasis on the environment of the organization and the organizational stance in relation to the environment.[38] Such an emphasis is captured in Huntington's criteria of adaptability and coherence and in Pfautz's criterion of viability. Such an approach suggests that organizational goals, and the means employed to achieve those goals, will be important in an institutional analysis of an organization.

The analysis of goals and goal-seeking activity figured importantly in the development of the institutional approach to studying complex organizations. Robert Michels, in *Political Parties*, discussed the tendency of organized groups to become oligarchic over time.[39] Philip Selznick, writing in 1943 and citing Michels, emphasized the failure of organizations to achieve their stated goals.[40] Bureaucratization involved the delegation of functions. But a delegation of authority resulted in a bifurcation of interests between the formal leadership of an organization, those with high positions, and those subordinates with responsibility for carrying out the functions. Since persons participating in organizations participated as whole persons, not merely in terms of their official statuses, every organization created an informal structure which modified the professed goals of the organization. "The day-to-day behavior of the group becomes centered around specific problems and proximate goals" as opposed to the professed or "original" goals of the organization, Selznick concluded.[41] Consequently, the operational goals of an organization and the control of goal-seeking behavior were central problems for the theory of bureaucracy.[42]

Selznick emphasized the factors of displacement of goals and the penetration of elements of the environment into the organizational structure in his influential case study, *TVA and the Grass Roots*, published in 1949. The Tennessee Valley Authority's professed goal of democratic planning was subordinated to the immediate technical goal of providing electric power, in his view. This goal displacement resulted from the TVA's decision to incorporate elements of the environment into its decision-making structure to avert threats to the organization's survival. In the process, the TVA abandoned the idea of a decentralized, "grass roots" approach to administration.[43]

In a brief essay, *Leadership in Administration*, Selznick organized his ideas about the informal structure and the influence of the environment into a conception of institutionalization. He defined an organization as "an *expendable tool*, a rational instrument engineered to do a job." An institution, in contrast, was "more nearly a natural product of social needs and pressures—a responsive, adaptive organism."[44] The sources of institutionalization included the relation of the organization to its environment and the internal social world of the organization's members. Institutionalization resulted from the development of an organizational mission, the defense of institutional integrity, and the ordering of internal conflict.[45] The definition of mission involved the development of operational goals, a process in which the organization negotiated with such elements of its environment as constituencies, clients or customers, and competing organizations.[46] The defense of institutional integrity directed attention to the organization's boundaries, in particular, the orgainzation's control of its membership and its autonomy in setting goals.[47] An organization's ability to order internal conflict could be measured by its ability to coordinate members' goal-directed activity. Achieving coordination involved achieving organizational control, whether by sanctions, which implied formalization, or by socialization, which implied the informal organization's commitment to organizational goals and a high level of communications.[48]

Selznick's view of institutionalization involved clear organizational goals which could provide an institutional mission, organizational integrity or boundedness, and the ability to elicit the coordination of the activities of organizational members. A fourth element, which he called "the institutional embodiment of purpose'' involved building organizational goals into the social structure of the organization. The formal and informal organizational structure, Selznick argued, should reflect the institutional mission.[49] He identified professionalism, the commitment of an institutional elite to the organization's goals and characteristic methods of achieving them, as the basic means for achieving an embodiment of purpose, which would infuse the organization with commitment to its mission.[50]

Selznick empahsized the positive consequences of institutionalization. In his essay, he placed great stress on the creativity of institutional leadership as a prerequisite for the institutionalization of an organization. In a different context, however, he remarked that too much institutionalization could be pathological.[51] Such pathology might result from a ''premature'' consensus on organizational goals, from an insensitivity to the needs of elements of the environment, or, as Charles Perrow suggests, from the implementation of institutional goals of which the analyst does not approve.[52] Since one consequence of institutionalization was thought to be increased organizational independence, institutions might well be impervious to attempts on the part of constituents to influence them.

Analysts such as these present a variety of approaches to defining indicators of institutionalization. Selznick's discussion is the most extensive; in addition it addresses the phenomenon which I discuss in this study, the institutionalization of a formal organization.[53] Some of the differences between Selznick's criteria and those of the other analysts are instructive. While Huntington, Polsby, and Pfautz used complexity as an indicator of institutionalization, Selznick emphasized the extent to which the internal social structure of the organization reflects the organization's operational goals.[54] Thus, in his view, institutionalization involved in part the extent to which an organization's internally differentiated structure reflected its goals.

Selznick also put more emphasis on the distinctiveness of organizational goals as a criterion for institutionalization than did the other analysts. He suggested that ''adaptability'' or ''viability'' were outcomes of institutionalization rather than criteria.[55] ''Institutional integrity'' appears to combine Huntington's criteria of autonomy and coherence and to be related to Polsby's criterion of boundedness; indeed the robustness of an organization's boundaries, particularly the organization's control of entry, may be a partial indicator of an organization's integrity.[56] The use of universalistic and automatic decision rules, indicated by formalization and a system of sanctions to enforce the formal rules, is one way to achieve coordination in an organization. In some complex organizations, it is the primary method.

Selznick suggested that institutionalization is a process: ''no organization of any duration is completely free of institutionalization.''[57] For the purposes of this study, the following indicators of institutionalization are used.

1. The selection of organizational members was important in determin-

ing the extent of the institutionalization of the Indian Office. Two categories of personnel are considered: Indian agents and agency personnel. The selection of personnel was significant for the organization's "boundedness"; as such, changes in the selection of personnel provide a measure of changing organizational integrity (Chapters III and IV).

2.   The control structure of the organization provides a second indicator of institutionalization. The strategy of control employed, the centralization of control, and the relationship of the control structure to the hierarchical structure of the organization determine the control structure's ability for coordinating the activities of personnel (Chapters V, VI, VII, and VIII).

3.   The evolving organizational goals, the means for attaining goals, and the reflection of the goals in the organization's formal structure provide a third indicator of institutionalization (Chapters II and IX).

During the late nineteenth century, the Indian Office centralized the appointment of field personnel, the control system, and the organization's goal-setting activities. While centralization was not viewed as a necessary component of institutionalization by Selznick, the centralization of the Indian Office increased its institutionalization. A decentralized structure, which characterized the organization prior to 1880, was associated with highly permeable boundaries. Consequently, the centralization of the functions of personnel selection, organizational control, and goal definition provided a means for institutionalizing the Indian Office. Centralization is a major theme in the chapters which follow.

Similarly, my emphasis on centralized organizational control, particularly inspection and formalization, is greater than a reading of Selznick would suggest is indicated. Selznick, in common with other organizational theorists of the twentieth century, appears to lay greater stress upon the commitment of personnel to the organization as a means for transforming an organization into an institution; the "professionalism" of organizational members becomes a crucial variable in his analysis.[58] Socialization of personnel, the intensity of the communication system, and the formal structure of the organization are other variables which may produce coordinated effort in organizations.[59] This emphasis on non-coercive methods for achieving coordination reflects in part the conviction that "voluntary" sources of control, especially commitment to organizational goals, are more effective than those based on the threat of negative sanctions. I also stress the increasing routinization of work, the increasing reliance on universalistic and automatic criteria for decision-making, an emphasis which may seem at variance with Selznick's "organic" model of institutionalization.

It is likely, however, that such elements as negative sanctions, the use of automatic decision rules, and formalization promote institutionalization at an early stage in an organization's development. Surely, such is the case when the organization begins from a position of weakness and must be moulded into an effective tool before it can acquire value. For the Indian Office in the late nineteenth century, centralization, control, and routinization were adaptive responses. Beginning the period with vague goals and an adherence to a removal and concentration policy which was outmoded, the organization had highly permeable boundaries and was threatened by other organizations in its environment. By centralizing the selection of personnel and the control of their behavior and by routinizing the functions of the field and inspection staffs, the Indian Office was able to become an organization which was relatively well-bounded, self-controlling, and well-integrated.

The Indian Office emerged from the Civil War as a weak organization. Washington officials, who were supposed to control organizational activity, did not control the appointment of field or supervisory personnel. They had few reliable sources of information regarding the distant field units and engaged in little activity designed to direct or coordinate the behavior of subordinates. Policy, during a period of short tenure for Commissioners of Indian Affairs, was made by a series of Commissions, by the Congress, and often by the Army.

The period of drift continued through the Grant administration. The administrative reforms of the 1870s replaced political patronage with religious patronage and created a control system which was external to the organization and ineffective. However, the creation of Indian Inspectors in 1873 laid the groundwork for a centralized system of control. Experiments on the reservations during the 1870s, reviewed in Chapter II, provided the basis for the integrated set of goals for Indian policy which emerged in the 1880s.

Carl Schurz, President Hayes' Secretary of the Interior, initiated the administrative reforms which would eventually centralize the organization and provide it with a control system and a set of goals around which Indian Office activity could be organized. A decade later, T. J. Morgan, Benjamin Harrison's Commissioner of Indian Affairs, made Indian education the primary focus of the Indian Office's work. Morgan also presided over the introduction of the classified civil service to positions in the Indian Service.

By 1900, the Indian Office could be described as a unified organization. The Washington office shared the appointment power for most field positions with the U.S. Civil Service Commission, insulating appointments, to a certain extent, from political pressures. The organization possessed an inspection system which was relatively routinized and which yielded predictable results. The education of Indians and their integration into American life provided the office with a goal which was widely accepted and around which it was organized.

These developments, which I describe in greater detail in the chapters which follow, resulted in an organization with a clearer sense of purpose, stronger boundaries, and more integrity than had been the case in 1865. By 1900, the members of the Indian Office knew what they wanted to achieve and believed they possessed the means for achieving it.

CHAPTER II

UNITED STATES INDIAN POLICY:
FROM THE CIVIL WAR TO THE BURKE ACT

United States Indian policy changed greatly between the end of the Civil War and the passage of the Burke Act in 1906. Although policy-makers experimented with the establishment of a reservation policy in the decade before the Civil War, the old objectives of removal and concentration still dominated most official plans for dealing with the "Indian problem" in 1865. During the next forty years, Congress and the Indian Office established a reservation system for American Indians and subsequently created a mechanism for destroying it. Education and the allotment of Indian lands, they thought, would end the reservation system and assure the assimilation of the Indians.

Whether described as an "assault on Indian tribalism," a "movement for Indian assimilation," or simply as "Americanizing the American Indian," the new system envisioned the integration of American Indians into the mainstream of white American life.[1] Since the Indians were a rural people, and most whites subscribed to a land ideology which favored small holdings of land which could be worked by an individual and his family, the cornerstone of the policy change involved "breaking up" Indian lands into individually owned allotments on which the former tribesmen would learn to produce subsistence and cash crops.[2] Since whites assumed that Indians were an uncivilized people, Congress and the Indian Office introduced such "civilizing" agencies as police forces, courts, and schools.[3] Since no one disputed that Indians occupied land which whites wanted, the effect of Indian land policy was to permit white intrusion into what had been "Indian country."[4] Ironically, the assimilative measures which evolved during the late nineteenth century defined a separate and unique status for many American Indians during the first three-quarters of the twentieth century.

As in other areas of public policy, Indian policy responded to changes in the environment. The most salient elements for policy-makers included white pressures on Indian lands and the military equation on the Western plains. The completion of the first transcontinental railroad in 1869 and the subsequent expansion of rail routes brought an increasing number of whites to the fringes of "Indian country" while it altered the military equation in favor of the Army, by making the rapid deployment of troops possible. Improved transportation increased the pressure on Indian land while it reduced the Plains Indians' capacity to resist.[5]

While improved transportation and communication increased white pressure on Indian lands, an Indian reform movement exerted pressure for a humanitarian policy toward the American Indians. Originating in isolated efforts by missionaries and Christian laymen to influence Indian policy during the Civil War, Indian reform received institutional expression with the creation of the Board of Indian Commissioners in 1869.[6] The formation of the Indian Rights Association in 1882 provided reform-minded whites with a membership organization which would promote their objectives.[7] Annual meetings, such as the annual conference of the Board of Indian Commissioners with the representatives of missionary associations and the Lake Mohonk Conferences of Friends of the Indian, provided the reformers with forums and access to legislators and Indian Office officials.[8]

While the reform movement was not monolithic, most Indian reformers of the period agreed on the objective of Indian acculturation, or "civilization" as they would have put it. Such an objective required opposing despotism—first the despotism which the reformers often perceived in the behavior of the chiefs and later the despotism of the "old-time Indian agent," who had earlier served as a model for others to emulate. The reformers opposed despots, along with communal land-holding, Indian religion, and such "Indian" economic practices as hunting and trapping, in order to individualize the Indian—in essence, to accomplish his separation from an aboriginal culture and later from a pauperized culture, based on the dole or ration system of the agencies of the 1870s.

Expanding white population and power in the West and a maturing reform movement in Eastern and other urban areas provided the context for the evolution of Indian policy in the late nineteenth century. Changing policy provided the context for organizational development. Indeed, a sense of organizational purpose or "mission" was a necessary condition for the institutionalization of the Indian Office.[9] Consequently, I begin with a review of policy changes during the period covered by this study.

Prior to the Civil War, the objectives of removal of Indians from the path of White settlement and concentration of the tribes in isolated areas guided United States Indian policy. The acquisition of territory in the southwest following the American victory in the Mexican War and in the northwest following settlement of the Oregon question provided the United States at the beginning of the 1850s with an expanded Western empire and a large number of Indians who were increasingly likely to conflict with whites. Western expansion resulted in the beginning development of a reservation "idea," an attempt to limit the geographic territory of Indians to defined reserves. On the reservations, Indians would be protected from whites and helped by Indian agents to adapt to white civilization.[10]

The early reservation system depended upon the presence of the Army to enforce compliance with the new boundaries and prevent armed conflict between tribes and between Indians and whites. It also required an efficient administration of the Indian Office, whose responsibilities for administering the reservations and providing rations to substitute for hunting grounds given up by the tribes increased as result of the many treaties negotiated during the 1850s.[11] However, little improvement in Indian Office administration followed the rash of treaty-making of the 1850s. The coming of the Civil War exacerbated the administrative problem. Although the pace of white westward movement hardly slowed, the Army withdrew troops from frontier areas to fight the Confederacy and Congress and the President devoted primary attention to the War rather than to questions of Indian administration.[12]

Spurred by the Indian Office's failure to fulfill treaty obligations and by continuing encroachments on Indian land, and perhaps conscious of a diminished military presence in the West, Indians from Minnesota to New Mexico made war on frontier whites. Despite a military response which was quick and brutal, often involving local "volunteers" rather than the regular Army, warfare continued and increased after the conclusion of the Civil War in 1865.[13] By 1867, Indian affairs had reached a crisis, according to Commissioner of Indian Affairs Nathaniel G. Taylor. After summarizing reports of warfare throughout the Great Plains, he concluded, "In my judgment we have war, general, prolonged, bloody, and ruinous, with all its accompanying barbarities and atrocities, and peace, speedy and durable, its concomitant, and consequent blessings, in our own hands and at our own option."[14]

An Indian reform movement began during the Civil War, led by missionaries and other Westerners who were able to observe the factors contributing to the outbreak of warfare on the prairies and plains of the West. Henry B. Whipple, Episcopal Bishop of Minnesota, urged reform in the administration of Indian affairs throughout the 1860s. After the Sioux Uprising of 1862, he was influential in persuading President Lincoln to commute the execution of nearly three hundred Santee Sioux ordered by a military tribunal.[15] John Beeson, an Englishman of Quaker sympathies who moved to Oregon in 1853, defended the northwestern tribes throughout the 1850s and '60s, securing a promise from Lincoln of reform in Indian affairs after the conclusion of the war.[16] Members of the Society of Friends, motivated no doubt by their tradition of fair dealings with the Indians of Pennsylvania, as well as former abolitionists seeking new fields for reform, soon joined the reform cause.[17]

In part because they focused on the failures of implementation of Federal policy which led to the western outbreaks, the reformers promoted administrative reforms, rather than changes in basic policy. A strict adherence to obligations incurred in the treaties, improvement of the nascent reservation system and the selection of good men to implement policy in the field would result in improvement of Indian affairs, the reformers believed. Many westerners and military men, however, favored an expanded role for the military in Indian affairs, exemplified in the movement for the transfer of the Indian Office from the

Interior to the War Department. While increased forcefulness in the implementation of policy was implicit in such a shift, its proponents envisioned no shift in basic policy. Transfer would permit improved communications between military men and administrators. Transfer would improve administration, as the patronage-ridden, corrupt Indian Office was replaced by the War Department. However, the objectives of concentration and removal would continue to guide administrators.[18]

In 1865, Congress created a joint special committee "to conduct an inquiry into the condition of the Indian tribes and their treatment by the civil and military authorities."[19] The "Doolittle Committee," so named after its chairman, Senator J.R. Doolittle of Wisconsin, was a congressional response to the Indian wars and the political turmoil resulting from them. The committee's findings reflected the political interests of its members, and Doolittle delayed making a final report until 1867, after the press acquired and published portions of the testimony.[20] The committee members found that the Indians were decreasing in population due to disease, wars, and loss of hunting grounds; they recommended against transfer but favored the creation of boards of inspection to oversee civilian administration.[21]

Later in 1867, reporting to the Senate on "Indian hostilities on the frontier," Commissioner Taylor recommended consolidation of the warlike tribes

> On large reservations, from which all whites except government employés shall be excluded, and educating them intellectually and morally, and training them in the arts of civilization, so as to render them at the earliest practicable moment self-supporting, and to clothe them with the rights and immunities of citizenship.

Taylor recommended the creation of Northern and Southern Indian territories, to be located on the Great Plains north of Nebraska and south of Kansas, for the Plains tribes, and of "one or more reservations of ample size" west of the Rocky Mountains for the Indians of the Pacific slope.[22] The Indian Peace Commission, created by Congress in 1867 and headed by Taylor, endorsed this suggestion and recommended that a clear line be drawn between civil and military responsibilities. The Commission opposed transfer, but recommended a revision of the laws regulating intercourse with the Indians and administrative reforms to insure "competent and faithful" personnel.[23]

The end of the Civil War resulted in an increase in the pace of Indian removals from the states of Kansas and Nebraska and from the Western Great Plains. Congress authorized the removal of Indians from Kansas to the Indian Territory in 1863.[24] However, action was not possible until after the war. In the decade and a half following the end of the Civil War, the Indian Office removed a large number of tribes to Indian Territory, including such Plains tribes as the Kiowas, Commanches, Cheyennes and Arapahoes, and tribes formerly settled on reservations in Kansas and Nebraska, including the Sac and Fox, Pottawatomies, Wichitas, Osages, Pawnees, Iowas, and Otoes. Warfare resulted in the removal of some tribes. Portions of the Modoc and Nez Perce tribes were settled on the Quapaw Agency in the 1870s following their defeats by the Army. The Indian Office removed the Poncas from Dakota Territory after their reservation was mistakenly included in the Sioux Reservation.[25] A northern Indian territory was defined by a series of treaties and agreements with the Sioux and other Northern Plains tribes, beginning with the Fort Laramie Treaty of 1868 and culminating in the Sioux agreements of 1876 and 1889.[26]

The recommendations of the Peace Commission, together with the ongoing processes of removal and concentration, provided the Grant administration with its Indian reform policy. Hailed by contemporaries as a new departure in Indian affairs, the Grant reforms were attempts to improve administration rather than to reformulate the goals of Federal activity. Two of the major elements of the Grant administration's program, church nomination of Indian Service officials and the creation of the Board of Indian Commissioners, were administrative changes. The third element was expressed as "Peace on the reservations, war off."[27] Indians remaining on the reservations were to be subject to a purely civil administration; those leaving without permission were assumed to be at war with the United States and were to be subject to military discipline.[28]

Congress ended the treaty relationship with the tribes in 1871.[29] While the precipitating cause for the action was the unwillingness of the House to be left out of the process of treaty-making, the action was consistent with the spirit of the reservation policy. The ending of the treaty relationship symbolized the government's objective of breaking up the tribal relationship and individualizing the Indians. Eli Parker, Grant's first Commissioner of Indian Affairs, had earlier requested an end to the "fiction" of treating the tribes as independent nations.[30]

The Grant administration was a period of administrative reform and of continuation and perfection of the reservation policy, rather than a period of policy innovation. Because the administration encouraged missionary involvement in administration, the practice of assigning denominations exclusive rights to proselytize on the reservations became an element of the administration's program. The reservations were to be schools for civilization; reservation administration was characterized by "the segregation of the Indians . . . the issuance of rations, and the endeavor to exercise complete control by the agents."[31] Segregation would protect the Indians from the contaminating influence of bad white men, including, in the eyes of many reformers and Indian Office personnel, soldiers. Most of the treaties of the late 1860s provided for the issuance of rations to Indians remaining on the reservation.[32] Commissioner of Indian Affairs Francis A. Walker frankly described this practice as bribery in his annual report for 1872. Rations were the means to keep potentially hostile Indians away from whites until an alternative economic system could be developed.[33]

The provision of rations inherent in the reservation policy was never a source of comfort to reformers or Indian Office officials. The military frequently condemned the policy, and the Indian Office never described it as anything but a temporary expedient. Congress never provided adequate appropriations for rations during the reservation period.[34] In 1875, Congress attempted to make Indian labor a requirement for the receipt of rations. The Indian Appropriation Act provided that

> For the purpose of inducing Indians to labor and become self-supporting . . . the agent . . . shall require all able-bodied male Indians to perform service upon the reservation . . . and the allowances provided for such Indians shall be distributed to them only upon condition of the performance of such labor.[35]

However, the act's effects were uneven. Agents on some reservations attempted to keep to the letter of the act; elsewhere, the work requirement was virtually ignored.

The exercise of complete control of reservation Indians by the agent was deemed essential for two reasons. One result of the penetration of whites into Indian country had often been to divide Indian communities into factions favoring or opposing the adoption of elements of white culture. In a seminal monograph, Robert F. Berkhofer, Jr. described this process for tribes which received Christian missionaries before the Civil War.[36] Most of the reservations established after the Civil War included "progressive" and "conservative" factions; the agents attempted to encourage the progressive, or pro-white, faction.[37]

Bureaucratic rivalry provided a second reason for the agents' attempts to maintain complete control of the reservation Indians. Pressure for the transfer of the Indian Office to the War Department continued throughout the 1870s. Indeed, the House of Representatives approved transfer bills in 1868, 1876, and 1878.[38] On the reservation level, the Army frequently established military posts on or near reservations, and sometimes the local commanders attempted to control reservation administration. Indian Agent John P. Clum arrived at the San Carlos Reservation in 1874 to find the agency under the control of Lieutenant J.B. Babcock.[39] At Standing Rock Agency in Dakota Territory, a succession of agents and military commanders engaged in a struggle for control of the reservation in the late 1870s and early '80s.[40]

Pressure for removals, rivalry with the Army, the attempt to exert total control, and the objective of civilization provided the context for a series of policy innovations which originated at the reservation level in the 1870s. Some agents proposed allotting Indian lands as a means of forestalling planned removals. Indian police forces, initiated on a number of reservations during the decade, provided agents with a means for exerting control over their Indians without calling on the Army. While many agents developed boarding schools on the reservations during the decade, the Carlisle Indian School, founded by Richard Henry Pratt toward the end of the decade, was to have the greatest impact.

Allotment, the division of Indian lands held by a tribe in common into individually-owned tracts, had a long history. The allotment of Indian lands was practiced as early as the seventeenth century in the American colonies.[41] Before the Civil War, reservations in Alabama and Mississippi were allotted as a means for facilitating the sale of Indian lands to whites.[42] After the Civil War, the allotment of Indian reservations was employed as an expedient to prevent the removal of tribes to more remote areas, by demonstrating the willingness of tribal members to become civilized. Thus, the Santee Sioux of Nebraska, threatened with the loss of their reservation on the Niobrara River and removal to Indian Territory, petitioned the Commissioner of Indian Affairs in 1869 to allot their reservation so that they might hold secure tenure on it. They were supported in this effort by their Agent and his brother, the Northern Superintendent, both nominees of the Society of Friends. There is some evidence that the allotment idea originated with them.[43] Similarly, when the Omaha Tribe of Nebraska was threatened with removal to Indian Territory in 1882, Alice C. Fletcher proposed allotment as an alternative. Miss Fletcher, the pioneer American ethnologist, was visiting the Omahas. She went to Washington to argue against the tribe's removal, carrying a petition requesting allotment. Successful in her mission, Miss Fletcher returned to supervise the allotment of the reservation. After the passage of the General Allotment Act of 1887, she was to supervise the allotment of several other Plains reservations.[44]

The frequency of special allotment acts applied to specific tribes both before and after the passage of the General Allotment Act led William T. Hagan to suggest that the course of policy development was little affected by the act. In his view, reservations would have been allotted with or without a general allotment law.[45] Most of the treaties negotiated in the 1860s included provisions for eventual allotment; similarly, Congress in 1875 provided that Indians severing their relations to their tribes could homestead on public lands under the provisions of the Homestead Law.[46] The possession of private property, especially the separate farm, came to be viewed as the key to Indian civilization and to the maintenance of an Indian land base.

Indian agents occupied an anomalous position in dealing with "a people without law."[47] President Grant promised that Indians remaining on reservations would not be interfered with by the Army. Further, while agents could request assistance from the Army in times of crisis, it was not in the interests of the Indian Office to involve this competing organization in the management of Indian Affairs. However, because of the factionalism endemic on the reservations, intra-tribal conflicts were frequent, often escalating to the level of personal violence. It was also frequently difficult to determine whether a tribe was at peace or war with the whites, given the unguarded reservation boundaries and the guerrilla warfare characteristic of Indian-white conflict. Prior to the development of the Indian Police, the Agents had no armed force other than the Army at their disposal to enforce order. Consequently, it is not surprising that in areas experiencing a great deal of conflict between whites and Indians, the Army was in effective control of Indian Affairs, despite nominal Indian Service control.

Such was the case at the San Carlos Apache Agency in Arizona in 1874, when John P. Clum, the twenty-two year old "boy agent," assumed control of the agency.[48] In his first annual report, written three weeks after his arrival at the agency he wrote,

> On taking charge of the agency, I found that the mixture of civil and military rule was still working detriment to the Indians. I therefore immediately assumed entire control of all affairs appertaining to the Indian service, in order that the Indians might understand that there was but one administration and one administrator. . . . Should the military desire to remain on the reservation, I shall not object. Yet I should strongly oppose a nearer residence than five miles from the Indian camp, as the effect of the association of the soldiers with the Indian is very demoralizing.[49]

Clum reminded the local troop commander at Camp Apache that the Army's role was to assist him, but only if he called on them. To provide an alternative to military control of the reservation, the Agent organized an Indian police force, originally consisting of four men, which grew in time to number over a hundred. He also engaged in a running battle with Colonel August V. Kautz, commander of the Military Department of Arizona, over the need for a military presence on the reservation and the effectiveness of the Indian police. Clum was supported by Indian Inspector William Vandever, sent to San Carlos in 1877 to look into the dispute. Clum was "the best agent for wild Indians that I know of in the service. Despite persistent and bitter opposition from the military authorities . . . by the aid of his Indian Police force [he had] accomplished far more than [Kautz] with his two regiments of regular soldiers to assist."[50] Claiming that his Indians were now civilized, Clum left the Indian Service in 1878. In the same year, Congress authorized the creation of Indian Police Forces.[51] By the end of 1878, about a third of the agencies had police forces. Two-thirds of the agencies had police forces two years later, and virtually all of the agencies had police forces by 1890.[52]

The first off-reservation government boarding school for Indians was founded by Captain Richard Henry Pratt at the Carlisle Barracks in Pennsylvania in 1879. In 1875, a regular Army officer with eight years of service on the Plains, Pratt received the assignment of escorting seventy-two Indian prisoners of war to exile at Fort Marion near St. Augustine, Florida. At Fort Marion, he was able to teach the Indians the rudiments of speaking and writing English and to get some of them jobs in St. Augustine. When the three-year period of exile was over in 1878, some of the Indians expressed a desire to remain in the East, and Pratt was able to get seventeen of them admitted to General S.C. Armstrong's Hampton Institute, an institution for freedmen in Virginia. At first assigned to direct an Indian program at Hampton, Pratt, who had attracted a great deal of attention as a result of his success at Fort Marion, was able to persuade the Army to turn over the Carlisle Barracks to him and to persuade the Indian Office to finance an experiment in Indian education. Pratt remained at Carlisle until his forced retirement in 1903. A man of strong convictions, Pratt was dedicated to the assimilation of the Indians. He advocated the mingling of Indians with whites as the best means for bringing about assimilation. Thus, Indian schools should be located in the east, far from the reservations. Pratt regarded the boarding school as a temporary expedient, until Indian students could be integrated into white institutions. He is reported to have told his Carlisle students, "If I were sure you would fall into the public schools, I would burn these buildings tonight!"[53] Pratt was proudest of his invention of the "outing system," whereby Indian students were sent out from Carlisle in the summer to work for white employers, thus presumably acquiring habits of industry and thrift.[54] However, his most lasting contribution probably was the idea of the large boarding school. The Indian Office established numerous off-reservation boarding schools in the 1880s and '90s, none of them as distant from the reservations as Carlisle, but all of them based on Pratt's philosophy of separating the Indian student from his family ties and cultural roots as a prerequisite to acculturation.[55]

Land allotment and Indian education came to dominate discussions of Indian policy. Indian police, while perhaps viewed as a temporary expedient, were the single largest personnel classification in the Indian service during the 1880s. Carl Schurz, Secretary of the Interior during the administration of Rutherford B. Hayes, supervised the integration of these elements into a unified Indian policy. Schurz pushed for the adoption of a general allotment law, supported Pratt's experiment in off-reservation education, and promoted the extension of police forces.[56] His successor, Henry M. Teller, authorized the creation of reservation courts of Indian offenses in 1883.[57]

In the decade preceeding the passage of the General Allotment Act, the diminution of the Indian land base, which William T. Hagan argued was the underlying goal of all Indian policy of the period, continued unabated.[58] The policies of removal and concentration contributed to this reduction. However, by the early 1880s, the concentration policy had to be abandoned as unworkable. There were fewer truly isolated regions to which Indians could be removed. Further, the results of removals, particularly of northern Plains tribes to the Indian Territory, were unacceptable. Unaccustomed to the climate, Indians died at an increasing rate on the new reservations. When tribes, like the Poncas, resisted removal, they found an increasingly sympathetic audience from reform groups.[59]

After the abandonment of removal as a policy, diminutions in the Indian land base resulted from such factors as the discovery of mineral resources on reservations and from the early experiments in allotment, in which surplus land remaining after each Indian had received an allotment was opened to settlement by whites. The discovery of gold in the Black Hills of Dakota Territory resulted in the Sioux Agreement of 1876, which removed the hills from the Great Sioux Reservation, opening them to white exploitation.[60] Similarly, the discovery of gold and silver on the Ute reservation in 1879, combined with an uprising against their agent, resulted in the removal of the Utes from their Colorado home. While some reformers protested the Ute removals, they ultimately acquiesced. Albert B. Meacham, a prominent Indian reformer, served on the Ute Commission which supervised the removal.[61] Reformers supported land-reduction schemes in part because they believed the Indians, in William Hagan's words, "would have to give up most of their land to retain title to any."[62]

If a tribe held good farm land, white pressures for removal led reformers to advocate allotment even where mineral resources were not discovered. They viewed allotment as doubly beneficial. The experience of property ownership would encourage civilization and Indian acquisition of the habits of hard work, thrift, and acquisitiveness which were presumed to characterize the white population at its best. In addition, by providing protections for the Indian title—commonly, a prohibition against alienation for a twenty-five year period—allotment would forestall efforts at removal and enable the tribesmen to retain at least a portion of their homeland.[63]

On the reservations of central and western Indian Territory, which were better suited to cattle grazing than to cultivation, a different pattern of white intrusion developed. The contractors who supplied the agencies with beef allowed the issue herds to graze on Indian lands. Texas cattlemen who began driving their herds north to Dodge City, Kansas, in the 1870s similarly exploited reservation grasslands. In the late 1870s, agents at the Cheyenne and Arapahoe and Kiowa-Commanche reservations began to charge ranchers grazing fees, using the proceeds to supplement meager Congressional appropriations for supplying the Indians with rations. While the grazing fees were of doubtful legality, sporadic attempts by Washington officials to regulate their collection were ineffective until Congress legalized the practice in 1891.[64]

Expenditures for Indian education increased dramatically after 1880. While the frequently stated objective of universal schooling for the Indians was not achieved during the nineteenth century, the increased organizational emphasis on Indian education was quite dramatic, whether measured by the absolute amount spent to support schools, the proportion of the Indian service budget devoted to educational matters, or the number of educational workers employed in the field.[65]

The General Allotment Act, also known as the Dawes Act, which Congress approved in 1887, gave the President the power to allot reservations at his discretion, with heads of families to receive a quarter-section of land and unrelated individuals to receive one-eighth of a section. The "surplus," if any, was to be sold to settlers in units not to exceed 160 acres. The title to the allotment was held in trust by the government for a twenty-five year period. At the expiration of the trust period, the allottee, who was expected to have become competent to manage his affairs, received a title in fee simple to his allotment. The act made special provisions for railroad rights-of-way across reservations and for modifications in areas suitable only for grazing. Upon receiving his allotment, the Indian became a citizen of the United States.[66] The passage of the act may have accelerated the process of allotment, even though in many cases special legislation was necessary to carry out allotments. The Sioux Agreement of 1889 provided for the allotment of the Sioux reservations of North and South Dakota.[67] The Dawes Commission, established by Congress in 1893, attempted to negotiate the allotment of the Indian Territory reservations of the Osages and the five civilized tribes, which were excluded from the provisions of the Dawes Act. The tribes resisted until the passage of the Curtis Act in 1898, which required the allotment of the Indian Territory lands.[68]

The Dawes Act made no provision for the leasing of allotments. However, in 1891 Congress approved the leasing of allotments made to children, old people, and others judged to be incapable of farming.[69] A series of additional Congressional actions in the 1890s extended the scope of leasing. In 1894, Congress authorized the leasing of unsold surplus lands for farming, as well as for grazing purposes.[70] The Curtis Act of 1898 authorized the leasing of Indian Territory allotments and provided for mineral leases in the territory.[71] Congress broadened the criteria for permitting the leasing of allotments in 1900, providing "inability," in addition to age and disability, as a ground for leasing.[72] The leasing provisions, combined with the surplus land provisions of the Dawes Act, permitted extensive white intrusion into what had been reservation lands.

The Burke Act of 1906 modified the citizenship provisions of the Dawes Act by deferring citizenship until expiration of the trust period. However, the Secretary of the Interior could authorize the issuance of a fee simple patent to allottees he found to be competent before the end of the twenty-five year trust period. For allottees found to be incompetent at the end of the twenty-five year trust period, the trust period could be extended upon the order of the Secretary. The immediate effect of the Burke Act, however, was probably to hasten the end of the trust period for many allottees. Particularly during the Wilson administration, competency commissions were active in ending the trust period ahead of schedule.[73]

Changes in Indian policy provided the Office of Indian Affairs with shifting objectives during the forty years following the Civil War. The shifting objectives provided the context for organizational development and for the institutionalization of the Indian Office. In 1865, the goals of Indian policy were containment and removal of the Indians from the path of white emigration. Acculturation, or the "civilization" of the Indians, while a stated goal, did not receive organizational expression in terms of the allocation of funds or personnel to the task.[74] By the end of the century, however, Indian civilization was both a stated goal and one which received organizational expression. Land allotment, education, and citizenship were the mechanisms for integrating Indians into American life. By 1900, the Indian Office had acquired a mission around which the organization had unified and become coherent.

As Indian policy became more coherent and focused during the nineteenth century, the organization with the responsibility for implementing that policy also became more coherent, more autonomous, and better-bounded. The maturation of policy and the maturation of the organization were reciprocal, mutually-reinforcing processes. The development of an organizational goal, which could provide Indian workers with a sense of mission and organizational purpose, was essential to the institutionalization of the Indian Office.

Ironically, the procedures developed to assimilate the Indian in the late nineteenth century would define a unique Indian experience for many in the twentieth. The Indian boarding schools provided several generations of Indians with a unique socialization and contributed to the development of twentieth-century Indian leadership.[75] Allotment and leasing deprived Indians of the control of reservation resources and created on many reservations a system of peonage unique in North America.[76] Indian police and tribal courts became a symbol of tribal sovereignty when a new generation of assimilationists attacked these institutions in the 1950s.[77] Most fundamentally, the reduction of the Indian land base in the late nineteenth century deprived Indians of much of their heritage, and a possible basis for economic revitalization in the twentieth century.

CHAPTER III

INDIAN AGENTS: THE SEARCH FOR A SELECTION PROCEDURE

The organizational structure of the Office of Indian Affairs was deceptively simple in 1865. At its head, the Commissioner of Indian Affairs directed a Washington office of clerks who received reports from the field and processed requests for funds. The Commissioner, who reported to the Secretary of the Interior, in theory supervised the superintendents and agents who controlled the Indians on the reservations. The agents, in direct control of one or more tribes, reported to the Commissioner through their respective superintendents, except for a few "independent" agents, who reported directly to the Commissioner. The agents supervised the work of the subordinate agency employees, including an interpreter, manual laborers and craftsmen, and often one or more teachers. (See Chart I.)

The control of entry into the positions in the Indian Office was important in determining the organization's boundedness. If the officials with supervisory control appointed their own subordinates, they could select the subordinates most likely to comply with supervisory directives, whether because of a shared commitment to organizational goals, previous socialization in the organization, or personal loyalty.[1] However, such was the case only for the agents, who appointed their own subordinates.[2] The agents and superintendents, like the Secretary of the Interior and the Commissioner of Indian Affairs, were Presidential appointees. Some superintendents were territorial governors who served as *ex officio* superintendents.[3] In addition, all of the Presidential appointments to Indian office positions were subject to confirmation by the Senate; even after the Johnson administration, the confirmation power provided the Senate with considerable power over office holding. Consequently, the formal Indian Office hierarchy had little control over entry into the organization. (See Chart II.)

Since the Indian agent was the official in direct contact with the Indians, he determined the extent to which organizational goals, whether of containment of the Indians or of their civilization, were met. Most commissioners viewed the Indian agent as the central figure in accomplishing the stated goals of the Indian office. In 1883, Commissioner of Indian Affairs Hiram Price wrote, "The civilization and elevation of the Indians depends more upon the agents who have their immediate care and management than upon any and all other instrumentalities combined, and hence none but the best class of men should be selected for this service."[4] In his previous *Annual Report*, Price outlined the characteristics of a good agent. "If the agent is an *honest, industrious*, and *intelligent Christian* man, with the *physical* ability and disposition to endure hardship and courageously encounter difficulty and disappointment, or, in other words, if he is morally, mentally, and physically above the average of what are considered good men, he will work wonders among these wards of the nation," the Commissioner wrote.[5] Yet the character of the men appointed to this position was never satisfactory, and commissioners frequently complained that they had nothing to do with the selection of the men who served as Indian agents, since they were Presidential appointees, requiring confirmation by the Senate.

In practice, Presidential appointment meant initial selection by the Secretary of the Interior. After the creation of the Department of the Interior in 1849, the Appointments Division of the Secretary's office carried out the processing of applications and appointments to positions.[6] Senate confirmation gave senators a voice in the selection of agents; indeed, as with other presidential appointments, the Secretary consulted senators of the administration party from the state in which the office was located in making Indian Office appointments. With Indian agents as with other appointments, certain positions came to be regarded as the property of individual senators. The practice of senatorial courtesy meant that a senator of the majority party could block the appointment to an office in his state of an individual who was not acceptable to him.

Political control of appointments, combined with the isolation of Indian agencies and the slowness of communication, reduced to a great extent the power of the central office to control affairs at the agencies. Indeed, many of the mechanisms of control devised by Commissioners of Indian Affairs and Secretaries of the Interior were the result of frustrations resulting from a lack of ability to influence field officials. For example, Indian Inspectors, who worked under the direction of the Commissioner until 1880 and under the direction of the Secretary of the Interior after that date, could suspend agents when there was a suspicion of impropriety. The power of appointment, however, was preferable to the power of suspension and removal. The power of appointment could prevent difficulties from occuring beforehand; suspension and removal necessitated explanations to aggrieved politicians or religious bodies when their protege was removed.

Attempts at reform in the late 19th century operated against the backdrop of a political appointment system. Political appointment resulted in home rule, the practice of appointing as agents men who resided in the vicinity of the reservation. Francis Leupp, Washington agent for the Indian Rights Association, branded home rule as "ring rule" in Indian Affairs.[7] The attitude of commissioners and secretaries toward home rule varied during the late nineteenth century, with advocates of home rule opposed by those who wished to create a career service within the Indian Service. Three major attempts at reform resulted from the situation during the late nineteenth century. Beginning in the Grant

Chart I

Organizational Structure of the Indian Office

1865-1873

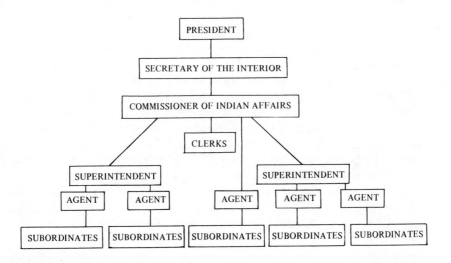

administration, and extending into the Hayes and Garfield Administrations on an attenuated scale, missionary associations nominated persons to be appointed to the position of agent by the President. The President appointed Army officers as Indian agents in emergencies throughout the period. Early in his administration, President Grant filled most agency and superintendency positions with Army officers. At the beginning of President Cleveland's second administration Congress encouraged the President to appoint army officers as agents. Finally, Commissioners W. A. Jones and Francis Leupp gradually abolished most agent positions between 1897 and 1905. Bonded school superintendents, appointed under civil service rules, replaced the agents as the chief administrative officers at the agencies.

The Indian Service was probably as disorganized and chaotic in the years immediately following the Civil War as at any time during the nineteenth century. During the Civil War disruptions in government services and an absence of troops resulted in a rash of Indian outbreaks, most notably in Minnesota and on the Great Plains. Troubles with the Sioux and Navajoes continued to trouble administrators after the Union victory.[8] Four Commissioners of Indian Affairs served under President Johnson during his brief administration. Because of the high turnover, the chief clerk, Charles E. Mix, provided what continuity there was in administration. Turnover among Indian agents was high during the period. The practical administration of Indian policy and planning was delegated to Congressional committees, such as the Doolittle Committee, and to the Indian Peace Commission, appointed by the President to negotiate treaties of peace with the warring tribes on the western plains.

The Peace Commission, in its report to the President on January 7, 1868, recommended that Congress fix a day within the next year,

> When the offices of all superintendents, agents, and special agents shall be vacated. Such persons as have proved themselves competent and faithful may be reappointed, those who have proved unfit may find themselves removed without opportunity to divert attention from their own unworthiness by professions of party zeal.[9]

The commissioners advocated this rather drastic measure as a means of rooting out corruption and incompetence; fundamentally, the Peace Commission addressed itself to the problems resulting from political appointments to the service. The Indian Service appointments, like those of other federal agencies, were highly politicized in the late 1860s. The election of Abraham Lincoln, at the beginning of the decade, resulted in an almost complete turnover of federal positions, because of the need to hold the new Republican Party together and to build political support for the Union cause.[10] Subsequently Lincoln's successor, Andrew Johnson, appointed political allies to federal positions to gain support in his fight with the Radical Republicans in Congress.[11]

When Ulysses S. Grant took office in 1869 he implemented the Peace Commission's recommendation to perhaps a greater extent than envisioned by its

Chart II

Appointment to Positions in the Indian Office

1865-1873

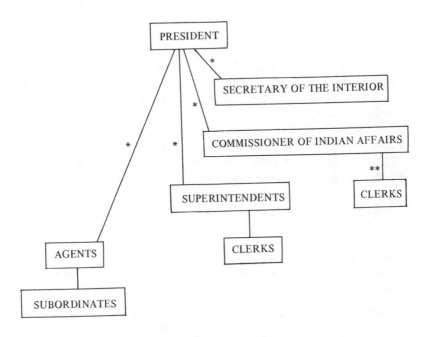

Key: —— appointment power
    * —— subject to Senate confirmation
    **—— subject to approval by the Secretary of the Interior

framers. He replaced the political agents with non-political appointees. His appointment policy, along with the creation of the Board of Indian Commissioners, was the administrative side of his famous "Peace Policy." In implementing this policy, the President took proposals which had been made before and extended them further. The Indian Intercourse Act of 1834 provided that the President could appoint army officers as Indian agents at his own discretion.[12] Under the authority of this act Grant filled all superintendencies and agencies with army officers who were detailed for such duty, with the exception of those in Oregon, Nebraska, Kansas, and the Indian Territory. In the Central and Northern Superintendencies, embracing Kansas, Nebraska and the Indian Territory, the President appointed nominees of the Society of Friends to fill the major field positions. The Oregon superintendent and agents were not changed. The Commissioner of Indian Affairs, Eli S. Parker, Grant's aide-de-camp during the Civil War and a Seneca Indian, commented, "There was doubtless just ground for it, as great and frequent complaints have been made for years past, of either the dishonesty of inefficiency of many of these officers."[13] The objective of the new appointment policy was to reform the administration of Indian Affairs by placing better men in the position of agent. In addition, Grant may have been motivated by a sentiment which favored transfer of the Indian Office to the War Department and by the need to find places for career Army Officers affected by the recent reduction in force of the Army. However, the new appointment policy was a piecemeal reform; D. C. Poole, an army officer detailed to duty as the Whetstone agent in Dakota Territory, found that Washington and Dakota Superintendency officials knew little about the Sioux Indians at the agency. He noted

> That those who had been some time associated with Indians assumed to know little of their character, and usually had no plans for their management, or fixed views as to how our government should treat them.[14]

In 1870, displeased by the removal of patronage, Congress prohibited detailing army officers to any position on the civil list, thereby effectively ending Grant's military appointment policy.[15] In reply, Grant is supposed to have said, "Gentlemen, you have defeated my plan of Indian management; but you shall not succeed in *your* purpose, for I will divide these appointments up among the religious churches, with which you dare not contend."[16] In any event, the blocking of the military appointment policy, combined with the popularity and apparent success of the Quaker appointment policy, resulted in a decision to extend the "Quaker Policy" to other denominations and to implement it throughout the Indian Service. Parker commented in 1870, regarding the superintendents and agents of the Society of Friends, "Their course and policy has been highly promotive of the welfare and happiness of the tribes under their charge."[17] Indeed, the plan of appointing Friends to superintendencies and agencies proved such a success "that, when Congress had its last session, prohibited the employment of Army Officers in any civil capacity . . . the President at once determined still further to carry out the principle by inviting other religious denominations of the country to engage in the great work of civilizing the Indians."[18]

The early implementation of the religious appointment policy involved many problems, several of which continued throughout the next decade. One relatively minor problem involved the question of who within the denominations should have the power to nominate agents. In most cases involving the Protestant denominations, the Mission Boards of the major churches could exercise this responsibility. With some smaller Protestant denominations such as the Unitarians and particularly with the Roman Catholic Church, whose missionary activities were carried out by a number of orders in a variety of Dioceses, the location of responsible individuals was not so easy. However, denominations responded to the need by creating structures to deal with the government, most notably in the case of the Catholic Indian Bureau, created in 1873 with Charles Ewing as Commissioner.[19] Ewing was appointed after Father Pierre DeSmet was prevented from serving in such a capacity as a result of ill health. The Unitarians, a relatively small group, did not have a Mission Board as such and there was some confusion on the part of government officials as to whom they should address.[20]

The assignment of agencies to denominations proved to be a more lasting source of contention than other concerns, however. Vincent Collyer of the Board of Indian Commissioners made the initial assignments. Collyer was not familiar with the previous mission activity of the denominations, which the assignment of agencies to denominations was supposed to reflect. Consequently, he made several errors in assignment. However, given the denominational rivalry which characterized Indian Mission work in the 1870s, it is unlikely that any selection would have been free from controversy. The major trouble spots were in Dakota, where the American Board of Commissioners for Foreign Missions, an organization of Congregationalists and Presbyterians, and the Episcopal Church had been competing for converts since the 1850s and where both groups were allied against the Catholics, in the northwest, where a conflict between the Catholics and the Methodists soon developed, and in the southwest, where the Reformed Church and the Catholics were in controversy.

A second problem had to do with the control of superintendencies. In the initial Quaker experiment, two superintendencies had been given to the two branches of the Friends Church, with the denomination appointing both the superintendent and all agents within the superintendency. In Dakota Territory, where the Episcopal Church received a number of agencies, the denomination initially demanded as a condition of participation that the Dakota superintendency either be abolished or be assigned to them.[21] Similarly in Arizona, where the

Reformed Church had several agencies, that denomination attempted and finally succeeded in gaining control of the superintendency.[22] Similarly, the Methodists gained control of many of the agencies and the superintendency in Washington Territory.

The Catholic Church, which had been more active in the Indian Mission field than any other denomination, complained that its interests were neglected by the government. The anti-Catholicism of many government officials and the lack of a national structure to represent the Church hampered efforts to gain a more equitable distribution of agencies. The Catholic Indian Bureau was established in large part to correct what, to the Church, was an unfair distribution of agencies.[23] However, the creation of the Bureau failed to resolve the problem; Catholic complaints about the assignments continued until the end of the religious appointments period.

Perhaps an even more significant problem involved the relationship between the Missionary Board or denomination and the agents appointed by it. The Quakers maintained a close relationship with the agents appointed by them, establishing an internal committee to supervise and support agents in addition to the government's control structure. Individual yearly meetings had general charge of individual agencies assigned to the denomination. The meeting was responsible for appointing agents and subordinate personnel, as well as for providing support for other activities. Sometimes nominations were cleared with the denominational Executive Committee before being sent to the Interior Department.[24] Initially, Church appointment nominally involved the delegation of all supervision of the agents to the nominating denomination. Eli Parker wrote to an Episcopal official in 1870 that the Indian Office made no inquiry ''as to the fitness, efficiency, or character of the persons designated for Indian agents by the different religious societies, the society making the designation in each case being held responsible for the proper conduct, good behavior, honesty, and efficiency of the person named.''[25] While Mission Boards could recommend the removal of agents nominated by them, however, the Interior Department first investigated the charges which the Mission Board brought.[26] In such a situation of divided responsibility, the authority and responsibility of Mission Boards was not clear. A persistent question was whether the Mission Board's responsibility ended with nomination or whether it extended to the agent's conduct after appointment.[27] While the government position was that the relationship between an agent and the nominating religious society should be a close one,[28] the details of the relationship were not defined and the Indian Office at times intervened without consulting the Mission Societies. In some cases, the Indian Office removed agents without consultation. When differences occurred between the agent and his denomination the Indian Office sometimes took the agent's side, particularly in the case of Quaker agents, where the denomination objected to the use of force against Indians.[29] At times, commissioners recommended individuals to religious societies for nomination as agents, possibly attempting to gain control over which individuals would hold the positions.[30]

Complaints about Indian Agents continued during the Grant administration, despite the innovations of the Peace Policy. In part, these were the result of disagreements between local whites and the denominationally-nominated Indian agents, who were not as a rule from the region in which the agency was located. In part, the complaints reflected the difficulty which the denominations had in finding and supervising good men to serve as agents. Throughout the Grant administration agents were paid $1,500 a year, a salary which the churches argued was inadequate. "It is not easy to find such a man as is needed, to go to Arizona for $1,500 a year," the Reformed Church secretary wrote in 1872.[31] Such difficulties resulted in delays in filling positions, complicating the work of day-to-day administration.

Requests for an increase in the salary paid to agents had been made by the Indian Office since at least 1865; the low pay (less than that paid to a third class clerk in Washington) was cited as an explanation for the corruption which prevailed in the Indian Service.[32] Most Commissioners, in their *Annual Reports* in the '60s and '70s, requested an increase in the maximum salary of Indian agents and a gradation in salaries, since the cost of living and the difficulty of the work varied from agency to agency. The low salary, combined with the difficulty of the work, led agents to lobby for appointment as superintendents or as Indian Inspectors, both more highly paid and seemingly less arduous positions.[33] A gradation and increase in the maximum salary of agents was achieved in 1878. However, the maximum salary was set at $2,200. Even by 1890 the average salary of Indian agents was only slightly above $1,500, too low in the opinion of the Commissioner of Indian Affairs. The salary range at that time was between $800 and $2,200, per year.[34]

Criticisms of the religious appointments policy during the Grant Administration made the missionary boards anxious about the new administration of President Rutherford B. Hayes. In his first annual report, Hayes' Secretary of the Interior, Carl Schurz, stated that religious appointments were an improvement on the previous political appointments, but were by no means perfect. Schurz suggested that the Indian Service should have the power to shift agents from posts of minor importance to more important ones, and that the pay of agents should reflect the difficulty of the position. Such a system would have destroyed the principle of religious appointment and substituted a system of central office control.[35] In January of 1878, the Senate failed to confirm four of the six agents nominated by the Quakers for the Nebraska Agencies, on the basis that they did not reside in the State. This action was at the request of the two Republican Nebraska senators and Schurz considered abandoning denominational appointments.[36] According to Commissioner of Indian Affairs E.A. Hayt, he did not do so because abandonment of the policy would have incurred the opposition of the churches and would have made political pressures for control of appointments too intense.[37]

Schurz's approach to the religious appointment policy was cautious, yet a change in attitude was clear. Agents were occasionally appointed without consultation with the churches. Frequently, they were removed without consultation. During the first year of the Hayes Administration, thirty-five of the seventy-four Indian agents were replaced.[38] Commissioner Hayt told the Joint Transfer Committee that about two-thirds of these removals had been due to incompetence or corruption.[39] In part the removals stemmed from the conviction that the denominationally-appointed agents lacked sufficient business experience. Hayt told the Joint Transfer Committee that he accepted ministers as agents only if they had had previous commercial experience; experience in the ministry was insufficient for the proper management of an Indian Agency.[40] Such a view was a common part of the Western and military attack on the religious appointment policy. Early in Schurz's administration, General John Pope wrote to the Secretary, "It must be said that what we have gained in honesty we have lost in practical knowledge and usefulness." Religious agents, wrote Pope, were not good business managers; nor were they really knowledgeable about the Indians.[41]

In the Fall of 1877, Hayt told a gathering of Quakers that he found the agents in the Central Superintendency to be inefficient and at times dishonest. The Quakers were disturbed, but after a meeting with President Hayes they agreed to continue their relationship with the Indian Office. However, problems with the government continued. In 1880, B. Rush Roberts wrote to Carl Schurz to ask him whether a decision had been made to "return to Grant's original agreement for the appointment of agents and employés by the denominations."[42] The Unitarians and the Episcopalians also complained.[43] As the churches found interference with their appointments growing, they began to withdraw from formal association with the Indian Office. Many individual denominationally nominated agents stayed on at the agencies, however. The Methodists, for example, had withdrawn from the Peace Policy by 1880, after the removal of the Methodist agent John L. Burchard from the Round Valley Agency and the appointment of a successor without consultation with the Methodist Mission Board.[44] Yet Methodist agent James H. Wilbur remained at the Yakima Agency until 1882.[45] Others had a much longer tenure.

One of the expressed purposes of the Peace Policy was to promote cooperation between the Indian agent and the religious bodies doing missionary work on the reservation. To this end, during the Grant Administration and the first part of the Hayes Administration, the Missionary Society which nominated the agent was considered to have exclusive rights to engage in missionary activity on the reservation. The Catholics resisted this restriction most strongly. They had the most to lose, since Catholic missionary activity was far more extensive than the number of agencies assigned to the denomination implied. The Protestant churches generally supported the restriction until 1880 when the Catholic agent at Devil's Lake Reservation in Dakota Territory expelled Daniel Renville, a Sioux Indian and a missionary of the Amerian Board of Commissioners for Foreign Missions, from the reservation on Schurz's orders. Following the expulsion, the Board of Indian Commissioners, at their joint conference with Mission Society Boards in January, 1881, petitioned Hayes for religious liberty on the reservations. On February 11, Schurz issued an order revoking the exclusive religious jurisdiction on the reservations.[46]

Late in the Hayes administration the churches attempted to regain control of the agent appointments. At the joint meeting of Mission Societies and the Board of Indian Commissioners in 1882, some of the conferees made an appeal for the agencies to be redistributed based on the denominations' actual missionary endeavors on the reservations, an acknowledgement of past bickering among the denominations.[47] At the same gathering, Rush R. Shippen of the American Unitarian Association described the change in procedure which led to the appeal:

> Eight years ago, under General Grant, when vacancies occurred my intimation was directly from Secretary Delano. He would say: "There is a vacancy, and your Board is invited to nominate a man." The nomination came primarily from us. Skip eight years, and the difference is this: as the Secretary for the Society, I heard nothing about a vacancy occurring. My first word would be a letter from some man, saying, "I am trying to get such an agency that is vacant. Two or three others are also trying, and I think I can get it if I have Unitarian influence." [48]

With the change in administration, other changes were made. Prior to the Hayes administration, agents, both political and religious, had the power to appoint all of their subordinates. Thus, during the Grant administration, churches were responsible not only for appointing agents but, through the agents, for appointing all of the field personnel of the Indian Office. Some denominations, such as the Quakers, appointed subordinate agency employees directly. In most cases, however, the agent himself appointed his subordinates. Many appointed wives and other relatives to subordinate positions as a means of supplementing their meager salaries. Early in the Hayes administration the Indian Office began appointing agency clerks and physicians. Not surprisingly, the religious agents regarded these individuals as spies who would undermine their authority. At the 1882 meeting of the Board of Indian Commissioners with the Mission Societies, a Congregationalist official commented, "Under President Hayes and the administration of Secretary Schurz a good many things crept into the Peace Policy . . . the agency clerk was appointed by the department, and was supposed to have a kind of power behind the throne greater than the throne itself."[49]

The new Garfield-Arthur administration brought a definitive end to the religious appointment policy. President Garfield died on September 19, 1881, and Vice President Chester A. Arthur succeeded to the Presidency. He appointed

Henry Moore Teller Secretary of the Interior, the first westerner to hold the office. In his first annual report, Teller wrote that the literary and moral education provided by the missionaries had proved a failure. He called for practical industrial education for the Indians.[50] In the Commissioner's *Annual Report* for 1882, the list of agencies showing denominational assignments was headed, "List of Indian Agencies Formerly Assigned to the Several Religious Denominations."[51] Teller, in a letter to a Methodist official, declared that the religious appointment policy had ended. "On taking charge of the Department of the Interior," Teller wrote, "I announced that I should not consult the religious bodies who had heretofore been allowed to name the persons to be appointed Indian agents." If religious bodies appointed agents, Teller continued, "the agent will, in the nature of things, owe fealty to that body and not to the government, and in his efforts will be controlled, not by what is the policy of the government, but by the policy of the church organization." Teller cited the need for "unity of action" and said that an Indian "Peace Policy" and the appointment policy of the Grant Administration were not necessarily connected.[52]

In summary, the religious appointment policy never worked smoothly. The early understandings regarding the joint responsibility of churches and the government had to be clarified periodically and the government exerted influence on the churches for the appointment of agents. Senate confirmation of agents was a frequent problem. Sometimes the Indian Office replaced church nominees without consultation, even during the Grant administration. At other times appointments were made without consultation. Throughout the period the struggle between denominations for official sanction made the policy difficult to carry out. The distribution of agencies to various denominations, based on criteria which were less than clear, resulted in denominational jealousies. The Baptists complained that the assignment of only five agencies to them, while the smaller Presbyterian and Episcopal denominations had eight or nine each, was unfair.[53] The Catholics contended that the assignments did not reflect their superior record of support for Indian Missions.[54] Small denominations, particularly the Lutherans, felt excluded. More favored denominations pressed for a consolidation of influence through the capture of a Superintendency. In Arizona, the Reformed Church eventually appointed the superintendent; in the Pacific northwest the Methodists appointed both Washington and Oregon Superintendents. At times, denominations requested superintendencies as a means of increasing the number of agencies under their control. When the Catholics lost the right to appoint the Fort Hall agent in 1872, some Catholics requested the right to nominate a Superintendent of Indian Affairs for Utah Territory saying, "The Catholic Church would be better satisfied with the Superintendency than with the Agency."[55]

Most accounts of the demise of the religious appointment policy emphasize the lust of the politicians for political patronage.[56] Probably of equal importance was the organizational requirement for central control of agent behavior, a requirement which church appointment made difficult to achieve. Church appointments blurred the boundaries of the Indian Service, delegating the selection of personnel to a group of outside organizations which became increasingly well organized during the Grant administration. The religious appointment policy was, from the perspective of the Indian Office, ultimately disintegrative. The diffusion of the power of appointment created a bifurcation of control over agent behavior, enabling denominations to pursue independent policies. Secretary Teller cited the requirement of organizational integrity in his justification for abandoning the policy.

The Hayes administration has been hailed as a turning point in the administration of the Indian Office.[57] However, the conclusion, while accurate, is true for reasons other than those usually advanced, which emphasize programmatic innovations, such as the extension of Indian police, most of which were actually begun in the Grant administration. The contributions of the Schurz-Hayes administration involved strengthening the inspection service, the first attempt to extend Indian Office control over agents' subordinates, and the systematic extension of the innovations of the Grant years. In this context, the change from religious nominations back to political nominations can be understood as an effort to strengthen the authority of the Indian Office in Washington.

In part, the Galpin affair, at the beginning of the Hayes adminstration, reflected the disintegrative tendencies built into the Peace Policy. S.A. Galpin came to the Indian Office from the Census Bureau in 1872, a protégé of Francis A. Walker, the director of the 1870 census who served briefly as Commissioner of Indian Affairs. Galpin rose quickly to the position of Chief Clerk. As Chief Clerk, Galpin was identified with the religious appointments policy; he was particularly close to the Quaker administration of the Central Superintendency. When the Board of Indian Commissioners attempted to investigate the distribution of annuities in the Central Superintendency during the last years of the Grant administration, Galpin defended the Quaker administrators. In 1877, Carl Schurz convened a Board of Inquiry to investigate the administration of the Indian Office, which, while failing to prove charges of corruption against Galpin, led to the ouster of the Chief Clerk and of Commissioner of Indian Affairs, J.Q. Smith. While the affair is discussed in more detail later, one of the major concerns uncovered by the Board involved the delegation of the authority for making purchases and inspections of goods from the Washington Office to the office of the Central Superintendent in Lawrence, Kansas. The delegation, engineered by Galpin, was justified on the basis of improved efficiency and flexibility. Thus, denominational administration could lead ultimately to organizational decentralization, a consequence which neither the Board of Inquiry, nor Schurz or E.A. Hayt, his Commissioner of Indian Affairs, was able to tolerate.

In the final analysis, the delegation of personnel functions to the churches worked no better than the delegation of personnel functions to the political system. Church appointments, like the detailing of Army officers to serve as agents, reflected a distrust of the Indian Office and of the political appointment system. However, as Teller pointed out, religious appointments, like political and military appointments, did not result in harmony of action since they introduced an element of outside influence into the operation of the Indian Office.

During the 1880s and '90s, the political appointment system prevailed. However, the Indian Office increased its control of other areas of administration, through the elaboration of an inspection system and through the extension of Indian Office appointment of subordinate agency employees. Later, in the 1890s, Civil Service regulations gave the Washington Office control of the appointment of the chief executive officer on the reservations, as well as his subordinates.

The Indian Appropriations Act of 1892, passed after the Ghost Dance uprising in South Dakota, required the President to detail officers of the United States Army to act as Indian agents at all agencies where vacancies occurred except when in his opinion the public service would be better promoted by the appointment of a civilian.[58] Combined with a consolidation of agencies, this requirement reduced the number of political agents, but the Commissioner of Indian Affairs joined the reformers in expressing his apprehensions. Indian work was civil and not military. The appointment of military men reduced the extent of political interference in the Indian Service but was not thought to be well-suited for preparing Indians for civilized life.[59] Further, the Army officers who served as agents did not owe their personal loyalty to the civilian administrators of Indian policy.[60]

Another provision of the 1892 Appropriations Act had a more lasting influence. The act authorized the Eastern Cherokee School Superintendent in North Carolina to act as agent for the remnants of Cherokees who had not removed to the Indian Territory.[61] The following year, Congress authorized the Commissioner of Indian Affairs to abolish any agent's position and devolve his duties upon the reservation school superintendent.[62] The Commissioner requested this change in 1892, citing the example of the Eastern Cherokees and arguing that as reservations were allotted and as the Indians became less of a potential danger to neighboring whites, the powers of the agent would diminish. The Indians would still, however, need guidance, which should be educational. The decreased responsibilities of agents, then, could best be exercised by school superintendents.[63]

A Presidential order of April 13, 1891, brought the school superintendents, along with agency physicians, teachers, and matrons, under Civil Service regulations.[64] By converting agents into school superintendents, the local administrative leadership of the Indian Service was brought under Civil Service regulations without the need to confront the issue of political versus merit appointments directly. Generally, political agents were brought into the classified service without an examination when the shift from agent to school superintendent was made, insuring that there would not be a direct protest at any point.[65] Even in the early twentieth century, individual Indian agencies were still regarded as the political perquisites of Senators.[66] The shift from agent to superintendent, begun in 1892, was carried on with most vigor during the Roosevelt administration by two Commissioners of Indian Affairs, W. A. Jones and Francis Leupp. By 1908, the last of the agent positions was abolished and all of the agencies were under the control of school superintendents appointed under Civil Service regulations.

The operation of the Civil Service Law gave Commissioners of Indian Affairs, for the first time, substantial power over the selection of Indian agents. When a vacancy occurred, the commissioner notified the Civil Service Commission of its existence and requested that the Commission certify three candidates who had passed the examination for the position. From the three eligibles certified, the Commissioner could appoint one to the position, or he could request a recertification. Thus, for the first time, the local officials in charge of agency affairs owed their appointment to the official in charge of the Indian Office. School superintendents were much more likely than political, military, or religious agents to have previous experience in the Indian Service. The result of changing the appointment system for agents, then, was a better-bounded organization, one in which the formal leadership controlled the entry of personnel into the key local administrative positions.

The superintendents were likely to have been socialized into the organization, as a result of previous service in the Indian schools. They knew the Indian Office's norms, were familiar with its culture, and were identified with its mission and characteristic methods of work. They owed their appointment to their administrative superior, the Commissioner of Indian Affairs, rather than to any outside institution. The devolution of the agent's duties upon the superintendent thus resulted in a better-bounded organization. This development was mirrored in the changing selection procedures employed with subordinate agency staff, in the development of centralized inspection, and in the development of methods of work with the Indians which exemplified the Indian Office's emerging goals.

CHAPTER IV

THE SELECTION OF AGENCY PERSONNEL

During the late nineteenth century, reformers and Washington administrators focused their attention on the selection and behavior of Indian Agents. The agent was the chief administrative officer on the local level. He supervised the work of a varying number of subordinate agency employees. During the reservation period, when agents attempted to gain complete control of the Indians on the reservations, the focus seemed warranted. Between 1867 and 1897, however, the proportion of field employees in the agent and agency clerk categories declined as the education and police categories accounted for an increasing percentage of the positions.[1] Further, several Commissioners of Indian Affairs, in particular E.A. Hayt, J.D.C. Atkins, and T.J. Morgan, succeeded in extending Indian Office powers of appointment over subordinate agency personnel during their administrations.

In some ways, the agency staff was perhaps as significant as the agent for organizational development. Shifts in the composition of the agency staff between 1867 and 1897 reflected the changing emphasis placed on education and social control by the organization. Only ten percent of the field positions were identifiable as educational positions in 1867; nearly half were in the education service in 1897. Agency employees performed most of the actual work of the Indian service: they distributed rations, educated Indian children, provided medical services, and exercised social control, under the direction of the agent or the reservation school superintendent and his clerks.

Prior to 1877, agents and superintendents were the only field officials appointed from Washington. They were also the only employees provided with travel expenses to the agencies. The agents appointed their own subordinates.[2] Prior to 1876 agents also appointed agency traders. When the Indian Office began to appoint some subordinate employees from Washington during the Hayt administration, agents and denominational officials objected strenuously. Prior to the extension of civil service regulations to the Indian Service in 1891, the power to appoint agency employees shifted from the Washington office to the agents with changes in administration. Beginning as an effort to limit the autonomy of the agent, centralized appointment of his subordinates ultimately made possible the creation of a career service in Indian affairs.

During the 1860s and '70s, every agency had an interpreter and a trader; most agents could appoint craftsmen, such as blacksmiths, carpenters, and millers, personal assistants (agency clerks), and teachers and physicians to assist in the work of the agencies. Some of these individuals were whites from the territory in which the agency was located. As a consequence of the religious appointment policy of the Grant administration, most of these positions tended to be filled by the agent's co-religionists, especially in the Quaker agencies. Under both political and religious appointment policies, nepotism was widespread. In an investigation of the Quapaw agency in 1878, Arden R. Smith reported that all agency positions were held by members of the agent's immediate family "or their relatives or near connections," with the exception of one of the teachers and the blacksmiths and interpreters. The former agency trader was a cousin of the agent's wife and of the Central Superintendent.[3] In his first annual report, Commissioner Hayt reported that nepotism in the Indian Service was "a public scandal."[4]

Nepotism was not the only problem associated with the agent's selection of agency employees. Agents were at times charged with selling subordinate agency positions.[5] Most seriously, collusion between Indian agents and agency employees could result in defrauding the government through the diversion of supplies intended for the Indians into the agent's hands.

In addition to the appointment of subordinates, agents had the power to appoint Indian traders. As early as 1865, Commissioner D.N. Cooley complained of this practice. "Agents are too often interested with or for the trader," he wrote. Calling for new regulations on Indian trade, Cooley contended, "Such combination of interests . . . can only exist to the injury of the Indians, and consequently of the government."[6] In 1866, however, over Cooley's objections, Congress liberalized the trade laws, permitting any loyal citizen to trade with the Indians, upon posting bond.[7] Acting Commissioner Charles E. Mix laconically commented in 1867 that the law was "rather a disadvantage to the Indians than otherwise."[8] Eli S. Parker, a member of the Commission investigating Western Indian hostilities, went further. He recommended abolishing the system of licensed Indian traders in favor of a government-run monopoly, similar to the factory system of the early nineteenth century.[9]

Fundamental reform in the trading system was not to come until 1876. The Indian Appropriations Act, approved on August 15, gave the power of appointing Indian traders to the Commissioner of Indian Affairs. Congress also empowered the Commissioner to make regulations governing the activities of traders and to specify "the kind and quality of goods and the prices at which such goods shall be sold to the Indians."[10] Commissioner J.Q. Smith promulgated regulations governing Indian trade on September 1. The regulations required traders to obtain permission to replenish their stock from the Office of Indian Affairs. Further, the regulations required agents to maintain copies of all invoices and records of all sales so that overcharging could be checked and controlled.[11]

In a laudatory report on conditions in the Indian territory, Smith's Chief

Clerk, S.A. Galpin, found the traders to be "of far higher standards and character than I had been led from common repute to expect." He recommended that Smith relax the regulations; in particular, the requirements for maintaining invoices and obtaining Indian Office permission prior to purchasing replacement supplies should be replaced "by occasional inspections made by the agents, under your special direction. . . . [Thereby] much needless annoyance will be avoided," Galpin predicted.[12]

However, the Board of Inquiry appointed by Secretary of the Interior Carl Schurz to investigate Galpin's management of the Indian Office found that the 1876 regulations failed to meet the requirements of the law; further, the traders ignored the requirements for maintaining invoices and obtaining permission to purchase replacement supplies.[13] While Galpin had reported that "a healthy competition" prevailed in the Indian trade,[14] the Board found such to be the case only at the Union Agency to the five civilized tribes. More than half of the licenses issued by Smith, 71 out of 128, were for trading at this agency; indeed, there was one trader for every 803 Indians at the Union Agency. In contrast, Smith had licensed only 57 traders for the remaining 69 agencies. At a ratio of one trader for every 3,158 Indians, these traders possessed a virtual monopoly.[15]

The new Commissioner, E.A. Hayt, moved quickly to remedy these presumed abuses. He accused some Indian traders of illegally selling guns, ammunition, and liquor to the Indians, of cheating them (often with the cooperation of agents) through the use of tokens and tickets in lieu of money, and of charging higher prices to Indians than to whites.[16] During his first year in office, Hayt made many changes in the traderships. He ordered that traders conduct their business in cash only and that Indians and whites pay the same prices for goods.[17] In 1879, he prohibited the granting of credit to Indians, observing, "It is not unusual for Indian traders to give Indians credit to an amount not only sufficient to absorb their whole year's crop, but also to demand, in payment for debt, even the amount left over for seed."[18] On occasion, Hayt ordered traders to modify the prices charged, threatening revocation of the license for non-compliance.[19] Hayt revised Smith's pamphlet of regulations for Indian trade in 1879. Traders were licensed for one year only; their license could be revoked at any time by the Commissioner. No employee of the Indian service could have an interest in a tradership. All employees of the trader were to be approved by the Indian Office. The trader was required to exhibit the original invoices for the goods to be sold to the agent, together with the price, to insure "fair and reasonable" prices.[20]

To reduce the possibility of collusion between agent and trader, as well as to combat the evil of nepotism, Hayt also turned his attention to the agency employees. He instituted a review of subordinate agency position-holders, ordering the dismissal of relatives of agents who were over-paid.[21] At many of the agencies, he appointed the agency clerk, and sometimes the farmer and physician, directly, ordering the agent to dismiss the incumbent.[22] Within a year, Hayt and his chief clerk, William Leeds, had made Washington office appointment of subordinate agency employees an established policy. "This office only has the right to name clerks and other employees, or at its discretion, to accept those nominated by [the] agent," wrote Leeds to Acting Crow Creek Agent William E. Daugherty.[23]

In most cases, agency clerks appointed by the Indian Office had to pay their own transportation to the agency, since the Indian Office had no funds for this expense.[24] At times, as a result, Indian Office appointees performed other services for the Indian Office *en route* to their assignments, such as conducting investigations of other agencies and carrying messages.[25] Exacting such double duty made it possible to secure payment for travel expenses for the appointee.[26] However, such additional duties probably increased the suspicions of their superiors, Indian agents who had been nominated by the churches during the Grant administration. The Quakers regarded the Indian Office appointees as spies;[27] their investigative activities supported such suspicions.

Agents sometimes attempted to remove the Indian Office appointees, claiming that mutual confidence was necessary between the agent and his employees, especially his clerk. In some cases, the appointees themselves seem to have experienced discomfort. Hayt wrote to Arden R. Smith, whom he had appointed clerk at the Kiowa and Commanche Agency, that "confidence and intimacy" between agent and clerk was not required; "each should discharge his duty independently."[28] There was "no question about an agent being at the head of his agency," as Hayt wrote to Pawnee Agent Samuel S. Ely, who objected to an Indian Office-appointed clerk, "but that will not warrant him in the exercise of a hot temper or arbitrary power." The Indian Office had the power to appoint subordinates; the clerk could not be removed.[29]

Other Indian Office appointees seemed unwilling to accept the authority of the agents. T.P. Pendleton, appointed Assistant Farmer at Rosebud Agency, seems to have spent most of his brief stay advising the agent on changes in agency administration.[30] H.L. Henry, appointed Superintendent of Farming at Yankton Agency in April, 1878, was discharged in June with Indian Office permission, for refusing to obey the orders of Agent John W. Douglas.[31] Hayt dismissed the clerk at the Omaha and Winnebago Consolidated Agency after the Quaker Agent, Howard White, complained to Secretary Schurz that he was inattentive to business.[32]

Washington office appointment of agency employees placed a large number of positions at the disposal of the commissioner. Perhaps inevitably, some of these positions became political appointments. Thus, for example, in 1878, Hayt corresponded with Senator J.B. Gordon of Georgia regarding candidates for the position of agency physician and farmer.[33] Appointment from Washington was always unpopular with agents. Hayt's successor, Hiram Price, partially abandoned the policy in the Garfield and Arthur Administrations. Price allowed agents to select their own subordinates, with the exception of the physician.[34]

Early in Price's administration, Dr. M.E. Streiby, Secretary of the American Missionary Association, complained that Indian Office administration was "a little like the British constitution—unwritten. . . . We have one Commissioner who rules one way and another who rules another way."[35] Price's successor, J.D.C. Atkins of Tennessee, returned to the Hayt policies of Washington office control of subordinate agency appointments and a close control of trader licenses. Probably, this assertion of Indian Office control was a consequence of the great demands for office occasioned by the victory of Grover Cleveland, the first Democratic president since James Buchanan. Both the traderships and such subordinate agency positions as clerk and physician were the subject of a busy correspondence between the Indian Office and Capitol Hill.[36] Atkins seems to have interpreted the requirement that traders' licenses be issued for one year as a provision for rotation in office. Citing the one year term of the license, he told Congressman John O'Neil of St. Louis that changes were frequent in the agency traderships.[37] There was "no life tenure" in traders' licenses, he wrote Republican Senator William B. Allison. The Act of 1876 gave the Commissioner "the sole authority to appoint traders." In response to Allison's complaints regarding the appointment of traders from Mississippi and Atkins' home state of Tennessee, Atkins somewhat plaintively replied, "I am convinced there are as good people in those States as in any other states of the Union, and . . . I am unaware they are disqualified to hold any position under the government to which other citizens are eligible."[38]

Inevitably, the return to Indian Office appointment of subordinate employees resulted in conflicts between agents and the Indian Office. Representative J.B. Weaver was asked to tell his protégé, S.S. Patterson, just appointed Navajo Agent, that both the clerk and carpenter at the agency were Democratic appointees and were to be retained in their positions.[39] Atkins instructed Siletz Agent J.B. Lane not to interfere with the agency trader, Mrs. C.G. Chambers, an appointee of the Indian Office.[40] The Commissioner told an Indian Territory trader not to complain about the management of his agency; such complaints were "very annoying." He instructed the trader to "confine yourself to the business for which you are licensed."[41]

The most celebrated conflict arising from the return to agency appointments involved the Pine Ridge agent, Valentine T. McGillycuddy. McGillycuddy refused to accept Henry Clarke, whom Atkins had appointed as Pine Ridge Agency clerk. Clarke had served as clerk at Standing Rock under Agent James McLaughlin, and was "one of the best, if not the best, clerk [sic] in the service," according to Atkins. Despite support from the Indian Rights Association, McGillycuddy was suspended for his "insubordination" in refusing to accept the clerk.[42]

Atkins defended the policy of Indian Office appointment based on "collusion between the Agent and his clerk" at many agencies. Such collusion resulted in widespread "corruption and fraud. . . . By divorcing the Agent and his clerk, and thus not making the clerk feel dependent upon the Agent for appointment and continuance in office, the opportunity for this collusion is materially lessened," wrote the commissioner.[43]

The passage of the Pendleton Act, during the Arthur administration, provided the Indian Office with an additional rationalization for the appointment of agency staff from Washington. The Act created a classified Civil Service, initially confined to a small proportion of the government employees at Washington, and in the larger customs offices and post offices.[44] Positions in the classified service were filled by competitive examination. A Civil Service Commission, appointed by the President, administered the examinations. The duties of the position examined for provided the basis for the examinations, necessitating the writing of job descriptions for the positions included in the classified service.

In announcing the policy of Washington office appointment, Atkins cited the problems of corruption and nepotism; collusion between agents and subordinates "rendered fraud easy and its detection by inspectors, special agents, and this office almost impossible." Consequently, the Indian Office would appoint all clerks, physicians, and additional farmers from Washington. Such a ruling, alone, would have gone no farther than the Hayt policy. However, Atkins also announced that "the plan has been adopted of plainly laying before all applicants for positions a statement of the duties that will be required of them, and of informing them that if they are found, on trial, to be incompetent, they will not be retained." Applicants for physician positions had to show evidence of graduation from "some reputable medical institution," clerks had to file a sample of their writing, and skilled workers had to demonstrate their proficiency to the Indian Office.[45] Prodded by his Indian School Superintendent, John Oberly, who was subsequently appointed to the Civil Service Commission by Cleveland and served briefly as Indian Commissioner in the closing months of the first Cleveland administration, Atkins stated that no removals would be made from the Indian School Service on political grounds. He ordered agents and school superintendents to explain the cause for removal when requesting a change in a school position.[46]

While the extension of Indian Office power over appointments was cloaked in the garb of reform, Indian reform organizations charged that the appointees were the recipients of political spoils. The *Nation* charged that Atkins was too simple-minded and good-natured for his position. "The real Indian Commissioner" was A.B. Upshaw, Atkins' Assistant Commissioner. Upshaw made nearly every appointment in the Indian service, managing Indian affairs, "for the benefit of his party and himself." The *Nation* called for the extension of the civil service rules to the Indian Service.[47] The Indian Rights Association cited the complaint of a military agent that Indian Office control of appointments made the agent a "mere figurehead." The President had the power to extend the Pendleton Act to the Indian Service without further Congressional action, the association noted.[48] The Indian Bureau was "managed in the interest of a party," the National Civil Service Reform League concluded. An extension of the civil service rules was needed.[49]

Despite the objections, Atkins' successor, Thomas J. Morgan, continued Washington office appointment of physicians and school employees, as well as of traders.[50] Agents were allowed to recommend persons to be appointed as agency clerk, although in some cases, the agent was overruled by the Indian Office.[51] At times, Morgan was guided in his personnel actions by the agent's recommendation, although he often supported his appointees to the school service when conflicts with the agent occurred.[52]

In his selections, Morgan was often guided by the recommendations of Republican members of Congress.[53] A Union general in the Civil War and a committed Republican partisan, he defended such political guidance as a means for insuring that appointees would be loyal to his policy. A strong proponent of Indian education, the Commissioner fostered the growth of non denominational, government-controlled schools for the Indians. Morgan and his Superintendent of Indian Schools, Daniel Dorchester, were subject to particularly severe criticism from Catholics for their removals of Catholic school employees.[54]

Reform groups continued to agitate for the extension of civil service rules to positions in the Indian service. In March 1890, Morgan wrote to Herbert Welsh, of the Indian Rights Association, that he had endeavored "to extend the spirit of the civil service rule to all the subordinate places in the Indian service, including physicians, teachers, farmers, etc." However, no further formal extension of the rules seemed practical, because of the limited number of employees at any given location, the wide geographic disperson of the agencies, and the practical difficulties involved in constructing competitive examinations.[55] However, a year later, after President Harrison ordered the extension of civil service coverage to the Indian field service, Morgan suggested classifying physicians and three categories of personnel in the school service, superintendents, teachers, and matrons.[56] President Harrison followed Morgan's suggestion in his executive order of April 13, 1891, which added 626 positions to the classified service.[57] The Civil Service Commission promulgated Indian Rules, covering the qualifications for office and the content of examinations, to take effect on October 1, 1891; their implementation was subsequently postponed until March 1, 1892.[58]

In 1893, Civil Service Commissioner Theodore Roosevelt toured Indian reservations in South Dakota, Nebraska, and Kansas. Several of the agents complained to him about Washington office appointees; Roosevelt suggested instituting non-competitive examinations for such positions as farmer and blacksmith, and for positions held by Indians.[59] In 1894, the Civil Service Commission sought and obtained Presidential approval for instituting non-competitive examinations for Indians nominated for positions in the classified service. The Commission ruled that graduation from an off-reservation Indian school was equivalent to passing the examination.[60]

The 1891 order resulted in the classification of slightly over one-third of the field positions in the Indian Service. By 1892, there were 641 individuals in the classified Indian Service, and, excluding agents, 1,169 individuals in the unclassified service. However, the total salaries of individuals in the classified group exceeded the salaries paid to the unclassified group, $471,340 vs. $444,817. This discrepancy reflected the relatively high pay received by the classified physicians, superintendents, and teachers.[61] This supports Ari Hoogenboom's observation that classification tended to be extended to elite positions first and only later to be extended downward.[62] Virtually all of the Indian School Service was classified by the 1891 order. In 1893, Democratic Indian Commissioner D. M. Browning attempted to have school superintendents removed from the classified service. However, the Indian Rights Association successfully lobbied to prevent this.[63]

Although the classified service dominated the Indian school service, most other employees were unclassified, including all agency personnel except physicians. Clerks were excluded from classification because of their confidential relationship with agents; in Cleveland's second administration, Commissioner D.M. Browning returned the priviledge of appointing clerks to the agents.[64] Only minor changes in the coverage of civil service rules were made between 1891 and 1896. On March 20th of the latter year, however, President Cleveland classified all field employees of the Indian Service, except those requiring Senate confirmation and laborers. Indians, however, normally were exempted from competitive examinations.[65]

The operation of the civil service regulations gave Commissioners of Indian Affairs increased power over subordinate agency employees. Upon the occurrence of a vacancy, the Civil Service Commission provided the appointing officer, the Indian Commissioner, with the names of three eligibles. The Commissioner could appoint one of the three, or request a recertification if he had some objection to any one of the eligibles certified. Further, the Commission had no power over promotions and transfers. In 1894, the Indian Office transferred a physician at Yakima Agency, who had been appointed during the Harrison administration, to Idaho after he refused to contribute to the Democratic campaign.[66] W.A. Jones, McKinley's Commissioner of Indian Affairs, had the Crow Creek Agency physician, Howard L. Dumble, transferred to Standing Rock to

Chart III

Appointing Power and Supervisory Power

1877-1891

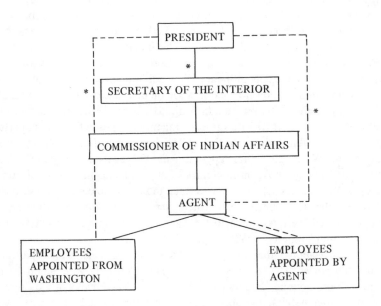

Key: ---- appointment
    * ==== appointment subject to senate confirmation supervision

create a place for Dr. Charles Eastman, who, it was expected, could help the Republicans in the 1900 elections in South Dakota. Since Republican Senator Richard F. Pettigrew, popular with the Indians, had bolted to the Populists, only Eastman, himself a Sioux and a native of Flandreau, South Dakota, could hold the Crow Creek voters in the Republican column.[67]

The shift to appointment of subordinate agency personnel under the civil service system was a significant advance in centralization and organizational maturation. By centralizing the appointment of agency employees, the Indian office became better-bounded and more unified. Washington appointees at the agencies could be expected to be loyal to the Indian Office, rather than to the agent. Agents opposed the attempts of Commissioners Hayt, Atkins, and Morgan to centralize the appointment of their subordinates, because they saw the loss of the appointment power as a limitation on their autonomy. However, after 1877, every Commissioner retained the right to name at least some categories of subordinates. (See Chart III.) Reformers sometimes opposed the policy, particularly during the Atkins administration, when they detected the spoils system as the motive for Washington office appointment. Yet, as the three commissioners pointed out, leaving the Agent in control of appointments made central control more difficult to achieve. Not only was fraud more easy to conceal under the old system, but the development of a career service was difficult when agency employees owed their positions to the agents, who came and went with the changing administrations in Washington.[68]

The organization of the early Civil Service Commission gave the departments considerable power. The commission concerned itself only with appointments, seldom with promotions, demotions, or transfers.[69] The powers of the Commissioner of Indian Affairs, the appointing officer for the Indian Service, were actually increased by the extension of the classification to the Indian field service, especially as the reservation school superintendents replaced the agents as chief local administrator after 1892. (See Chart IV.) Significantly, when practical farmers and stockmen were removed from the classified service in 1901, the Commissioner, W. A. Jones, kept the power of appointment to these positions in the Washington office. While expressing a preference for appointing local men "who were conversant and familiar with the local conditions," Jones used some of the positions to reward Republican politicians in his home state of Wisconsin and elsewhere.[70]

The extension of the civil service classification increased the formalization of the organization, by requiring that job descriptions and minimum entrance requirements be established for the positions. Most significantly for the institutionalization of the organization, the new system of appointment made possible the development of a career service, protected by the civil service laws and committed to an organizational career. Hoogenboom refers to the develop-

CHART IV

Appointing Power and Supervisory Power

1891-1905

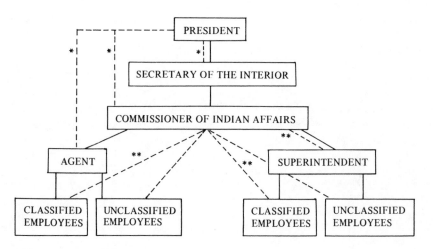

Key: ----appointment
     * ----appointment subject to Senate confirmation
     ** === appointment from list of three eligibles certified
          by USCSC supervision

ment of this commitment as the "professionalization" of the civil service. Its consequences were to increase the morale of employees, to increase their social status, and, perhaps to decrease the "missionary spirit" of Indian workers in favor of an "organizational spirit," a committment to the Indian Bureau as an organization which would have been inconceivable thirty years earlier.[71]

CHAPTER V

THE BOARD OF INDIAN COMMISSIONERS

Changes in the procedures for selecting Indian agents and their subordinates between 1865 and 1900 resulted in a better-bounded organization. Employees appointed by the Washington office, who could expect to spend a career in the Indian Service, would be more likely to share a commitment to the organizational mission and to respond to changes in goals and procedures. Thus, the changes in the personnel system enhanced the ability of the Washington office to control events in the field.

Control was important in determining institutionalization because it made possible the coordination of the activities of the members of the organization. Arnold S. Tannenbaum hypothesized that amount of control in an organization determines its effectiveness in achieving its goals.[1] The most salient elements of the control system of the Indian Office during the period included which officials had the power to impose sanctions on organizational members, the communications structure of the organization, and the location of the control system, particularly whether control was internal or external to the organization.[2]

During the period between the end of the Civil War and 1900, the control system of the Indian Office changed. Congress and the Grant administration created an external control mechanism, which proved to be ineffective. Subsequently, the nature and role of the "men in the middle," the officials who mediated between the Washington Office and the field units of the organization, changed. The new middle-level officials, the Indian Inspectors, provided the organization with its major control device for the last quarter of the nineteenth century. Loyal to the central organization and committed to its objectives, the inspectors provided the Indian Office with a predictable and reliable system of control. Before the creation of the inspection system, however, the Board of Indian Commissioners represented an attempt to control the organization from outside of its formal boundaries.[3]

Indian affairs, like many other governmental activities, were in a particularly chaotic state after the Civil War. During his presidency, Andrew Johnson had four commissioners of Indian affairs, including Lincoln's Commissioner, William Dole, who served for a time after the assassination. Both Congress and the President (and the Interior and War Departments) were preoccupied with the struggles of reconstruction. At the same time, beginning a few years before the end of the Civil War and continuing into the late 1860s, there was an unusual amount of warfare on the Great Plains, as the Indians observed the departure of soldiers to fight in the South and as the emigration of Whites into the West increased after the close of the Civil War. The direction and control of Indian Affairs was a major problem. Yet reform efforts were not directed at the administration of the Indian Office, generally viewed as a corrupt, patronage-ridden machine. A series of Congressional committees and special commissions, in effect, made Indian policy; if the commissions could not affect administration, the Indian Office could be circumvented by delegating activities of the Indian Office to the Army.

In the last days of the Civil War, Congress created a joint special committee to visit the West and report on the condition of the Indian tribes.[4] Headed by Senator James Doolittle of Wisconsin, the Committee made its report in 1867. Indians were decreasing in number, the committee found, and Indian Wars were usually due to the aggressions of lawless White men. The decline in Indian population and strength was the result of the wars and the loss of hunting grounds. On the question of transfer of the Indian Bureau to the Department of War, the Committee members could see arguments on both sides. "Many agents, teachers, and employees of the government are inefficient, faithless, and even guilty of peculations and fraudulent practices upon the government and upon the Indians," the committee found. However, the committee favored the retention of the Bureau in the Department of the Interior because the Indian question was seen as primarily a public land question, thus falling within the jurisdiction of the Interior Department. The high cost of Indian wars fought by the Army, combined with the prevailing sentiment against a large standing Army, also contributed to the committee's recommendation against transfer. Further, the conflict between the Department of the Interior and the Department of War over Indian affairs was beneficial. "To some extent, they serve as a check upon each other," the committee reported; "neither are slow to point to the mistakes and abuses of the other." The evils of Indian affairs were not so much to be found in the system of Indian administration, the committee concluded, as in the abuse of the system. They recommended the creation of five inspection districts, each with a board of inspection, to consist of one assistant commissioner of Indian Affairs, one Army officer, and one visitor, nominated by the religious societies of the United States. The duties of a Board of Inspection would be to visit each tribe within its district at least once a year, to "preserve peace and amity," to examine the accounts and conduct of the officials in both the Indian Bureau and the military, and to suspend and remove any Indian Office employee found guilty of fraud or mismanagement.[5]

Despite the Doolittle Committee's conclusions, events in 1866, particularly the attack on Fort Phil Kearney and the Fetterman Massacre, convinced some that more fundamental reform was in order. Early in 1867, President Johnson appointed a special commission to inquire into the reasons for the outbreak at

Fort Phil Kearney. The commission was to negotiate with the Indians and to make recommendations which would secure a lasting peace on the frontier. The commission consisted of Generals Alfred Sully, J.B. Sanborn, and N.B. Buford, Colonel Eli S. Parker, and two private citizens, Judge J.F. Kinney and Mr. G.P. Beauvais. The commissioners recommended the concentration of the Indians into a small number of large reservations, a withdrawal of the Army from the Indian country defined by that concentration, and the development of a system of laws and government for the Indians. General Sanborn further recommended that the Indian Bureau be made a separate department of the government.[6]

Colonel Parker, a Seneca Indian and General Grant's aide-de-camp, had previously made his recommendation for "the establishment of a permanent and perpetual peace" between the United States and the Indian tribes. Parker favored the transfer of the Indian Office to the War Department. He advocated the prohibition of private trade with the Indians in favor of a return to government-run trading houses. Early in the nineteenth century, the government operated a number of such trading houses, or "factories," to control Indian trade and to insure fair dealing with the Indians. The system of government-licensed Indian traders which replaced the "factory system" was corrupt and unfair to the Indians, Parker contended. Like the other commissioners, Parker favored concentration, and the creation of a territorial government for the Indians. He recommended the creation of an inspection board, or commission, to serve until a transfer of the Indian Office to the War Department had been effected. The commission would

> Examine the accounts of the several agencies, see that every cent due the Indians is paid to them promptly as may be promised in treaties, and the proper and suitable goods and implements for agriculture are delivered to them when such articles are due, [and would] make semi-annual reports, with such suggestions as in their judgment, might seem necessary to the perfect establishment of permanent and friendly feeling between the peoples of the United States and the Indians.

An additional Indian Commission composed of Whites and educated Indians would visit all of the Indian Tribes, make peace, and promote consolidation and civilization.[7] Parker's proposals revealed his distrust of the Indian office, not unusual for a military man. The proposals of Parker and the other Commissioners for inspection boards revealed a widespread lack of trust in the Indian Office.

Unlike the military men, officials of the Indian Office tended to blame problems in Indian administration on the interference of the Army. Commissioner of Indian Affairs Nathaniel Taylor proposed early in 1867 that treaties be made with the warlike Plains tribes, that Congress appropriate funds for the making of such treaties, and, finally, "that all military operations within the Indian country be subject to the direction and control of the Indian Department."[8] Thus, Taylor's proposals revealed the bureaucratic rivalry noted by the

Doolittle Committee in its report, based on the conflicting claims of the Interior and War Departments for dominance in Indian affairs.[9]

Both the Army and the Indian Office agreed on the desirability of consolidating the Indian Tribes. Consolidation, from the military point of view, made the control of the potentially warlike Indians easier. For the civilian administrators, it both removed the Indians from the path of White settlement and concentrated them in a place where efforts directed toward their civilization could be focused.

In response to Taylor's suggestion, Congress created an Indian Peace Commission in July of 1867.[10] The commission was to inquire into and, if possible, remove the causes of Indian wars, to negotiate treaties with the warring tribes, and to propose a plan for the civilization of the Indians. Congress emphasized the objectives of consolidation and pacification in creating the Commission. President Johnson appointed Taylor president of the Commission. In addition to the Commissioner, the Peace Commission included three Army generals and two private citizens. In its first report to the President, the Commission recommended a revision in the Indian Intercourse Laws. If the objective of Indian policy was to be "to civilize the Indians," the Office of Indian Affairs should not be transferred to the War Department. Because of widespread corruption in the Bureau, the Commission recommended that, by February of 1869, "the offices of all superintendents, agents, and special agents" should be vacated. "Such persons as have proved themselves competent and faithful may be reappointed. Those who have proved unfit will find themselves removed without an opportunity to divert attention from their own unworthiness by professions of party zeal." The commission also suggested that the Office of Indian Affairs be made an independent department, responsible directly to the President. The Commission recommended a regular system for the inspection of Indian agencies and either the continuation of the Commission or the appointment of a new one to continue to negotiate with the Indians.[11]

The Commission spent most of the fall and early winter of 1867 traveling on the Great Plains. It negotiated treaties with the Kiowa-Apaches, Cheyennes, and Arapahoes at Medicine Lodge and with the Sioux and other northern plains tribes at Fort Laramie.[12] The treaties "embodied the principles of the concentration policy."[13] They specified reservations and off-reservation hunting grounds and provided for schools, assistance in farming, and subsistence for a fixed period of years.

Delays in obtaining Congressional approval of the treaties, combined with disputes between civilian and military administrators over the distribution of fire arms for hunting, led to further outbreaks in the southern plains during the summer of 1868. In October, the Commission, reacting to the fighting on the southern plains, called for immediate provisions to feed and protect the Indians who had been party to the Medicine Lodge and Fort Laramie treaties. The government's failure to provide the provisions promised in the treaties had occasioned the outbreak, the commissioners concluded. The treaties should be considered to be in force, the Commission argued, whether approved by the Senate or not. However, the Commission suggested that Indian tribes should no longer be recognized as "domestic dependent nations." Indians should be "individually subject to the laws of the United States," implying an end to the treaty relation. (Congress ended the treaty relationship with the tribes three years later, in 1871, as a result of a conflict between the House and the Senate over an Indian appropriations bill.)[14] Because of the outbreaks on the southern plains, the Commission recommended abrogating the provisions of the Medicine Lodge treaty which permitted the Indians to hunt off the reservation. Military force should be used to compel Indians to go to reservations after provisions to feed and protect them had been made. Finally, the Commission now recommended the transfer of the Bureau of Indian Affairs to the Department of War.[15]

Only Samuel F. Tappan, a civilian member of the Peace Commission, opposed transfer. He wrote to Taylor blaming the outbreaks explicitly on the failure of Congress to make appropriations to fulfill the treaties made by the Peace Commission. He recommended concentration and "justice, protection, and good faith," toward the Indians. To bolster his argument, Tappan enclosed a communication from E.W. Wynkoop, the Cheyenne and Arapahoe agent, suggesting that the war would have been prevented had the government furnished supplies to the Indians.[16]

A bill providing subsistence for the tribes that signed the treaties of Medicine Lodge and Fort Laramie had been passed in July. Congress, sharing the widespread suspicion of the Indian Office, specified that the funds appropriated for these tribes were to be spent under the direction of General William T. Sherman, Commander of the Military Division of the Missouri.[17] Sherman created two new military districts to implement the law.[18] Transferring the distribution of funds to the Army left the civilian agents on the Great Plains essentially without a function, since Congress had placed Indian affairs under the direct control of the military. Sherman had sought such authority in a letter to General Grant on May 8, in which he recommended making the Army responsible for the subsistence of the tribes until the Indian Bureau had made provisions for them.[19]

During the immediate post-war period, then, reformers, military men, and politicians doubted the capacity of the Indian Office to discharge its duties honestly and efficiently. The Army, of course, was motivated in part by its organizational rivalry with the Indian Office, but the policy innovations of 1867-68 reflected more widespread suspicion. The creation of commissions to make peace with the Indians and to plan future Indian policy, the delegation of Indian Office responsibilities to the Army, and the proposals for removal of the Indian Office from the Department of the Interior, through transfer to the

Department of War or through the creation of an independent agency, all implied a lack of confidence in the existing organization's ability to deal with Indian affairs.

Even if the employees of the Indian Office had been honest and efficient, the Washington office faced grave problems in achieving concerted action. Indian Agents were political appointees, as were the Superintendents, many of them territorial governors, who directed their work. As such they owed their primary allegiance to the political system, not to the organization itself, and had some freedom in carrying out directives from Washington. Further, the reservations and superintendencies were scattered. Geographic dispersion resulted in formidable communication problems. The strategy proposed for improving Indian administration in the late 1860s was to bypass the Indian Office, either through transfer to the War Department or through the imposition of a regulatory inspection body to oversee Indian Office operations. In the short run, Congress delegated Indian Office functions to an outside organization, the Army. At the beginning of the Grant Administration in 1869, Congress created a regulatory inspection body, the Board of Indian Commissioners.

In his history of post-Civil War Indian policy, Loring Benson Priest argued that the purposes of the Board of Indian Commissioners were to study Indian problems and recommend improvements, to stimulate popular interest in the Indian, and to promote closer cooperation between Indian administrators and the public.[20] A study of the legislative history of the creation of the Board, however, suggests a different conclusion. The Indian Appropriations Act of 1869 included an appropriation of $2,000,000 to "maintain peace and promote civilization among the Indians." It was not usual for such a large amount of money to be appropriated for such a general object. The President was authorized "to organize a Board of Commissioners . . . who may, under his direction exercise joint control with the Secretary of the Interior over the disbursement" of the funds. A separate appropriation of $25,000 was made for the Commissioners' travel and subsistence and for the pay of a clerk.[21] The original wording of the bill gave the board the power to "supervise and control the disbursements" and the power to suspend agents, superintendents, and traders, and to appoint replacements, under the President's direction.[22] The section had been introduced by Senator James Harlan of Iowa; William Pitt Fessenden of Maine offered an amendment, which the Senate accepted, substituting the words "joint control" for "supervise and control" and removing the power to suspend officials. Fessenden commented, "As this is an experiment, we had better let them try it at first and any powers that may be found necessary afterward, if the experiment proves successful, may be conferred hereafter."[23] Thus, the initial wording of the section gave to the Board powers similar to those which had been held by the Army in the disbursement of the 1868 appropriation, in addition to supervisory powers over field employees of the Indian Office. Despite the weakening of the Board's powers provided by the Fessenden amendment, some questioned the effect of the measure. Senator John Thayer of Nebraska asked, "Does that mean the Indian Office cannot exercise control unless this commission shall cooperate . . . ?" Fessenden replied that the Board would be under the direction of the President and he expected "the President will order probably under the advice of the Interior Department."[24] The bill, including the Fessenden amendment, became law on April 10, 1869.

The words "joint control" were to create problems for the new Board. Its first President, William Welsh, resigned within a month after his appointment because the Board was refused full supervision over accounts. However, some of the other commissioners did not view the Board's powers as broadly as Welsh did. Board member Nathan Bishop wrote to Secretary of the Interior J.D. Cox a few days after Welsh's resignation, "that our commission had *no powers* at all conferred upon it by the Act—that we could exercise joint control *only after* the President had directed us to do so, and that the Secretary ought not to allow any commission to become a coordinate power with him as such a *double-headed power* would soon lead the department into confusion."[25] Cox assured the Board that its powers would be adjusted to meet its needs. He regretted Welsh's resignation. The Board of Indian Commissioners was to counsel and advise the Interior Department, "upon personal investigation of the condition of the Indians, what improvements and changes in our system of dealing with them would better promote their civilization." Welsh had overlooked the problem of a "double-headed organization from which nothing but confusion could come" and the criticism when the board was first proposed that it would become a new "ring."[26] Therefore, Cox thought it best that the Board's role be advisory at first:

> While great regard for their advice would give them such weight in the direction of affairs as would be made by a practical control, [the members of the Board] would be freer and easier without the responsibility for the actual disbursements of the public funds with all the contingencies of hostile criticism involved.[27]

The first members of the Board of Indian Commissioners, with some justification, regarded themselves as superior to the Commissioner of Indian Affairs.[28] The Board was the heir of the administrative makeshifts of the Johnson administration, which were designed to bypass the Indian Office. It combined, in the original language of the Appropriations Bill, the policy-making powers of the Indian Peace Commission with the disbursing powers delegated to General Sherman in 1868. In addition, the Board had broader powers to inspect agencies and to remove field officials and appoint temporary replacements than either the Peace Commission or the Army had had. The language of the section, as proposed by Senator Harlan, would have, in effect, made the Indian Office an independent agency, run by an unpaid Board under the direction of the President. However, the potential powers of the Board were reduced by the Fessenden amendment and by the interpretation of the act by the Secretary of the Interior.

Welsh's interpretation of broad powers was not justified by the language of the act; other Board members took a much more limited view of the powers of the Board. Congress gave it supervision over expenditures, but not over field officials.

The 1870 Indian Appropriations Act provided "it shall be the duty of said commissioners to supervise all expenditures of money appropriated for the benefit of Indians in the United States, and to inspect all goods purchased for said Indians in connection with the Commissioner of Indian Affairs, whose duty it shall be to consult said commission in making purchases of said goods."[29] However, the continued failure of Congress to provide the Board with control over field officials frustrated efforts to improve administration. The Board complained that it could accomplish little while the government failed to be bound by its pledges to the Indians. Such complaints continued throughout the 1870s.

In 1871, Congress gave the Board the power to examine the Indian Office's vouchers and accounts. The Indian Appropriations Act provided that "no payments shall be made to contractors . . . beyond 50% of the amount due until the accounts and vouchers shall have been submitted to the executive committee [of the Board] . . . for examination, revisal, and approval." However, the Secretary of the Interior had "the power to sustain, set aside, or modify the action of said board."[30] The Board's power to examine and approve vouchers was extraordinary; some Congressmen viewed it as a censure of the Interior Department.[31] However, the power of the Secretary of the Interior to set aside the Board's decision rendered its power of little effect. In 1872, Congress decided that payments could be made to contractors without the Board's approval.[32] This limitation on the Board's authority further weakened its power. In 1873, the Indian Office withheld payment on accounts amounting to only two per cent of the total value of the accounts to which the Board objected.[33] Despite its lack of power, the Board continued to examine Indian Office accounts until 1881.[34]

A decline in the Board's ability to influence Indian administration mirrored the erosion of the Board's statutory powers in the early 1870s. In 1871, the Board forced the Commissioner of Indian Affairs, Eli S. Parker, to resign. Parker had approved bids from the Erie Railroad and the Northwestern Transportation Company for transporting annuity goods to the West. The Board rejected these contracts in favor of lower bids, but Parker, supported by the Secretary of Interior, overruled the Board.[35] The Commissioner, already under criticism from William Welsh for alleged administrative laxity, resigned in July, although a House committee cleared him of any wrongdoing.[36] Grant appointed Francis A. Walker, director of the 1870 census, to the Commissioner position. Despite this seeming victory, Interior Secretary Columbus Delano forced the resignation of Board Secretary Vincent Collyer early in 1872. Collyer was a frequent critic of the Secretary of the Interior.[37]

In 1873, the Board conducted an investigation of Agents John J. Saville and Edwin A. Howard of the Red Cloud and Spotted Tail Agencies in Dakota Territory, whom Professor O.C. Marsh, a geologist, had accused of providing goods of bad quality to the Indians at their reservations. The Board's investigator confirmed the Yale professor's charges.[38] However, a subsequent Indian Office investigation, widely suspected to be a "whitewash," cleared the two agents of the charges.[39] In May, 1874, the six remaining original members of the Board resigned. The commissioners did not make a public announcement of the reasons for their resignation, but some speculated that the resignations were the result of the alleged "whitewash" of the Saville investigation. In their letter of resignation, the members cited the progress made under the Board of Indian Commissioners. They wrote,

> It is not claimed that honesty and right dealing have been secured through all the ramifications of the Indian Service, but many corrupt practices have been corrected and enough has been accomplished and demonstrated that with proper organization it is possible to secure at least as great a degree of honesty in Indian Affairs as in any other department of the government.

The Board members regretted that the Secretary of the Interior had not recommended legislation to make the Indian Office an independent department, which they argued was crucial for the perfection and perpetuation of President Grant's Indian policy. They objected to a bill in the House of Representatives which would require the Board to perform all duties mandated by law in the City of Washington. Previously, the Board had instituted the practice of conducting bidding for Indian supplies in New York City. Concluding with the observation that the independence of the Board was essential, the commissioners resigned.[40] According to the biographers of two of the members, they did so primarily because of the President's failure to make decisions of the Board of Indian Commissioners binding upon the Department of the Interior.[41]

The resignations had a momentary effect on the Board's powers. A month after the six resigned, Congress approved the Deficiency Act, providing that "none of the monies hereby appropriated for the payment of deficiencies in the Indian Service shall be paid until the necessity for the expenditures shall have been examined into by the Secretary of the Interior and any existing Board of Peace Commissioners."[42] The Act materially expanded the powers of the Board for that one appropriation. However, the Indian Appropriations Act, approved the same day as the Deficiency Act, did not change the powers of the Board with regard to the Indian Office's regular appropriations.[43]

Following the resignations, Grant appointed six new members to the Board, including Clinton B. Fisk of St. Louis, who became Chairman. Fisk, a noted philanthropist and founder of Fisk University, was the Secretary-Treasurer of the railroad running through the Indian Territory.[44] Grant invited the denominations participating in his religious appointment policy to nominate candidates for the Board. B. Rush Roberts of the Friends recommended Samuel M. Janney, who had been the Quaker Northern Superintendent. Janney was not appointed; Grant named Roberts himself to the Board. Other appointees included Ezra M. Kingsley, nominated by the Presbyterians, and E.A. Hayt, nominated by the Reformed Church.[45]

Loring Benson Priest concluded that compliant men were appointed to the Board after the resignations of 1874.[46] However, some of the appointees, in particular Hayt, would give the officials of the Interior Department a great deal of difficulty during the remainder of the Grant administration. A year after the resignations of May 1874, Secretary Delano asked the Board to appoint a commission to investigate Marsh's charges again.[47] This commission recommended the removal of Agent Saville and the referral of the Red Cloud agency accounts to the Department of Justice.[48]

Throughout the Grant administration, the appropriation for the Board was relatively substantial, generally around $15,000 a year. This enabled members of the Board to travel, to inspect agencies, and to meet with Indian groups. On occasion, Washington officials asked Board members to investigate questions on which the Indian Office needed to make a decision. For example, in 1874, Commissioner E.P. Smith asked F.H. Smith, a member of the Board, to investigate the possibility of allotting lands to the Indians in Washington Territory.[49]

In 1876 and 1877, the Board's purchasing committee, headed by E.A. Hayt, sent agents to the Indian Territory to investigate the distribution of annuity goods to Indians in the Central Superintendency. The Board's agents clashed with the Quaker agents and Central Superintendent William Nicholson. In May, 1876, Commissioner J.Q. Smith wrote to Hayt that his agent, W.R. Barnum, had been accused of "selling, or attempting to sell, to the Indian traders *bogus jewelry* which by them was to be sold to the Indians." Smith suggested that Barnum was "a very improper person to act as the confidential agent of the Board of Indian Commissioners."[50]

Hayt and Smith also clashed over the Indian Office's decision to accept bids for Indian supplies at St. Louis. Perhaps influenced by Board Chairman Clinton Fisk, a resident of St. Louis, the Indian Office began accepting bids there as well as at New York. Hayt, a New Yorker, objected, but the bids were received anyway and St. Louis accounted for a substantial percentage of the contracts awarded in 1876.[51] Commissioner Smith attempted to circumvent Hayt's influence by having other members of the Board go to St. Louis to observe the lettings. Smith wrote to Commissioner A.C. Barstow that he wanted Barstow to go to St. Louis to observe the lettings. Hayt was to go, wrote Smith,

But you know he was very much opposed to the arrangements and it may be that he will be a little too much disposed to find fault. In all events it would be most agreeable to me to have you and one other member of your Board at least joined with Mr. Hayt as advisors. I say to you in strict confidence that I think Mr. H. is a little too much disposed to be dictatorial. I fully appreciate the fact that he knows many things which I do not, and I believe him to be a perfectly honest man, very desirous of giving me his best aid, and in many respects that aid must be valuable. But as, after all, I am the man who must necessarily be held responsible, I would rather not yield any clear opinion I may have on any subject within my proper provence to Mr. Hayt's opinion alone. . . . I am still confident that it is wise to try St. Louis. We are almost sure to get a better class of bidders than we ever had before. I am not sure whether the plan of having the contracts and the bonds filed with the bids will work well or not, but hope it will. We have spent a great deal of time and labor in trying to get everything in good shape for the lettings and trust we have done it with reasonable correctness.[52]

By late summer, Hayt's agent in the Indian Territory reported that the government was issuing poor quality flour to the Indians. The Quaker agents were interfering with his attempts to inspect the flour. Commissioner Smith preferred to trust inspection to the agents in the Indian Territory but in September he wrote to Hayt that he had no objection to "the most rigid scrutiny of the matter." Hayt could send "reliable men on a tour of inspection" if he wished. However, Smith objected strenuously to the presence of Barnum in the Indian Territory.[53] A month later, Barnum was in New York. He had similar difficulties with William J. Morris, an Indian Office Clerk sent to New York to supervise the annual letting of contracts.[54] To Morris, Smith wrote, "What *is* the matter with Mr. Hayt? . . . I am afraid every letter I get from him that he is going to pitch in."[55] A few days later Smith wrote, "If Mr. Hayt does *pitch into you*, he will find there are blows to take as well as blows to give." He promised Morris his support should any disagreement develop.[56]

In the Fall of 1876, Hayt kept Barnum in New York, but sent his confidential clerk, William Leeds, on a tour of inspection of the Central Superintendency. Like Barnum, Leeds complained that the Indians were receiving bad flour and the agents were blocking his attempts to inspect it. Commissioner Smith advised Hayt that he hesitated to overrule Central Superintendent William Nicholson in the matter of inspections. "I do not know what reason Dr. Nicholson had for advising the agent not to permit Mr. Leeds to examine invoices and quantities of annuities," wrote Smith, "and before I interfere I think I ought to hear from Dr. Nicholson the reasons for his advice. Dr. Nicholson is a man of superior judgment and always has a strong, if not sufficient, reason for what he does. . . . Evidently the prudent thing to do is to wait until I hear from the Superintendent before I give any directions to the agents."[57]

During the winter of 1876-77, S.A. Galpin, the Chief Clerk of the Indian Office, also made a tour of inspection of the Central Superintendency agencies. Leeds charged that Galpin was a member of an "Indian ring" and part of a plot, which involved Zachariah Chandler, the Secretary of the Interior, and the Quaker agents, to bring the Bureau under his control. Galpin conveyed these charges to the Commissioner, asking for a "full and searching inquiry" of Leeds. He accused Leeds of making serious charges against the Commissioner, the Secretary of the Interior, and against Galpin himself. Specifically, Galpin said Leeds charged that goods purchased in New York City after inspection were shipped by Indian Office clerks and might have been changed by them after inspection. Further, Leeds charged that Galpin might arrange for goods at the Sac and Fox Agency to be issued to Indians before Leeds could reach the agency to inspect them. Galpin said Leeds also charged that the Commissioner and Galpin were both anxious to avoid the disclosure of frauds. Leeds had characterized the Secretary of the Interior as a "trickster," a dishonest man, but influential with the President because of his position as Chairman of the National Republican Committee.[58]

William Stickney, the Secretary of the Board of Indian Commissioners, learned of Galpin's letter and wrote to Hayt urging him to come to Washington to answer the charges. "I think it well for you to come on," Stickney wrote, "that any differences may, if possible, be harmonized and the *entente cordiale* be restored."[59] Hayt replied that it was impossible for him to get away from New York, but telegraphed Stickney that "no statements as alleged have been authorized by me or known to myself."[60] On January 12, 1877, Hayt wrote to the Secretary of the Interior, Zachariah Chandler, denying that he bore Chandler any animosity or that he had expressed any such animosity to Leeds. On the contrary, wrote Hayt, he had expressed to Leeds his conviction that Chandler wanted to root out corruption in the Indian Office. He attacked Galpin, saying that his letters from Kansas seemed designed "to forestall the effect of any statement Mr. Leeds may have to make on his return in regard to matters in the territory."[61] On the same day, Chandler requested Hayt's resignation.[62]

Hayt resigned a week later, writing that Leeds' purported statements had been attributed to him unjustly. About a fourth of the flour, Hayt said, which had been delivered to agencies had been rejected by the Board's New York inspector, "the highest authority in the Corn Exchange in the City," as below the grade called for in the contract. In the Indian Territory, the Quaker agents had interfered with Leeds' investigation. He had been barred from making the kinds of inspections necessary to insure that the supplies issued to the Indians were of good quality. Hayt recalled Professor Marsh's earlier complaints regarding the bad quality of supplies received at Red Cloud Agency and suggested that only through thoroughgoing inspections by the Board of Indian Commissioners could the Indian Office be free of such charges.[63] John Ferris, the corresponding Secretary of the Reformed Church Board of Foreign Missions, wrote a strong letter to Secretary Chandler requesting the reasons "Why Mr. Hayt was requested to resign." Ferris suggested that the Reformed Church's future cooperation with the government would depend upon Chandler's answer.[64]

Despite Hayt's resignation, Leeds' allegations created problems for the Indian Office. Leeds charged that Commissioner Smith had encouraged agents in the Indian Territory to accept inferior beef for issue to the Indians in addition to the inferior flour which had been distributed. In reply to inquiries from the Board, Smith wrote to E.M. Kingsley that the beef and flour were adequate, that

Leeds failed to check his facts or consider extenuating circumstances and that Galpin's objections to Leeds did not result from any

> known hostility, [but from] Mr. Leeds' course as a government official. Such feeling as he has had in regard to Mr. Leeds, was induced by Mr. Leeds' large assumption of authority and by the belief apparently expressed by Mr. Leeds in all his acts that none of the executive officers of this Bureau were either honest or capable. So far as Mr. Leeds acted as a public officer, Mr. Galpin thinks that his acts were fairly subject to criticism. He can expect nothing more than to be judged by his official acts.[65]

However, some of the clerks in the Indian Office echoed Leeds' charges. In February, Smith wrote to three chiefs of divisions of the Indian Office inquiring whether they had charged that Galpin was in complicity with the "Indian Ring."[66] Smith dismissed one of the three, Dr. Josiah Curtis, Chief of the Medical Division. He subsequently attempted to have another, E.L. Stevens, Chief of the Land Division, replaced by his predecessor, C.C. Royce.[67]

When President Hayes entered office in March 1877, he appointed Carl Schurz, a liberal Republican and civil service reformer, Secretary of the Interior. At first, Schurz moved cautiously in regard to Indian Affairs. Soon after Hayes' inauguration, he asked Commissioner Smith to describe the operation of the Indian Office and to make recommendations for increasing its efficiency. In his reply, Smith emphasized the complexity of the work of the Indian Office and the need to maintain the size of the clerical staff. The work of the office was in arrears, in large part, Smith implied, because of the requirement that the Secretary's Office approve purchases in advance and because of the practice of submitting vouchers to the Board of Indian Commissioners prior to payment. Submitting vouchers to the Board was not required by law, Smith pointed out; further, Schurz could overrule any Board decisions. Smith suggested that the Board should be required to occupy a room in the Indian Office.[68] In May, Schurz sent his chief clerk, Alonzo Bell, to New York to observe the opening of bids for the Indian supplies. In addition, Bell reported to the Secretary on the members of the Board of Indian Commissioners. The Board members were "active and reliable businessmen," Bell reported. "All the members are good men."[69] E.M. Kingsley had succeeded Hayt as chairman of the Purchasing Committee. Smith corresponded with him in the spring regarding the inspection of goods.[70]

In his report to Schurz, Smith denied any wrong-doing in the Indian Office. "I know of no custom in the Bureau which can properly be termed an abuse," he wrote, "unless perhaps, the disposition manifested on the part of some of the clerks to enlarge the customary leave of absence given by the Department should be so construed."[71] However, allegations against Galpin persisted. In June, Schurz organized a Board of Inquiry, composed of three officials from the Interior, Justice, and War Departments, to investigate the charges against the Chief Clerk.[72] The scope of the Board's investigation soon expanded from the specific charges against Galpin to the methods of record-keeping and administrative control employed in the Indian Office. The Board met in secret, at Schurz's direction.[73] Inevitably, rumors about the findings of the Board spread. Commissioner Smith demanded to know whether the Board's investigation would be "one in which my character as an officer may become involved."[74] Francis A. Walker, who had first brought Galpin into the Indian Office, and former Interior Secretary J.D. Cox, both political allies of Schurz, objected to the manner in which the investigation was conducted. They charged that it was controlled by Schurz's chief clerk, a member of the Board, and that damaging information regarding Galpin was being leaked to the press. The investigation should be either truly secret, they argued, or public, giving Galpin an opportunity to face his accusers.[75]

By September, Smith's position was untenable. Schurz offered the Commissionership to E.A. Hayt, Smith's nemesis. Hayt asked to name his own chief clerk. "You are aware that . . . Galpin would so hamper a Commissioner that failure would assuredly result."[76] Hayt selected William M. Leeds for the chief clerk's position.

The report of the Board of Inquiry, published early in 1878, failed to implicate Galpin in any corrupt practices. However, the Board described an administrative chaos apparently engineered by the chief clerk. Letters to the Commissioner alleging corruption at Indian agencies were lost, official business was transacted by means of informal correspondence which did not become a part of the Indian Office files, and a lack of routine in the handling of official correspondence enabled Galpin to dominate the functioning of the office. The Board could find few published regulations and, other than a handwritten copy of regulations delegating great authority to the Central Superintendent, these were mostly outdated. A general animosity to the Board of Indian Commissioners prevailed. Galpin, Smith, and a few others, the board found, had formed a closed group which ran the Indian Office for its own ends.[77] In testimony before the board, Galpin had been belligerent and evasive. The Chief Clerk's removal resulted principally from his own testimony, *Harper's Weekly* concluded.[78]

The Galpin affair resulted in a more significant role for the Board of Indian Commissioners during the Hayes administration. With the former Chairman of the Board's Purchasing Committee as Commissioner of Indian Affairs, the Board took an active role in the annual opening of bids for Indian Service supplies. The Purchasing Committee employed a full-time clerk in the Indian Office's New York Warehouse. Board members examined all bids for furnishing supplies and annuity goods to the Indian Service.[79] Soon after Hayt became Commissioner, the Board again investigated the Central Superintendency, this time with official support.[80] Subsequently, President Hayes abolished the superintendency.[81]

Despite the Board's expanded influence during the Hayes administration, political problems remained. In the House-Senate Conference Committee on the

Indian Appropriations Act of 1880, the House conferees insisted that none of the money appropriated in the Act could be paid to or used by the Board of Indian Commissioners.[82] The House had attempted to abolish the Board, but the Senate conferees were successful in limiting the action to the removal of appropriations. In the Civil Bill, approved a month later, the Senate was able to secure an appropriation of $10,000 for the Board.[83] However, this was less than the $15,000 annual appropriation the Board had enjoyed during the 1870s and the appropriation was further reduced in 1882. For the first time, in that year, the Indian Appropriations Act specified how the Board's $4,700 appropriation was to be spent.[84] In 1883, Congress further reduced the appropriation to $2,000.[85] During the rest of the 1880s and '90s, the appropriation was usually $3,000 a year, permitting only very limited travel on the part of the Commissioners. The Board could now have only a very reduced impact on day-to-day administration. After 1880, the Board's impact on the Indian policy and administration became very different from what it had been.[86]

Since 1872, the Board had sponsored an annual conference with the representatives of the Mission Societies involved in Indian work. These conferences continued and provided an important opportunity for missionaries and Washington officials to get together. In addition, beginning in 1883, Board member Albert K. Smiley sponsored meetings of "Friends of the Indian" at his summer home at Lake Mohonk, New York.[87] The Mohonk conferences provided an important opportunity for Indian workers, including Board members, government officials, and missionaries, to get together and discuss questions of Indian Policy. The Mohonk Conference proceedings were printed in the Board's *Annual Reports*.

Initially designed to provide an external administrative check on the activities of the Indian Office, the Board of Indian Commissioners was never able to perform this function effectively. Nor did it ever become an integral part of the organization. Members of the Board continued to attempt to influence administration through the 1880s. Despite a few successes, not even when a former Board member became Commissioner of Indian Affairs did the powers of the Board materially change. Whether appointed by Grant or Hayes, and whatever their disposition toward the Board, officials found it in their interest to promote the centralization of the organization. As an outside group the Board threatened central control and most Washington officials resisted its efforts to oversee Indian Office activities.[88] Thus, the defense of the Indian Office against the Board of Indian Commissioners in the 1870s and early '80s may be seen as an example of successful boundary maintenance. Like the Army and the Peace Commission in the 1860s, the Board of Indian Commissioners in the 1870s presented a threat to organizational integrity. The Board was a check on the organization motivated by a basic distrust of the organization itself. Organizational regeneration demanded reform from within and the powers given to the

Board "could hardly have been intended as other than a reproach," as Senator Cornelius Cole said in the debate on the 1871 Appropriations Act.[89]

The Board of Indian Commissioners was an experiment in reform which did not succeed in its original goals. Composed of ten men, presumably selected for their philanthropy and benevolence, the Board served without pay. The Board suffered from a lack of clear definition of its purpose and authority. This lack of clarity made it possible for both officials of the Indian Office and Congressional opponents to reduce the Board's influence. After 1882, the Board may well have been significant for its role in channeling and focusing reform efforts, as some have argued.[90] However, channeling reform effort was far from the original purpose of the Board. The Board was created to supervise the Indian Office's expenditure of funds, to inspect Indian agencies and superintendencies, and to persuade Indians to agree to accept the government's civilization program. The Indian Office resisted efforts by the Board to exercise its supervisory and control functions. After the Board withdrew from the auditing of accounts and the inspection of supplies in the early 1880s, it never again exercised fiscal supervision over the Indian Office. The inspection of field units and the exhortation of the Indians to agree to the government's program were more acceptable to Washington officials, but these functions could be performed as well by internal units in the developing organization. After the creation of an inspection corps in 1873, officials of the Indian Office relied increasingly on these internal, paid functionaries. Inspectors, and later special agents and school supervisors, provided Washington officials with information on the functioning of the Indian agencies and schools. They also negotiated with the Indians and exhorted them to cooperate with the government's program. As the inspection services grew in size and scope, the Board's activities were increasingly displaced towards reform activities.

The function which the Board did fulfill, after 1880, was an important one. The infusion of an organization with purpose, the creation of a sense of destiny and mission, while not incompatible with centralization, required other kinds of skills, other kinds of emphases. It was this role which the Board, with its ties to reform organizations, its links to larger reform movements of the late nineteenth century, and its missionary zeal, could perform better than the organizational managers in Washington. Further, the Board provided a continuity which the short-tenured Washington officials could not provide. Clinton Fisk served as Chairman until his death in 1890.[91] Other members, including Kingsley, Smiley, and Wittelsey, had similarly long tenure. For organizational reasons, the function of the Board changed from that which was initially intended. The inspection and regulatory functions that the members of Congress envisioned in 1869 were ultimately provided by Indian Inspectors, full-time Presidential appointees who were subject to organizational directions and control. The definition of organizational purpose, while no less important, was less immediately threatening to the interests of administrators, whether their interest was to control the behavior of subordinates or to protect themselves against charges of corruption. It was this function which the Board performed for the Indian Office after 1880.

CHAPTER VI

THE CONTROL OF OFFICIAL BEHAVIOR:
THE MEN IN THE MIDDLE

The Indian Office used various methods to control the behavior of Indian agents and other local officials during the decades after the Civil War. Since the local units of the organization, the Indian Agencies, were many and far-flung, separated from each other and from the Central Office by considerable distances, and since transportation and communications were slow, obtaining information about activities at the agencies and exerting control over these activities presented a formidable problem for the Indian Office. The Agent's annual reports and his quarterly estimates or requests for funds provided the central office with one means of communication and control, particularly in the decision whether or not to grant the requested funds. Published regulations and circulars sent to agents, as well as specific instructions directed to individual agents, provided a means of direction. However, these mechanisms presented obvious difficulties. Regulations had to be written in general terms, to apply to a variety of situations. Specific instructions sent to individual agents could more closely reflect the particular conditions which prevailed at an individual agency, but the writers of the instructions in the Washington Office were far removed from the agencies and were generally ignorant of local conditions. It was up to the agent and other local officials to interpret and implement the directives. A third level of officials mediated between the Washington office and the field; these middle range functionaries, the "men in the middle," in theory checked the activity of the agents and provided Washington officials with information on developments at the local level. The way in which these middle-range positions were structured was crucial for organizational development. During the 1870s, the nature of the mediating positions changed. This chapter will be concerned with describing that change and indicating some of the reasons for it.

Before the 1870s, the Indian Office possessed a hierarchical structure based on the geographical dispersion of its operating units.[1] The local operating units, the Indian agencies in a given region, usually a state or territory, were parts of a superintendency which supervised all of the Indian Office's work in the region. The Indian Agent reported to the local Superintendent of Indian Affairs who was in some cases the territorial governor, serving *ex officio* as Superintendent. In other cases the Superintendent served full-time. The President appointed full-time

Superintendents, like agents and territorial governors, subject to the approval of the Senate.

During the 1870s, there was a shift from the Indian Superintendent to the Indian Inspector as the mediator between the Washington office and the agencies. Congress created the position of Indian Inspector in 1873; Interior Secretary Carl Shurz abolished the last superintendencies in 1878. This change reduced the identification of the "men in the middle" with the agents and consequently promoted the centralization of the Indian Office. Since the shift away from superintendencies was an early part of Schurz's rejection of the religious appointment policy, the move increased the boundedness of the organization.

Superintendencies originated in colonial times. British colonial administration differentiated Indian relations from the functions of provincial colonial government. The Crown appointed a northern and southern superintendent of Indian affairs to mediate and negotiate with the Indian tribes on the frontier of settlement. Royal control of Indian affairs, particularly the protection of Indian interests against the interests of colonists who wished to expand westward, was one of the precipitating causes of the American Revolution.[2] However, because the interests affected in negotiating with Indian tribes transcended purely state interests, the new nation delegated Indian affairs to the central government. Both the Articles of Confederation and the Constitution gave the Congress sole responsibility for regulating intercourse between whites and Indians.[3]

In the early years of the nation the government's interaction with the tribes was primarily diplomatic and economic. Indian superintendents, often territorial governors like William Henry Harrison, governor of Indiana Territory during the administrations of Jefferson and Madison, were responsible for regulating trade with the Indians and for encouraging Indians to cede lands to whites to permit white expansion. Frequently the territorial governors also served as military commanders when warfare broke out with the Indians.[4] During the early period of territorial administration, governmental functions were relatively undifferentiated. Administrative responsibility for a variety of governmental functions was concentrated in the position of the territorial governor. With the increasing development of the territorial system, and of the territories themselves, these functions increasingly came to be distinguished from one another.

The act "to provide for the organization of the Department of Indian Affairs," passed in 1834, established the system of Indian administration which existed at the close of the Civil War.[5] The Act established a number of specific superintendencies and agencies, which subsequent legislation was to modify. It also prescribed the duties of superintendents. Superintendents supervised Indian agents within a geographical area and were responsible for maintaining accounts and making payments to Indians. They had the power to suspend and remove agents. During the next thirty years, Congress changed the number and location of superintendencies and agencies as whites moved west, bringing the settlers in contact with new groups of Indians. Superintendents were initially very important in Indian affairs. They negotiated with Indian tribes, arranged for groups of Indians to be moved westward, and paid funds due to Indians under treaty stipulations. As late as the 1860s, superintendents had wide discretion in the management of government funds. An investigator of Indian affairs in the Pacific northwest reported in 1863,

> I freely confess my inability to understand the details of the expenditures made in Indian territory, except upon the general principle that the superintendent took the responsibility of applying the monies transmitted to him in such manner he deemed most advantageous to the Indians, without regard to funds, forms, or instructions. That he can explain the necessities which compelled him to adopt this course, satisfactory to the department and to Congress, I have very little doubt. The main difficulties have arisen from the intention of the monies required to meet the necessary expenses of the service, and the conflict between the regulations and the anomalous condition of the Indians.[6]

When a territory had been organized in an area in which Indian reservations or agencies were located, the territorial governor was usually assigned to act as superintendent of Indian affairs. Two patterns were likely when a territorial governor served as *ex officio* superintendent. The territorial governor might devote an inordinate amount of time to Indian affairs; alternatively, he neglected Indian affairs or delegated them to subordinates.[7] The combined functions of territorial governor and of superintendent of Indian affairs often proved to be incompatible with one another. The responsibility of the territorial governor, particularly in territories with considerable white settlement, was to promote development, meaning a further expansion of white population. This often conflicted with his responsibility as superintendent of Indian affairs to protect Indian rights, particularly land rights, against white intruders. Combining the offices of governor and superintendent, William M. Neil concluded, provided the incumbent with "irreconcilable objectives." Most governors saw their first duty due to the White settlers.[8] This incompatibility often led to conflicts between territorial governors and the Indian Office.

Prior to the creation of the Department of the Interior in 1849, the divided authority over the governor's responsibility complicated these conflicts. The Department of State was responsible for territorial affairs, while the Indian Office was a part of the Department of War. Even after the creation of the Interior Department, conflicts between Indian agents and governor-superintendents were not uncommon. In the Mormon territory of Utah, religious conflicts between Governor Brigham Young and the gentile agents, who were suspicious of Mormon missionary endeavors, further complicated the situation. In 1854, Commissioner of Indian Affairs George W. Manypenney recommended that the functions of Governor and Superintendent be separated in Utah, as well as in New Mexico, Washington, and Minnesota.[9] In 1867, the Acting Commissioner of Indian Affairs, Charles Mix, recommended a similar separation of functions in four territories, Colorado, Idaho, Montana, and Dakota. He noted that the territorial governors serving as *ex officio* superintendents were busy with other duties.[10]

Divided loyalties and the press of business provide a partial explanation for the separation of the functions of territorial governor and superintendent. Statehood, since it replaced territorial government with local administration, also led to a separation of functions. As western territories became states, full-time superintendents were appointed to supervise Indian agencies, as in California (1850) and Nevada (1864). A final motive for separation may have been to achieve greater Indian Office control over Indian Affairs in the territories. The Commissioner's 1867 recommendation followed by only three years the massacre of Cheyennes by Colonel John M. Chivington's Colorado volunteers under the ultimate command of Territorial Governor John Evans. The creation of several new territories following the Civil War resulted in considerable confusion, as agencies were reshuffled into new superintendencies. Finally, territorial governors appointed under the spoils system were frequently accused of fraud in their management of Indian funds.[11]

During most of the period before the Civil War, Superintendents were probably more significant than agents in directing Indian affairs in the field. They negotiated treaties, made payments required under the treaties, and controlled such aspects of administration as trade between whites and Indians. However, with the passage of time, particularly with establishment of defined reservations for Indians at mid-century, agents were increasingly likely to be permanently in contact with tribes. As superintendencies became larger and more remote from the Indians, agents became more significant than superintendents. While superintendents were legally responsible for distributing payments to Indians, the agents increasingly carried out this responsibility in the years before the Civil War. In some superintendencies, the superintendents were so remote from the reservations that any supervision of agents was impossible.[12]

After Grant's inauguration in 1869, legislation by an economy-minded Congress permitted the President to discontinue unnecessary superintendencies. Such laws were passed in 1870, in 1871, and in 1873.[13] The percentage of "independent" agencies, those reporting directly to Washington rather than through a superintendent, increased in the decade after the Civil War as a result of this legislation. The legislation grew out of the declining importance of the Superintendent in Indian affairs, the increasing importance of Indian agents and perhaps the increasing intensity of their contact with Indians, and from a drive for economy. The increasing decline in the influence of superintendents resulted also from a change in the objectives of Indian work, particularly after Grant's inauguration. Prior to the Civil War and even to a certain extent in the turbulent years between the end of the war and Grant's election to the presidency in 1868, Indian affairs were largely a matter of diplomatic relations and treaty negotiation. Concentration and removal were the major objectives. However, Grant's announcement in his inaugural address of 1869 that he would favor any course that tended toward the civilization of the Indians indicated a major shift in United States Indian policy. Now the emphasis was not so much on concentration and removal as primary objectives, although these might be advocated as the best means to an end. Increasingly, the emphasis was on teaching the Indians a new social role, that of White American. This change was symbolized by the action of Congress in 1871, ending the practice of making treaties with the Indian tribes. While the practical effect of this act was to replace treaties with "agreements," requiring the consent of both houses of Congress, the linguistic change signified a more profound shift in the objectives of Indian policy. The reservation system originated in the post-Civil War era, not at midcentury.[14]

During the early years of the Grant administration, the superintendency system was first reorganized and subsequently increasingly reduced in importance. In 1869, Grant invited the Society of Friends to nominate persons for appointment as Central and Northern Superintendents, as well as for appointment to the Indian agencies in those superintendencies. He detailed Army officers to serve as superintendents and agents everywhere else except in Oregon. However, in 1871, after Congress had blocked the appointment of Army officers to civil posts, the Acting Commissioner of Indian Affairs, H.R. Clum, reported that six superintendencies had been discontinued. "The agents [previously] subordinate thereto now report direct to the Indian Bureau," Clum reported. "No detriment to the service has been caused by this change. . . . a considerable sum, which was expended on account of salaries and office, incidental and traveling expenses, is thereby saved to the government."[15]

The law of 1873 required the President to abolish superintendencies when possible; under this legislation all of the existing superintendencies were discontinued by 1878. The same act authorized the President to appoint up to five Indian Inspectors, subject to confirmation by the Senate, at a salary of $3,000 per year, twice the pay of an Indian agent and equivalent to the salary of the Commissioner of Indian Affairs.[16] Congress reduced the number of Indian inspectors to three in 1875, but new legislation increased the number to five in 1880.[17] The legislation which provided for the discontinuation of the superintendencies also created a new kind of mediating official, the Indian Inspector. After five years of experience with the Indian inspector system, the last superintendency, the Central Superintendency, which the Quakers had lobbied to retain, was finally discontinued by an executive order of January 5, 1878.[18]

In the thirteen years following the Civil War, Congress and the Grant administration changed the superintendency system considerably. Originally an aspect of territorial administration, by the end of the Johnson presidency the functions of the superintendents were distinct from other aspects of territorial administration, as a result of the shift toward full-time superintendents, initiated by several Commissioners of Indian Affairs. While this change resulted in a better-bounded organization, the inclusion of the superintendents' positions in the religious appointments policy gave the power of nominating candidates for the superintendent positions to external organizations, the churches. When a denomination named both agent and superintendent it was likely that the superintendent would defend the agent in any conflict with the Washington office. Thus, when combined with the religious appointments policy, the superintendency system had a disintegrative potential.

While economy was purportedly the reason for the discontinuation of the superintendency system, its immediate replacement with an inspection system, staffed by highly-paid inspectors, makes this explanation alone doubtful. The Central and Northern Superintendents were nominated by two branches of the Society of Friends. Quaker lobbying kept the two superintendencies in existence for a time after the 1873 legislation.[19] The President discontinued the Northern Superintendency in 1876, while the Central Superintendency survived two more years. After the extension of the "Quaker policy" to other denominations in 1870, church groups attempted to control the nomination of superintendents as well as agents. The Episcopalians attempted to make appointment of the Dakota Superintendent a condition of their participation. However, the Superintendency was discontinued in 1870. When the superintendency was reestablished in 1877, the Commissioner of Indian Affairs wrote to Episcopal Bishop Hare to solicit his nomination for the position.[20] The Methodists gained control of the superintendencies in the Pacific northwest for a time, while the Reformed Church at one point secured control of the Arizona superintendency, apparently as a means of providing a position for a member who was unwilling to accept the lower paid job of Indian agent. The Catholics asked to nominate the Utah Superintendent after losing the right to nominate the agent at Fort Hall.

Even after the reestablishment of the Dakota Superintendency, the Indian Office attempted to persuade Superintendent William J. Pollock to accept a position as special Indian agent, an inspection position, rather than that of superintendent.[21] Pollock, whom Grant appointed Dakota Superintendent in February, 1878, became a Special Agent in June and the Superintendency was discontinued. In April, 1879, Hayes named him Indian Inspector. In the late 1870s, some superintendents performed many of the functions of inspectors. While Pollock was still Dakota Superintendent, Commissioner E.A. Hayt asked him to investigate Santee Agency in Nebraska, a Quaker agency which had been a part of the Northern Superintendency and for which Pollock was not nominally responsible.[22] Pollock also served briefly as Acting Agent at the Rosebud Agency in Dakota Territory, after he had removed the agent.[23]

The Central Superintendency, controlled by the Orthodox Friends and the superintendency which survived longer than any other, presented a special problem. Late in the Grant administration, the powers of the Commissioner of Indian Affairs over agencies in the Indian Territory were delegated to the Central superintendent. The Quakers and the administration of the Indian Office defended the delegation on the basis that Central Superintendent Enoch Hoag was closer to the field and could be more aware of the activities of his agents than the commissioner could. Hoag had special regulations for the Central Superintendency written and promulgated to his agents. Investigators, including an agent of the Board of Indian Commissioners, thought the increased powers of the Central Superintendent were designed to evade the normal inspection of supplies destined for Indian Territory agencies.[24] The Chief Clerk of the Indian Office, S.A. Galpin, had been instrumental in arranging for the delegation of authority. Galpin toured the Central Superintendency at the same time as the Board's representative and produced a report favorable to the Quaker administration and critical of the Board's investigation.[25] While no specific charges against Galpin or the Central Superintendent were proved, a Board of Inquiry charged by the Secretary of the Interior Carl Schurz with investigating the administration of Indian affairs found the delegation of authority to be illegal. President Hayes dismissed Galpin and Commissioner J.Q. Smith as a result of the inquiry. E.A. Hayt, the former chairman of the Purchasing Committee of the Board of Indian Commissioners, became Commissioner. He appointed William M. Leeds, the Board's investigator in Indian Territory, Chief Clerk to succeed Galpin. With the appointment of Hayt and Leeds, the subsequent abolition of the Central Superintendency was probably inevitable.

The Board of Inquiry in its report, published early in 1878, found that a superintendent's powers in law were limited. Section 2050 of the *Revised Statutes* provided that the superintendent could "exercise general supervision and control" and could suspend agents "for reasons forthwith to be communicated to the Secretary of the Interior." However, "certain powers, some of which, while legal, [are] either inherent in or alone attached to the Office of Indian Affairs as it exists in immediate connection with the office of Secretary of the Interior, [had] been delegated" to the Central Superintendent.[26] For example, under the regulations, the Central Superintendent could make purchases without sending the agent's estimates to Washington. The Board quoted a letter written by Galpin, as Acting Commissioner, to William Nicholson, who had replaced Hoag as Central Superintendent, giving Nicholson the same powers "within your jurisdiction as are possessed and exercised by myself over those agencies which report directly to me."[27]

There was no provision in the delegation of powers for a review of purchases by the Board of Indian Commissioners. Indeed, the Central Superintendent had resisted examination by Leeds of the Superintendency's financial records.[28] The proposed regulations approved by Commissioner Smith in February 1877, provided, in addition to independent purchasing, that all correspondence, including financial information, between the Commissioner of Indian Affairs and the agents in the Central Superintendency would be routed through the superintendent.

The Board of Inquiry found the delegation of authority to be illegal and commented, "One of the greatest difficulties which an administration of Indian affairs has to contend with is the practical inaccountability of the officers of the service to, and isolation from, the direct control of the Indian Bureau."[29]

The substantial delegation of powers to the Central Superintendent illustrates, in exaggerated form, the problem of the superintendency system in the management of Indian affairs. A typical problem of "men in the middle" has been whether to identify upward or downward—with superiors or with supervisees. With denominational appointment of both superintendents and agents, the likelihood was great that superintendents would identify with their subordinates. In the Central Superintendency, both Hoag and Nicholson defended the agent against charges made by inspectors. From the perspective of the central office, full-time superintendents represented an improvement over the governor-superintendents of earlier decades. Full-time superintendents internalized decision-making, making for a better-bounded organization. Yet superintendents were likely to identify with the agents. This centrifugal tendency might ultimately have weakened the integrity of the organization. The new group of middlemen, the Indian Inspectors, were unlikely to identify with the agents, since they were assigned to a broader geographical area and they received their instructions from Washington officials. Inspectors were removed from the chain of command; their role was to assist Washington administrators by checking the extent to which agents followed regulations. As inspectors replaced superintendents as the "men in the middle," the centralization and formalization of the Indian Office increased.

The early Indian Inspectors were selected from the ranks of the denominational mission boards, in harmony with the practice of the Grant administration to delegate personnel selection to the churches. For example, E. C. Kemble, among the first Indian Inspectors, was a member of the Protestant Episcopal Church's Domestic Missions Board. In June 1873, Commissioner E. P. Smith wrote to a mission board secretary that "the pressure from all sides" regarding the appointment of inspectors was "unparalleled."[30] Denominations attempted to influence the selections. Some of the denominationally-nominated agents sought the higher-paid inspector positions.[31] The new inspectors, who were to visit all Indian agencies in rotation, carried denominational infighting into their inspection reports. Kemble complained of a "politico-religious machine," run by the Methodists, in the Pacific northwest; he deprecated aspects of the Quaker administration of the Central Superintendency. Many of the early inspectors complained about the influence of the "Romanists."

After Hayes' election, there was an increasing tendency to select former agents and superintendents as inspectors. Two new inspectors and two special agents were appointed in 1878. "Good results must continue to follow the more active and thorough supervision which is being carried out," commented Commissioner E. A. Hayt.[32] Two former Dakota Superintendents entered the inspection service. J. H. Hammond left the superintendency for an inspector position in Feburary 1878; his successor as superintendent, William J. Pollock, served less than a year, becoming Special Agent in June and Indian Inspector in 1879. Hayes appointed James M. Haworth, who had served five years as Quaker agent at the Kiowa and Commanche Agency, Special Agent in 1878.

Haworth, who was to become the first Superintendent of Indian Schools in 1882, provided a link with the religious appointment policy of the Grant administration. He attended many of the annual meetings of the Board of Indian Commissioners with the secretaries of the mission societies, and appears to have presented the Indian Office position.[33] Hammond and Pollock, in contrast, appear to have been more representative of the political system which gained influence as denominational influence waned. Pollock was an ally of Governor William H. Howard of Dakota Territory and was considered for the position of territorial secretary in 1879.[34] Hammond complained that the position of Indian Inspector was a political dead-end. Despite the high pay, the position had ruined him financially. It was impossible to gain a following. A position in territorial government, or in a land office, was preferable.[35]

Some of the persons appointed to inspection positions lacked denominational or political backing. Their appointments reflected previous service in the Indian Office. These individuals were appointed from the corps of clerks in the Indian Office or were persons who had been appointed to agency positions under the policy of Washington office appointment of agency clerks initiated by Hayt. Arden R. Smith, a clerk in the Indian Office, was detailed to the Central Superintendency early in 1878 to investigate the records of the superintendency and in particular affairs at Quapaw agency.[36] After the conclusion of his investigation, Hayt appointed Smith clerk at the Kiowa and Commanche agency in Indian Territory.[37] In 1879, when William J. Pollock became an Indian Inspector, Smith succeeded Pollock as Special Agent.

Before the creation of an inspection service in 1873, the occasional investigations necessitated by complaints were conducted by specially appointed special agents, superintendents, and commissions. Thus most of the personnel engaged in the investigation of Indian agencies were the holders of temporary, *ad hoc* positions, who were engaged for a specific investigation. Because of political and boundary problems, the creation of the Board of Indian Commissioners did not result in a regularization of investigative activity, despite the Board's involvement in several important investigations during the 1870s. The appointment of full-time inspectors, however, regularized the practice of inspection. Ultimately, the full-time inspection system resulted in a more dependable, professional product, the inspection report.

The 1873 law which established the Indian Inspectors provided that inspectors would alternate in their inspection of agencies, with no inspector investigating the same agency twice in a row. However, inadequate appropriations for travel expenses led to the repeal of that provision in 1875, and the reduction in the number of inspectors from five to three. The Commissioner of Indian Affairs commented, "The use of the force has been thus placed at the discretion of the department, and the service of three made equivalent to that of five, as rendered under previous restrictions." However, he continued, "The force is not sufficient." He requested five Indian Inspectors and "sufficient" travel funds.[38] Congress added two Special Indian Agents in 1878 and increased the number of inspectors to five in 1880, after a board appointed by Schurz to investigate business methods in the Indian Office recommended strengthening the inspection service.[39]

Inspectors and Special Agents reported to the Commissioner of Indian Affairs until 1880, when Carl Schurz ordered inspectors to report directly to him. Since the inspection reports, under the 1873 legislation, were to be forwarded to the President, Schurz argued that reports should go to the Secretary, since, in legal effect, the Secretary acted as the agent of the President.[40] Special Agents continued to report to the Commissioner. Inspectors continued to report to the Secretary of the Interior until 1908 when the inspection service was reorganized. Inevitably, the separation of inspectors from the direct control of the Commissioner led to conflict. Removed from direct control of inspections, the Indian Office attempted to enforce accountability for the finances of inspectors.[41] While inspectors could remove Indian agents and appoint temporary successors, only Special Agents could serve as acting agents themselves.

Under the direction of Schurz and subsequent Secretaries of the Interior the inspectors' work became more regularized and routinized. Schurz required the inspectors to report to him twice a week, indicating their activities and their mail and telegraph address for the week following.[42] He required monthly reports of the inspectors' financial activities. After complaints from the Indian Office of meddling by the inspectors in agency affairs, inspectors were cautioned not to make promises to the Indians without prior authorization from the Secretary.[43] Under Schurz's successors as Secretary of the Interior, Samuel J. Kirkwood and Henry M. Teller, the volume and scope of instructions expanded.

In 1882, Teller requested authority to designate two inspectors for specialized duty. A medical inspector would inspect the medical facilities provided on Indian reservations, collect vital statistics, and direct the work of the physicians in the Indian Service.[44] An Inspector of Indian Schools would perform similar functions for education. While the position of Medical Inspector was not established, Congress approved the creation of the Inspector of Indian Schools position in the Indian Appropriations Act of 1882.[45] James M. Haworth became the first School Inspector, a position he held until his death in 1885. The creation of the Inspector of Indian Schools position, combined with the request

Chart V

Organizational Structure, Office of Indian Affairs

1880-1908

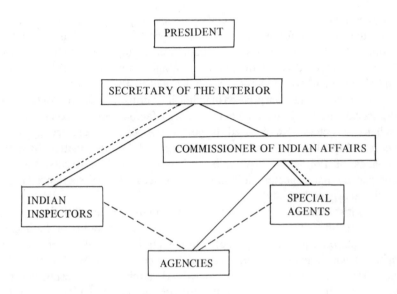

Key: ———— Supervisory Authority
      ---- Investigative Authority
      ------ Reports

for a Medical Inspector, suggests that specialized inspectors were to become responsible for the increasingly important functions of education and medical care. Inspection had become the major strategy for mediating between the Indian Office and the agencies. The control of inspectors by the secretary provided an external check on the activities of the Indian Office. (See Chart V.)

In 1883, the duties of Indian inspectors were codified in a departmental publication, which summarized the instructions issued to inspectors by Secretaries Schurz, Kirkwood, and Teller. The pamphlet was reprinted with a few modifications in 1885.[46] Special agents and inspectors continued to be drawn from the ranks of former agents. When Special Agent Arden R. Smith was dismissed in 1883, Commissioner Hiram Price appointed Cyrus Beede, a former Quapaw agent, to succeed him.[47] James A. Wright, former Montana Superintendent and Crow agent, was appointed Special Agent in 1882.[48]

Inspectors were often accused of political favoritism. Valentine McGillycuddy, the cantankerous agent at Pine Ridge, was famous for his complaints about Indian Inspectors. He accused Inspector Pollock of prejudice against him because McGillycuddy had been recommended for his position by political enemies of Pollock's.[49] As late as 1895, the Indian Rights Association complained that inspectors, as political appointees, were inexperienced in Indian affairs and gave bad advice.[50]

Political influence was never absent from government administration in the late nineteenth century. However, the creation and elaboration of the inspection system placed a group of men between the Washington administrators and the agencies whose loyalties were more likely to be with the Washington officials than with the agents. Removed from direct administrative responsibility and responsible to the Secretary of the Interior or the Commissioner of Indian Affairs, the Indian Inspectors and Special Agents performed a monitoring function in Indian administration. The growth of regulations governing agency administration and the inspection function itself resulted in a final product, the inspection report, which was increasingly routinized and predictable. With the increasing importance of education in the government's Indian program, the school inspector's position became increasingly significant. Eventually the title was changed to Superintendent of Indian Schools and the position became quasi-administrative.

The inspection of Indian agencies antedated the creation of the Inspection service in 1873. The 1873 legislation created the conditions for regularizing what had been an unsatisfactory, if necessary, activity. It also created a "man in the middle" whose activity would further the centralization of Indian administration in the coming decades. The change from Superintendent to Indian Inspector resulted in the creation of a group of "men in the middle" who were more likely to identify with Washington administrators than with agents, because they did not have direct administrative responsibility but only consultative and investigative responsibility for events in the local areas. It also provided a regular system for what had been a continuous but not very satisfactory activity in Indian affairs, the agency inspection.

CHAPTER VII

THE FORMALIZATION OF INSPECTIONS
AND AGENCY AFFAIRS

The transition from supervision to inspection as the organization's means of mediating between Washington and the agencies increased the centralization and boundedness of the Indian Office. The adherence of agents to the regulations of the Indian Office was, for the first time, systematically monitored. However, unpredictability and individual eccentricity marked the early years of the inspection system. The early inspections reflected the inspectors' extra-organizational allegiances, particularly their religious associations, and as such did not contribute to achieving a unified organization. If one of the hallmarks of bureaucratic organization is "purging particularism," focusing organizational effort on the accomplishment of a common organizational goal, the Indian Office of the 1870s could hardly be described as a bureaucracy.[1]

If the inspection system was to help to achieve greater coordination and unity of action in Indian affairs, inspections had to be predictable in terms of which problems inspectors would examine, what solutions they would propose for those problems and under what conditions they would recommend disciplinary action against agents and other subordinates. For inspections to be predictable, the standards for agency administration needed to be clear, to agents and to inspectors. Further, the behavior of the Indian inspectors themselves had to be made predictable. The alternative was a continuation of denominational or other particularistic conflict in the inspection process. During the 1870s, a paucity of regulations, denominational conflict, and the endemic disagreements between civilian agents and military authorities complicated the work of the inspectors.

Formalization, the process of creating rules and increasing the extent of rule-following in an organization, provided the means for regularizing agency administration and inspections during the 1880s. The volume of written regulations governing the activities of agents and agency employees expanded. Inspectors visited the agencies to determine the extent to which rules were followed. At the same time, written regulations made the inspectors' efforts increasingly useful to Washington administrators.

Acting Secretary of the Interior M.L. Joslyn, Teller's assistant, outlined the objectives of inspection in a letter of instruction sent to Inspector Samuel S. Benedict in 1882. Joslyn ordered Benedict to inspect several agencies in the Indian Territory. He instructed Benedict to "observe, examine, and report upon everything affecting the well-being of the Indians and the public service and make such recommendations as may seem to you to be proper." In particular, Joslyn asked for information about the extent of farming at the agencies, the names of Indians capable of doing any work performed by government employees, the quality of public buildings, the moral character of the agents, and the agents' practice regarding open market purchases. Joslyn closed by enjoining Benedict to "make no promises to Indians which have not first been authorized by the Department, nor direct any expenditures by the agents for supplies, services, or otherwise, unless authority for the same is first had from the Department."[2] These instructions, which summarized those previously made to other Inspectors by Secretaries Schurz, Kirkwood, and Teller, were codified in 1883 when the pamphlet outlining the duties of Indian Inspectors was published.[3]

The new inspection service resulted in a complicated set of administrative responsibilities for the Indian Service (Chart VI). After 1880, inspectors addressed their reports to the Secretary of the Interior. Clerks in the Indian Division of the Secretary's office prepared synopses of the reports, summarizing the inspector's conclusions and his recommendations for action. Copies of the synopses, which included a column for reporting the action taken on the inspector's recommendation, were routinely forwarded to the office of the Commissioner of Indian Affairs. The Commissioner's office returned the forms, with an indication of the action taken, to the Indian Division, usually after communication with the agent involved (Chart VII).[4]

In such a complicated communication system, the content of reports needed to be uniform and predictable if any action was to result. The synopses provided a way for the Indian Division clerks to reduce the comprehensive reports to a set of specific recommendations. For this to happen, inspectors needed to follow a consistent pattern in the material they presented and in the way they composed the reports. The regulations issued by Secretary Teller resulted in a standardization of the inspection reports.

The publication of the pamphlet, *Duties of Inspectors*, ten years after the creation of the inspection service, indicated a maturation of the inspection system. The pamphlet reflected an increasing demand for specificity in inspection reports which followed Schurz's decision to take charge of inspections in 1880. Before 1880, no general charge was made to inspectors. The inspection process was not routinized, and its consequences were not predictable. The situation had been even worse before the creation of a permanent inspection service in 1873.

Before 1873, the Washington office usually ordered inspections in response to crises or complaints. At times, Indian commissioners asked Army officers stationed in the vicinity of Indian agencies to make special inspections, as when Commissioner Francis Walker asked General John E. Smith to inspect Indian agencies in Wyoming.[5] Army officers were frequently the only reliable source of information, other than the agents, regarding agency affairs. However, because of the endemic conflict between the Army and the civilian administrators, at both the local and national levels, their reports were often not viewed as useful by the Indian Office. The results of investigations carried out by others in the vicinity were often unsatisfactory because of the suspicion that local whites had a personal interest in the results. Individuals appointed on an *ad hoc* basis to carry out specific investigations were often inexperienced in Indian affairs and were not sufficiently familiar with the Indians or with agency procedures to evaluate agency affairs.

The creation of a regular corps of inspectors was intended to alleviate these problems and provide Washington officials with a reliable source of information on affairs at the agencies. Inspectors were expected to be knowledgeable about Indian affairs and to devote all of their time to inspecting Indian agencies. They performed routine inspections in addition to special inspections when wrongdoing had been alleged. The combination of expertise and frequent inspection should have resulted in a greater usefulness of the inspection reports for administrators. However, the reduction in the number of inspectors from five to three and inadequate appropriations for travel expenses of the reduced force hindered attempts to achieve complete coverage in the 1870s. Only forty-four of the agencies were inspected in 1875.[6]

The nature of the work may also have increased the difficulty of inspections in the 1870s. The Indian Office failed to provide comprehensive instructions to inspectors. One of the major activities of inspectors during the 1870s was the investigation of specific complaints lodged against an agent or agency employee. These often came from white communities neighboring the reservations and sometimes reflected the disappointment of businessmen who wanted a greater share of agency business. The complaints were often vague and needed to be clarified in the process of investigation. As a result, the investigations of the 1870s tended to be particularistic, *ad hoc* affairs. In the absence of general rules governing inspections, the reports reflected the allegiances of the inspectors and the specific complaints against the agent.

Sometimes, persons were asked to make their complaints more specific even before an inspector was sent out. In 1877, Commissioner E.A. Hayt wrote to a person who alleged fraud in the management of the Michigan agency, "All facts should be stated with particularity. . . . subject matter being clearly stated, in order that I may be fully advised."[7] Often, the Commissioner asked to receive affidavits from persons with knowledge of alleged irregularities prior to ordering an inspection. Once a complaining individual had sent affidavits and detailed charges to the Indian Office, the Indian Office sent the information to the inspector who was to investigate the charges. Inspectors were to get in touch with the individuals making the complaints prior to their visit to the agency.[8] Frequently, charges of fraud or mismanagement were met with countercharges

Chart VI

Administrative Responsibilities For the Indian Service

1880-1900

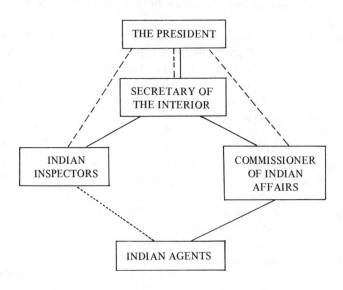

Key: ― ― ― Appointment
      ―――― Administrative Control
      ········ Inspection

Chart VII

From Inspection Report to Administrative Action

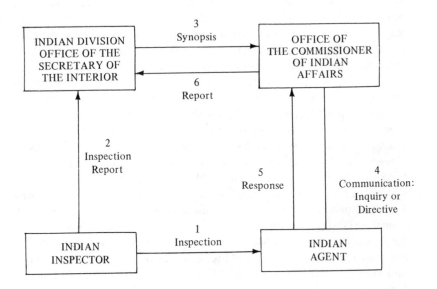

against the accuser. At Crow Agency, Montana, the agent and the trader each accused the other of defrauding the Indians.[9] Occasionally, inspectors arrived to investigate charges only to find that the persons who had complained were not available and the charges were apparently unfounded. In 1878, "James Smith" and "Mrs. Jane Ross" wrote to President Hayes and his wife charging the teacher and physician at the Wichita Agency with seducing Indian girls. The investigator found not only that there was no truth to the charges, but also that the individuals writing the letters could not be found.[10]

Ideally, inspectors were to spend most of their time making routine investigations, reviewing the programs of Indian agencies which were not the subject of specific complaint. During the 1870s, however, much of their time was spent investigating specific charges against Indian agents. In 1879, for example, Inspector W.J. Pollock was sent to Rosebud agency to investigate charges that Agent Cicero Newell had sold subordinate agency positions to friends in his home town of Ypsilanti, Michigan.[11] Inspectors also assisted in the removal of tribes to new agencies, a frequent occurrence in the 1870s. Inspectors J.H. Hammond and John McNeil assisted in the 1877 removal of the Poncas from their Dakota reservation to the Quapaw reservation in Indian Territory.[12] In the following year, when McNeil visited the new Ponca Agency to investigate charges against Agent Boone and his agency clerk, the Indian Office instructed him to report on the suitability of the Quapaw reservation for additional tribes. McNeil was to find locations on the reservation to which tribes could be removed and to estimate the probable cost of the removals.[13]

Frequently, the inspection reports did not address the details which were most useful to Indian Office administrators. Much of the work of the Indian Office involved making recommendations regarding personnel, particularly the transfer of an agent from one agency to another or the suspension or retention of an agent. Consequently, information about the adequacy of an agent's administration was crucial. When Agent Pyle, of the Cimmaron Agency in New Mexico, asked to be transferred to the Navajo Agency, Commissioner J.Q. Smith found that Inspector E.C. Kemble's inspection report on the Cimmaron Agency did not discuss Pyle's abilities as an agent. Smith wrote to Kemble,

> The enclosed nomination of agent Pyle to be transferred from the Cimmaron to the Navajo Agency has been referred to this office by the Secretary for report. There is nothing that I can find in this office which reflects at all on Mr. Pyle's administration of the Cimmaron agency affairs. In your report of the inspection of that agency in May, 1876, you confine yourself to discussing the abolition of that agency and the removal of the Indians elsewhere. The Navajo agency being one of considerable importance and difficulty, I should be glad to have your opinion not only as to Mr. Pyle's reliability, but also as to his ability to successfully manage so large a number of pretty headstrong Indians.[14]

At times, inspectors were reminded to keep their inspections to the point. While Inspector John H. Hammond was involved in a complicated investigation of affairs at Crow Creek and Lower Brule agencies in Dakota Territory, Commissioner Hayt ordered him to "Confine evidence to material points. Do not allow immaterial matters to be lugged in."[15] Sometimes the Indian Office lost track of the movements of inspectors, resulting in telegrams to agents requesting information on their movements.[16] In the more complicated investigations, the Indian Office sometimes hired detectives or other specialized personnel to assist the inspectors. E.C. Watkins investigated the agencies of the Five Civilized Tribes in 1875, with the assistance of a detective appointed by the Indian Office at Watkins' request.[17] On other occasions, particularly when theft of government supplies had been alleged, clerks were detailed to assist inspectors. In the 1876 investigation of Red Cloud Agent John J. Saville, accused of diverting rations to his own use, the Department of Justice detailed a clerk, Duncan Peyton, to assist Inspector William Vandever in his investigation.[18] Sometimes former government clerks with experience in handling accounts helped in investigations. In 1878, the Indian Office sent a former Navy clerk who had worked on quartermaster accounts to assist Inspector J.H. Hammond in his investigation of Crow Creek and Lower Brule Agencies.[19] In the same investigation, the chief of the accounts division of the Indian Office was also sent out to examine the accounts of the two agents, Livingstone and Gregory, who had been dismissed.[20] When inspectors uncovered evidence suggesting corruption, the Indian Office generally directed the inspector to provide the evidence to the nearest U.S. District Attorney.[21] Inspectors often themselves sought cooperation with the local District Attorney, as did Hammond in his investigation of the Crow Creek and Lower Brule agencies.[22]

Agents apparently became adept at managing inspectors. In 1878, Acting Indian Commissioner William M. Leeds ordered Inspector John McNeil to the Cheyenne and Arapahoe Agency to investigate charges made by the agency carpenter, G.J. George, against Agent Miles. George charged Miles with making a contract for the construction of the school at the agency and having the school constructed by agency employees after paying the contractor. Further, George asserted that the cattle at an off-reservation ranch, purportedly owned by Miles, were government cattle which Miles had appropriated for his own use. He also charged Miles with spending less than appropriated for agency expenditures and using the balance to supplement his own salary.[23] After ordering McNeil to conduct the investigation, Leeds sent him a long confidential letter warning him of the difficulties he would face.

At this agency, [Leeds wrote,] you will need all the shrewdness of which you are capable. You may find parties of the same agency who are able to put such a face upon matters as to entirely mislead you. Your attention will be drawn to things which are of very little account to you as an inspector; the school will doubtless be shown up in a very favorable light—and it no doubt is a good school. If there is truth in the charges, the agent will be most anxious to show you whatever will consume your time and draw you off from more important matters. The agent you will find to be a gentleman, and probably as good an agent as there is in the service, as far as business qualities are concerned. Nevertheless, it is desirable that the subjects which have been brought to the attention of this office, and are now placed in your hands for investigation, should be so thoroughly looked into that the agent can be freed hereafter from any suspicion, or the service can be relieved of an unfaithful servant.[24]

During the first years of the Hayes administration, Commissioner Hayt used inspectors extensively in clearing up the problems resulting from the dissolution of the old Central Superintendency, discussed in Chapters V and VI. McNeil was particularly active in the Indian Territory in 1878. Hayt sent him to the Osage Agency to assist the new agent there and to help eject the old agent, Cyrus Beede, who had been suspended by President Hayes but refused to leave the agency.[25] Beede and the former agency physician, a Dr. Duggan, had been among the Quaker appointees who had attacked the Board of Indian Commissioners investigation of the Central Superintendency in 1877, conducted by William Leeds, now Chief Clerk of the Indian Office. Hayt ordered McNeil to meet with Dr. Duggan to try to find out about any "crookedness which occurred under Beede's administration." Duggan had been physician at the Osage agency for seven years and was now being reassigned to the Quapaw Agency. McNeil was to persuade Dr. Duggan to disavow his attack on Leeds and to attribute it to pressure from Beede. The Indian Office had learned that Duggan had sent off from the agency a box containing quinine, morphine, and powdered opium. Apparently Duggan planned to appropriate these supplies to his own use. McNeil was to get Duggan to admit the theft. He then was to tell Duggan that Beede was liable for Duggan's misdeeds under Beede's bonds. "The Indian Office may charge the value of the goods to Beede. This may have the effect of making him [Duggan] open up to Beede. As you will have the doctor in a tight place," the instructions continued, "he may desire to turn state's evidence. No promises can be made to him. . . . Unless some facts can be shown which will put an entirely different appearance on this apparent 'petty larceny'. . . . Doctor Duggan need not expect any appointment to Quapaw agency."[26] McNeil's other duties included assisting Joseph Hertford and his wife with transportation to Pawnee Agency from the railroad at Wichita, Kansas. Hertford had been appointed by the Washington Office to serve as agency clerk at the Pawnee Agency.[27]

The investigation of the affairs of the Central Superintendency involved many individuals, including the agency clerks appointed by the Indian Office. Sometimes these clerks, called "Schurz's spies" by the Quakers, served in several capacities. For example, Hayt sent Arden R. Smith, a clerk in the Indian Office, to the Indian Territory to investigate several agencies. Smith served in a number of capacities. He first investigated the Quapaw Agency, where the Quaker Agent, Hiram W. Jones, had long been the object of complaints from the merchants of Seneca, Missouri. Seneca was the town closest to the Quapaw reservation, and the Indians traded there until Jones set up an agency store, run by Quakers, and ordered the Indians to trade at the agency. Smith worked under the supervision of Inspector J.H. Hammond, in charge of the Central Superintendency Office in Lawrence, Kansas, after the removal of Superintendent Nicholson.[28]

Smith went to Seneca, where he found the merchants of the town divided between supporters and opponents of Agent Jones. H.H. Gregg, leader of the faction opposing Jones, was married to the daughter of his predecessor. Jones had licensed two brothers named Newlin, cousins of his wife, as agency traders in 1874. After the Newlins had established their store, Jones ordered the Indians, who had previously traded at Seneca, confined to the reservation. Jones also introduced a system of trading cards, provided to the Indians instead of cash, which could be exchanged for merchandise at the Newlins' store. The Newlins left the agency in January, 1876, just after a large payment to the Shawnees had been spent. Jones transferred the trading privilege to J.G. McGannon, a merchant in Seneca and Jones' principal supporter there.

Smith found the quality of both the agent's and the trader's records to be extremely poor. Further, "unlimited fraud" was possible under the trading card system, which the Interior Department attempted to ban in November, 1877. The agency grounds were "in bad order," the Indians complained of Jones' neglect, and nearly all subordinate agency positions were filled by members of Jones' family.[29] From Quapaw, Hayt sent Smith to the Wichita Agency to investigate the charges, which proved to be unfounded, against the teacher and the agency physician of "illegal intercourse with three or four of the female pupils of the school" and of "producing abortions."[30] Smith, while functioning as an inspector, was nominally a clerk in the Indian Office. Apparently, his position had been created for the express purpose of supplementing the inspections already underway in Indian Territory. In recommending Smith's appointment, Hayt wrote to Schurz that Smith would "make certain investigations. . . . in the Indian Territory, under instructions from this office."[31] After he completed the Quapaw and Wichita investigations, the Washington Office appointed Smith agency clerk at the Kiowa and Commanche Agency, under Quaker appointee J.M. Haworth.[32] Smith sought, and eventually obtained appointment as a Special Indian Agent. A Schurz partisan, Smith lost his position with the change of administration in 1881.[33] Former Osage Agent Cyrus Beede succeeded him.

Many of the individuals appointed to subordinate agency positions performed an investigative function. The Washington Office appointed T.P. Pendleton of Berryville, Virginia, as Assistant Farmer at Rosebud Agency, "to do detective service and report on. . . . violations of law" at the agency.[34] Pendleton was at Rosebud from May 4 to July 4, 1879. He was paid at the rate of $1,200 per year, although the salary of the Farmer was only $900 per year.[35] Pendleton investigated the farming program, Indian trade, agency administration, and the distribution of rations. He found Agent Newell, who had been accused of selling subordinate agency positions, to be "an honest and energetic man." However, he deprecated the practice of holding frequent "councils" with the chiefs and the issue of beef cattle "on the hoof" to the Indians. The agent was too deferential to Chief Spotted Tail for Pendleton's taste; a trader married to a daughter of the chief was permitted to trade at the agency without license. Pendleton recommended providing the Indians with large work horses to enable them to break the tough Dakota sod. The promotion of intermarriage with whites and the provision of rations to individuals, rather than to bands, would hasten the civilization process, he thought.[36]

In the late 1870s, inspectors negotiated with tribes to secure rights of way for railroads wishing to build on reservation land. In 1879, Hayt instructed Inspector W.J. Pollock to negotiate for a ferry for the Dakota Central Railroad across the Missouri River into the Sioux reservation. From there the company wanted to construct a wagon road westward and eventually build and operate a railroad to the Black Hills. Pollock was to persuade the Sioux to accept compensation in the form of stock cattle for their herds.[37] In the following year, Secretary Schurz ordered Inspector Robert S. Gardner to negotiate a right of way for the Chicago, Milwaukee, St. Paul and Pacific Railroad across the Sioux reservation.[38]

Initially, the shift in the direction of the inspection service, from the Commissioner of Indian Affairs to the Secretary of the Interior, did not result in any changes in the organization of the inspection service. Instructions to inspectors were specific and were occasioned by complaints reaching Washington. However, Schurz instructed the inspectors to report their movements to him twice a week.[39] Further, inspection reports submitted to the Secretary's Office were to be considered confidential, as Acting Secretary Alonzo Bell instructed newly appointed Inspector Isaac T. Mahan.[40] Bell's first assignments to Mahan were specific and in response to complaints made to the Secretary. Mahan's first assignment was to investigate Mackinac Agency in Michigan, where a mixed-blooded Chippewa had complained to the Secretary about the actions of the agent.[41]

By 1881, more general instructions were being sent to the inspectors. In May, Alonzo Bell wrote identical letters to the five inspectors directing them to report their expenditures on a monthly basis.[42] Schurz's successor, Secretary of the Interior Samuel J. Kirkwood, asked early in 1882 that "the investigations, both special and general, to be made of the agencies. . . . shall be as thorough as possible upon all points that may come under your observation, as well as upon the matters specifically presented in the letters and memoranda or rules and regulations before noted." Inspectors were to make general investigations of all agencies and not merely to respond to specific complaints.[43] Kirkwood expanded these instructions in a letter to Inspector Gardner in March.

In making these inspections, [Kirkwood wrote], the most rigid scrutiny into the administration of affairs is earnestly enjoined. Any extravagence in the use of the appropriations may lead to a scarcity at a critical period, when the gravest results may ensue. The case of Indians at the Sioux agency, brave, fearless, warlike, and restless, requires not only energetic men for agents, but a firmness, quick perception, honesty of character, ability, and example beyond cavil. . . . Ascertain the needs of the Indians and the best and most speedy manner of supplying their necessities with the power and means of the service. Observe the progress made by them since your last visit and listen to what they may have to say without making them any promises. If there are any deserving ones among the Indians who have distinguished themselves by industrial or agricultural efforts, report their case to the Department, and if worthy of special attention it will be recognized through the proper channels. . . . The question of liquor drinking among the agents or employees should also be inquired into. Also the question of dangerous half-breeds and squawmen who breed discontent and insubordination among the Indians. Also note any dissatisfaction of the Indians with the agents and the causes leading thereto. . . .[44]

The Secretary's Office directed all inspectors to include recommendations for improvements in agency administration in every report.[45] In response to complaints from the Indian Office, Kirkwood warned inspectors to make no promises to the Indians "which have not first been authorized by the Department."[46]

Toward the end of his short tenure, Secretary Kirkwood outlined the desired content of the inspection reports. Inspectors should

carefully observe everything connected [with the agencies] affecting the interest and well-being of the Indians, and the public interest, and forward to this office the full and particular report in writing of your observations with such recommendations as may seem to you proper. . . . Your reports should give verbal photographic views of each agency. . . . It is particularly desirable that your reports shall contain a clear and accurate statement of the extent to which farming is carried out in each agency, distinguishing between what is done by government employés and what is done by Indians, giving in each case as nearly as may be, the crops raised for the last year.[47]

In 1882, Kirkwood's successor, H.M. Teller, wrote to the inspectors specifying the kind of paper to be used, the indexing, and format of the inspection reports.[48]

These increasingly specific instructions provided the background for Joslyn's letter of instructions to Inspector Benedict quoted above. In 1883, the Interior Department codified the instructions in the pamphlet, *Duties of Inspectors*. The pamphlet presented a summary of the instructions contained in the letters discussed above. Five inspection divisions were created, and provision was made for the inspection of agencies and schools in rotation.[49] The pamphlet was reprinted, with minor modifications, in 1885.[50] The publication of the pamphlet signalled the formalization of the inspection process. Henceforth, inspection reports would be uniform in terms of topics covered, providing the secretary's office with predictable information regarding affairs at the agencies. In the mid-1880s, forms on which inspectors could complete their reports were provided, resulting in an even more standardized report.

In 1889, R.V. Belt, who had been Chief Clerk in the Indian Division since Secretary Teller's administration, became Assistant Commissioner of Indian Affairs under the new Commissioner, Thomas J. Morgan. Belt had presided over the preparation of the synopses of inspection reports in the Indian Division;

he proceeded to write synopses of all of the reports on individuals who had served as Indian Agents during the past decade. These memoranda were evidently intended for internal use, to guide the new Republican administration in deciding which applicants to nominate for the agent positions. The memoranda provided the first personnel records of Indian agents; they usually reflected the inspectors' conclusions about the fitness of the individuals concerned.[51]

Inspectors continued to report to the Secretary of the Interior until 1908. Commissioners of Indian Affairs controlled the Special Indian Agents, another corps of inspectors. However, Commissioners appear to have been anxious to find other outsiders who could be used to gain information on the agencies. Missionaries and representatives of such organizations as the Indian Rights Association performed this function for some. For example, Commissioner Morgan wrote to the Corresponding Secretary of the Board of Home Missions of the United Presbyterian Church in 1890:

> I shall be very glad indeed to have you see for me during your anticipated trip and report anything to which you think my attention should be called. It is very difficult to get unprejudiced information, and I am often much embarrassed in my action by not knowing the exact truth. Mark your letters "Personal" and in case they contain anything in which your name should not appear they shall be considered confidential.[52]

The formalization of the inspection process, traced in some detail above, mirrored the formalization of other aspects of Indian administration. A volume of regulations of the Indian Bureau, published in 1850, was in use in the Indian Office until 1876. However, the rules were written in such general terms as to be useless to Indian agents. The experience of D.C. Poole, an Army officer detailed to Whetstone Agency, Dakota Territory, in 1869, was perhaps typical. Poole visited the Dakota Superintendency Office in Yankton before taking charge of his agency. The officials with whom he met were cordial, but seemed to know little about the Indians or about agency administration. From Washington, Poole received

> A few lines of vague generalities about the beneficence of the Government, and a book of regulations containing the theoretical rules for his guidance. With these he [was] expected to cope with difficulties and effect great improvements.[53]

He was "occasionally visited by parties following the scent of some supposed rascality," but his activities were not supervised, nor were his accounts inspected.[54]

While the inspection service matured, the Indian Office regulations proliferated and became increasingly specific. The Indian Office published a book of *Instructions to Indian Agents* in 1876, and revised it in 1877 and 1880.[55] The *Instructions* were superceded by the *Regulations of the Indian Department*, issued in 1884 and revised in 1894 and 1904.[56] These general regulations were issued to all agents. They contained appendices showing the forms used and instructed agents on how the forms were to be completed. The general regulations were supplemented by specific publications summarizing Indian Office regulations covering such areas as trade (1876), [57] courts of Indian offenses (1883),[58] and schools (1890).[59]

The field positions in the Indian Service were brought into the classified Civil Service beginning in 1891. Classification required further formalization, since job descriptions for classified positions were required before entrance examinations could be composed. The spread of formal regulations and the increasingly predictable nature of the inspection process combined to increase the influence of the Washington administrators over developments in the field. Agency activity itself became increasingly predictable, as written rules increasingly narrowed the options available to local officials, as inspectors monitored rule compliance increasingly effectively, and as a single activity, education, came to dominate work with the Indians.

CHAPTER VIII

THE INSPECTION PROCESS

The inspection report was the final product of the inspection process. In a letter to the responsible Washington official, inspectors reported upon the condition of the agencies they visited. Attached to the report might be affidavits from agency employees, traders, and Indians, transcripts of councils held by the inspector with tribesmen, and, particularly in the late 1880s and 1890s, separate lists of public buildings, employees, and textbooks used in the agency schools.

These reports provided Washington officials with their major source of information about developments at the agencies. After Schurz directed in 1880 that they be addressed to the Secretary of the Interior, the inspection reports provided the Secretary's Office with a means of monitoring events at the agencies and of gauging the extent to which agents obeyed Indian Office directives. The inspection process provided a complex system of control. Although the President appointed the Inspectors, they reported to the Secretary of the Interior after 1880. The agents whose activities they monitored were also Presidential appointees, but the Commissioner of Indian Affairs controlled the funds for agency operations and prescribed the rules which the agents were to follow.

In such a complicated administrative system, conflict was likely to occur. Agents and Commissioners could question the accuracy of the inspection reports; a report of dubious value was useless in extending administrative control over the many Indian agencies. If the inspection reports were to be usable, they needed to be predictable in terms of content (areas covered), format, and the kind of evidence presented. Improvements in the predictability of inspection reports increased institutionalization, since they made it more likely that information would be used, and used to achieve uniformity of action at the organization's many operating units—the agencies and schools.[1]

The typical routing of an inspector's recommendation is traced in Chart VII (See above, p. 91). After 1880, a clerk in the Indian Division of the Secretary's Office noted recommendations reported in inspection reports. Subsequently, the Indian Division referred recommendations to the Commissioner's Office for report and action. The Commissioner's Office might take action, might check the facts with the agent involved, or might protest the inspector's recommendation. In such a situation, reports had to be routinized for such recommendations to result in action; the greater the standardization of the reports, the greater the probability that the recommendations would be translated into action.

The two pamphlets prescribing the *Duties of Inspectors* promoted the standardization of the inspection reports. The 1883 pamphlet prescribed how reports and testimony should be written. Subject indexes and summaries of recommendations enhanced the ability of the Indian Division clerks to digest the reports and extract recommendations for action. The pamphlet required inspectors to report on "everything. . . . affecting the interest and well-being of the Indians," including "the extent to which farming, grazing or other industrial pursuit is carried on. . . . the condition of the schools," public buildings, the "moral character" of agents and employees, the condition of books and accounts, and whether open-market purchases made by the agents were justi-fied.[2] The 1885 pamphlet repeated these specifications; the standards for reporting on school activities were elaborated and the pamphlet required inspectors to report on schools in a separate section of the inspection report.[3]

In the three decades following the creation of the inspection service in 1873, inspection reports became increasingly specific and predictable. In the 1870s inspections were likely to be occasioned by complaints from surrounding whites, settlers or the Army. The inspection reports were partisan documents; they supported or deprecated agent activities. Because of this, they were relatively unlikely to result in administrative action. Later in the nineteenth century, the reports were more likely to present a balanced account of agency activities. The reports came to emphasize education, allotment and land use, and the abilities of individual employees.

To illustrate the changes in inspection reports during the period between 1873 and 1906, I inspected all inspection reports for three agencies. The agencies were Quapaw, in the Indian Territory, Standing Rock, in Dakota Territory, and the Puget Sound agencies, variously known as S'Kokomish, Puyallup, and Puyallup-S'Kokomish, in Washington Territory. While no three Indian agencies from the late nineteenth century can be said to be representative, the three do reflect a range of problems encountered by the Indian Office during the period.

The reservations differed greatly from one another, in size, in the nature of the tribes served, and in location and topography. The Quapaw Agency, located in the Northeastern corner of Indian Territory, had jurisdiction over a number of small tribes which had been removed to the area from elsewhere. The principal tribes included the Quapaws, Peorias, Ottawas, Shawnees, Wyandots, Senecas, and, after 1873, the Modocs. Assigned to the Quakers during the Grant adminis-tration, the agency was part of the Central Superintendency prior to its abolition in 1878.[4] Standing Rock, known as the Grand River Agency prior to December, 1874, was established in 1869 at the junction of the Grand and Missouri Rivers in Dakota. In 1873, the Indian Office moved the agency about fifty miles upstream to an island in the Missouri River. The agency had jurisdiction over several bands of the Sioux, principally the Yanktonais, Hunkpapas, and Blackfoot Sioux. Assigned to the Catholics during the Grant administration, the agency administered a large reservation extending from the Missouri River into the high plains of western Dakota Territory.[5] The Puyallup and S'Kokomish Agencies in western Washington had charge of numerous small tribes located on reservations around Puget Sound. Tribes under the agencies' jurisdiction included the Puyallups, S'Kokomish, Nisqually, Squaxin, Chehallis, and Clallams or Skallams. The reservations had been established by the Treaties of Medicine Creek and Point-No-Point in the mid-1850s. Perhaps because they were not removed from their original homes, many of the Indians had little to do with the government. On some of the Puget Sound reservations, less than half of the tribesmen lived on reservation lands. Many worked for whites in the hop fields or in the logging industry; others supported themselves by fishing or clam digging.[6]

Two of the agencies, Standing Rock and the consolidated Nisqually, Puyallup, and S'Kokomish Agency, had relatively stable leadership during the 1880s and '90s. James McLaughlin served as Standing Rock Agent from 1881 until 1895 when he resigned to begin duty as an inspector. Edwin Eells served as S'Kokomish Agent from 1871 until the consolidation of that agency with Nisqually in 1882. Appointed to head the consolidated Nisqually-S'Kokomish Agency, Eells served until 1895. The Puget Sound Agency, known as Puyallup Consolidated Agency by 1895, was placed under the control of a reservation superintendent in 1895. Quapaw's last agent was replaced by a superintendent in 1900. At Standing Rock, however, agents continued to control the agency until 1908.

The agencies differed in terms of administrative control, the stability of leadership, and the problems of the Indians they supervised. At Standing Rock, the Indian Office faced the problem of controlling the warlike Sioux into the 1890s; here, too, conflict with the military authorities was endemic. While few problems of social control confronted the agents at Quapaw and Puyallup-Nisqually, at both agencies white intrusion on reservation lands was a problem. In addition, allegations of fraud and collusion with white intruders were made against the agents at these agencies. Taken together the three agencies represented a broad range of problems with which the Indian Office had to contend in the late nineteenth century.

The inspection reports for these agencies for the period 1873-1880 are held by the National Archives and Record Service in Record Group 75, Records of the Bureau of Indian Affairs. The Indian Office maintained a register of Inspectors' Reports, making it possible to check the extant reports against the register for completeness.[7] Inspection reports for the period after 1880 are held in Record Group 48, Records of the Office of the Secretary of Interior. The Indian Division of the Secretary's Office prepared registers of incoming inspection reports, again enabling me to check the extant reports against the registers for completeness.[8] The inspection reports are listed in Table I; complete citations to these reports will be found in the notes to this chapter.

Table I shows that inspectors visited these agencies with relatively dependable frequency during the 1880s and 1890s—about one inspection per year was normal for the three agencies. During the 1870s and after 1900 inspectors visited the agencies less frequently, suggesting that the purpose of inspection may have been different during these periods. Inspection reports completed between 1880 and 1900 covered a wider variety of topics than those completed before 1880 or after 1900. The small number of inspectors before 1880, combined with the lack of central control of their activities, may explain the episodic and incomplete reports of that period. After 1900, with the Indian Service personnel largely in the classified civil service and with the potential for armed conflict with the Indians much diminished, the frequent and searching inspections of the previous twenty years may have been unnecessary.

The earliest inspections, those of 1873-75, reflected the tensions which characterized Indian affairs during that period. The inspection reports concerned such matters as interdenominational conflict, controversies over the control of Indian trade, and civilian-military disagreements. Perhaps the reports of E.C. Kemble, an Episcopalian layman and a member of the church's Mission Board, exemplified the early problems of the inspection system.

Kemble inspected Puyallup and S'Kokomish Agencies in 1873 during his general investigation of the Washington Superintendency. The Methodist Church nominated the Superintendent, as well as many of the agents serving in the territory. Kemble found few redeeming qualities in Methodist administration. He was soon embroiled in a controversy with Washington Superintendent R.H. Milroy.

At Puyallup, he found the farmer-in-charge, Byron Barlow, "living out of government supplies and keeping a sort of boarding house for parties living off the Reservation." In addition to his government duties, Barlow was in the dairy business with a farm near the reservation. Kemble accused him of subsisting his hired help on government supplies intended for the Indians. The barley raised on the reservation fed Barlow's private stock. Indeed, Kemble estimated that "not over 5% of the supplies brought out to the reservation were issued to the Indians." Prior to Barlow's appointment, the Puyallup Indians had a run a logging business on the reservation; Superintendent Milroy ordered Barlow to manage it, and the result was the wholesale defrauding of the Indians, Kemble charged.[9]

When Kemble reported Barlow's activities to Milroy, he promptly discharged the farmer.[10] Still, the inspector accused the superintendent of "complicity with frauds against the government." Milroy's failure to investigate earlier charges against Barlow, together with problems at other reservations, led Kemble to suspend him on November 7. A "politico-religious Ring . . . has unquestionably ruled the Superintendency," Kemble charged.[11]

In the absence of a confirmation of Kemble's order by the President, Milroy refused to surrender the funds of the superintendency to Marshall Blinn, the temporary successor designated by Kemble.[12] On November 13, Grant approved Kemble's action.[13] Kemble and Milroy began to trade charges against each other, in communications to Commissioner E.P. Smith and in the public press. Admitting that he could find "no evidence of defalcation or felonious abstraction of funds" against Milroy, Kemble charged him with surrounding himself with unsavory characters, one of whom charged Kemble with conducting a "star chamber" proceeding in an open letter published in the *Puget Sound Daily Courier*.[14] Milroy called Kemble "an egotistic, incompetent fool" and sent Smith a copy of a vituperative newspaper article by Kemble, which he characterized as slanderous.[15] Grant revoked his order approving Milroy's suspension in February, 1874, and restored the superintendent to office on March 4.[16] However, the Indian Office discontinued the superintendency in June, 1874, after Congress failed to appropriate funds for its support. In his last official letter as Superintendent, Milroy complained to Smith that his office had been "bombarded with serious damag [sic] by Kemble, Congress, and yourself."[17]

Milroy and the administrators Kemble charged with malfeasance were Methodists. The S'Kokomish Agency, while part of the Washington Superintendency, was in the hands of the Congregationalists. Rather than frauds, here Kemble found a want of energy. He arrived at the agency at nightfall and heard the Towana Indians' drum. The white employees were "assembled by themselves for a prayer meeting, scarcely an Indian being present." The agent, Edwin Eells, was "a conscientious and honorable man," but not an especially effective one. Three-fourths of the Indians refused to live on the reservation. The school, with twenty pupils, was "prospering both in numbers and in discipline." But the sick were "in wretched condition," unattended by the physician. The agent's father, Cushing Eells, was an old Northwest missionary, but had not organized an Indian Church. The old man needed support from his denomination, Kemble suggested.[18]

Kemble's inspection of Quapaw Agency in 1874 was one of a number of investigations of trading practices on that reservation during the 1870s. The Indian Office ordered him to investigate Quapaw Agency after merchants in Seneca, Missouri, complained of bias in a prior investigation ordered by Central Superintendent Enoch Hoag. Hoag had appointed William Hadley to investigate charges that the agent's son solicited bribes to direct Indian business to merchants in Seneca. Hadley, a Quaker like Hoag and Quapaw Agent Hiram Jones, ran the bank in Lawrence, Kansas, where Hoag deposited the superintendency's funds.

Hadley observed that most of the complaints of the Seneca merchants resulted from the establishment of a store at the Agency. While Endsley Jones, the agent's son, probably accepted bribes for influencing Indians to trade with specific merchants, Hadley could find no evidence that the agent's son had exercised his influence "in a manner prejudicial to the Indians' interests." The

Table I
Inspection Reports for Quapaw, S'Kokomish-Puyallup, and Standing Rock Agencies, 1873-1906

Year	Quapaw	S'Kokomish and Puyallup	Standing Rock
1873		E. C. Kemble	
1874	E. C. Kemble	W. Vandever	J. D. Bevier
			W. Vandever
1876			
1877		E. C. Watkins	
1878			J. H. Hammond
1879	J. McNeil		
1880			J. McNeil
1881		W. J. Pollock	
1882	B. N. Benedict		R. S. Gardner
1883	H. Ward		B. N. Benedict
	R. S. Gardner		
1884		H. Ward	M. R. Barr
		W. A. Newell	
1885	B. N. Benedict		H. Ward
			M. A. Thomas
1886	R. S. Gardner	E. D. Bannister	G. R. Pearsons
	E. D. Bannister		
1887	T. D. Marcam	F. C. Armstrong	E. D. Bannister
	R. S. Gardner	R. S. Gardner	
1888	M. A. Thomas		E. Mallet
	F. C. Armstrong		
1889	F. C. Armstrong	T. D. Marcum	A. W. Tinker
		J. H. Cisney	
1890	W. W. Junkin	R. S. Gardner	J. H. Cisney
			R. S. Gardner
1891			J. H. Cisney
1892	A. W. Tinker	B. H. Miller	J. H. Cisney
	R. S. Gardner		B. H. Miller
1893	C. C. Duncan		
1894	T. P. Smith	P. McCormick	J. W. Cadman
			T. P. Smith
			J. W. Cadman
1895	P. F. Faison	P. McCormick	
1896	C. C. Duncan	P. McCormick	J. McLaughlin
		J. Lam	
1897		W. J. McConnell	J. McLaughlin

Table I
(Continued)

Year	Quapaw	S'Kokomish and Puyallup	Standing Rock
1898	C. F. Nesler C. Beede		
1899		W. J. McConnell	A. W. Tinker J. McLaughlin
1900			
1901		W. J. McConnell	J. E. Jenkins (3)
1902			C. F. Nesler Levi Chubbuck
1903			
1904			
1905			J. McLaughlin
1906		Levi Chubbuck	

Number:	22	22	30
Number/Year:	.65	.65	.94

1880-99

Number:	20	16	22
Number/Year:	1.00	.80	1.10

Source: Registers of Inspector's Reports, NARS, RG 48 and RG 75
          (See notes 7 and 8).

agency store, run by two Quaker brothers named Newlin, was a benefit to the Indians, because it resulted in fewer trips to Seneca and less drunkenness.[19]

Kemble found that Hadley was not "an impartial commissioner." He had endeavored to "cover up and conceal the facts that would have shown a corrupt official [Endsley Jones] in his true standing." Jones admitted receiving fifteen percent of the money spent by the Quapaw Agency Indians at the stores where the agent allowed them to trade. Even though Hadley pronounced Endsley Jones guilty, the latter's father subsequently appointed him sub-agent for the Modoc Indians who had been removed to Quapaw after the Modoc War of 1872-73. Kemble believed that Hiram Jones knew of his son's activities even before Hadley's investigation.[20]

Kemble confined the official report of his inspection of Quapaw Agency to a discussion of trading and accounting practices. He found no "misapplication" of funds, but "such looseness and irregularity in [Agent Jones'] method of conducting business as to amount to serious error." The agent failed to advertise prior to letting contracts for supplying the agency. He did not weigh or examine beef or other issue supplies, made issues without "system or regularity," and "borrowed" supplies for use by his family. The agency store charged very high prices. The managers were "estimable young men," but had "only the business object of getting the best prices" possible "and of 'making money' by their dealings with the Indians." The agency store enjoyed a near monopoly of the Indian trade. However, the problem was not wilfullness or "an evil intention" on the agent's part, but "a want of proper instruction in his official duties" and a "lack of proper supervisory control" on the part of the Central Superintendent. Kemble recommended abolishing the office of Modoc sub-agent, held by Endsley Jones, and an abolition of the Indian order system, which restricted individual Indians in their choice of trading establishments.[21]

The other reports of the 1873-75 period were more routine than Kemble's. William Vandever visited the Puget Sound agencies in 1874, at the request of F.H. Smith, Secretary of the Board of Indian Commissioners. The Indian Office asked Smith and Commissioner John D. Lang, in Portland, Oregon, to supervise the purchase of goods for the Indian service, to visit Puget Sound and report on the advisability of allotting the reservations there. The Commissioners "considered the question one of sufficient magnitude to justify them in requesting the cooperation and advice" of Vandever and of General O. O. Howard, Commander of the Military Department of the Columbia. The four visited Puget Sound in October, 1874. Commissioners Smith and Lang recommended consolidating the scattered tribes of the Puget Sound region at an enlarged S'Kokomish reservation, with those not wishing to remove to S'Kokomish to be offered allotments at their old reservation.[22]

Like General Howard, Vandever endorsed the recommendation for consolidating the various Puget Sound tribes at the S'Kokomish reservation.[23] His two inspection reports on the S'Kokomish and Chehallis Agencies were confined to descriptions of councils that he held with the Indians and his observations on their complaints. The S'Kokomish Indians wanted their annuities paid in cash rather than in goods, which Vandever thought was contrary to the Treaty of Point-No-Point. They also complained, as they had to Kemble a year earlier, that the agency physician was "inattentive." However, Vandever, perhaps repeating what he had been told by the physician, said that "sometimes the indians [sic] require more than the Doctor thinks beneficial for them and then he withholds the supplies they ask." The physician had "never failed to render prompt treatment in case of sickness." Agent Eells and his six employees cared for only about two hundred Indians; an additional five hundred "never come about the reservation."[24] At Puyallup, a sub-agency of the Chehallis Agency, the major concern of the Indians was the expiration of the Medicine Creek Treaty in 1875; Vandever recommended allotment.[25]

Inspectors visited Standing Rock twice during the first three years of the inspection system. J.D. Bevier visited the agency, then known as the Grand River Agency, in August, 1874. In a four-page report, he described the Dakota agency, calling for the creation of a boarding school and instruction in farming techniques.[26] Vandever visited the agency a year later. Unlike Bevier, he discovered a great deal of internal conflict at the Missouri River agency. Captain J.S. Poland, the commander of the military post at Standing Rock, supported an unlicensed trader at the agency, an Indian woman named Mrs. Galpin, whose daughter was married to an ex-soldier. Poland had prevented Agent John Burke from shutting down Mrs. Galpin's store; he accused the licensed trader, H.D. Parkin, of charging exhorbitant prices. Vandever did not find Parkin's prices excessive; Poland, he wrote, was "disposed to exceed his legitimate authority, and to assume the management of the Indians and the supervisory controle [sic] of the affairs of the agency." Further, the military post at Fort Rice provided a source of whiskey for the Indians. In his official report, Vandever opposed War Department plans to build a large military post at Standing Rock. He repeated his attack on Captain Poland in a separate communication to the Commissioner.[27]

Religious conflict, civilian-military disagreements, and problems in regulating trade presented major difficulties for agents and Washington officials during the 1870s; the inspection reports completed at the three agencies between 1873 and 1875 generally were confined to one or another of these controversies. As such, they were partisan reports and were not useful for administrative control. Kemble's adverse report on R. H. Milroy's conduct as Washington Superintendent resulted in vacillating behavior by Washington officials. Kemble's investigation of Quapaw agency problems did not lead to a resolution of the difficulties; nor did Vandever's attack on Captain Poland and the Army at Standing Rock. Consolidation and allotment of the Puget Sound agencies did not follow the recommendations of Inspector Vandever, General Howard, and the

Board of Indian Commissioners. All three problems figured in inspectors' reports on these agencies during the early years of the Hayes administration.

During the remainder of the decade, inspectors who visited the three agencies similarly emphasized trade, conflicts with the Army, and allotment. Their reports were little more useful than the earlier ones, although the Indian Office removed one agent as the result of an inspection report. Arden R. Smith's 1879 special investigation of trading practices at Quapaw Agency was discussed above.[28] Smith worked in conjunction with Inspector John McNeil, who removed Agent Hiram Jones from office in April, 1879, after an exhaustive investigation.[29]

In July, 1878, Inspector J.H. Hammond reported that troops were gathering at Standing Rock with the intention of building a fort to replace Fort Rice. He asked Hayt to request that the troops be removed. The Indians were doing well, and "a large military post is inconsistent with agriculture and stock raising."[30] Despite Hammond's request, the Army established Fort Yates near the Standing Rock agency on December 30, 1878.[31] The military commander, Colonel W.P. Carlin, was soon in conflict with the Standing Rock Agent, Joseph A. Stephan, a Catholic priest. Inspector John McNeil went to Standing Rock in September, 1880, to investigate charges made against the priest-agent by Colonel Carlin. He found the agency books not maintained, because the agent was without a clerk. However,

> strict regard appears in all other matters to have been given to orders and regulations of the department. Issues were promptly made and attested, the public property was found in good order, and public money to have been prudently and judiciously expended for authorized objects. Even the close and prying attention of the Military Commandant at Fort Yates failed to discover any failure in duty that could be sustained or the least misappropriation or waste.[32]

In a separate report on Carlin's charge that the agent was implicated in weight frauds, McNeil charged the Colonel with personal animus against Stephan. He found "no shadow of suspicion" against the agent or his employees; most of Carlin's charges were frivolous.[33]

Inspector E.C. Watkins visited S'Kokomish and Puyallup Agencies in September, 1877. The Puyallup Agent, former Washington Superintendent R.H. Milroy, lived in Olympia rather than at the agency. He told Watkins that he had received no funds since July and had therefore closed the schools. (An Indian Office clerk claimed that funds had been sent.) Watkins recommended consolidation of the Indians at Puyallup followed by an allotment of the reservation.[34] At S'Kokomish, Watkins also recommended allotment. Agent Edwin Eells told him that allotment would encourage the Indians to farm, rather than subsisting on fish and timber sales.[35]

The inspection reports of the 1880s were both more comprehensive and more predictable as to content than those of the previous decade. In part, this was doubtless a result of the increasing formalization of the inspections, traced in the previous chapter. In addition, after the Secretary of the Interior assumed control of inspectors in 1880, the selection of agencies to be investigated was routinized. The 1883 pamphlet, *Duties of Inspectors*, provided that when an inspector was assigned to one of the five inspection divisions ''he will proceed at once to the agency nearest and most accessible from the point where he receives the instructions. . . . and when the work at that agency is completed he will proceed to the next agency nearest and most accessible to him, and so on.''[36] Such an instruction, if followed, would have resulted in less concentration on agencies where specific complaints had been made against the agent.

Even before 1883, the inspection reports addressed to the Secretary of the Interior regarding the Puget Sound agencies, Quapaw, and Standing Rock were evidently not the result of specific complaint, and provided, for the most part, greater detail than the earlier reports. Inspector William J. Pollock's reports on Nisqually and S'Kokomish Agencies in 1881 included estimates of the Indian population at each agency and the size of the reservations served by the agencies, in addition to information on the economic activities of the Indians and on school expenditures and enrollments. In both cases, Pollock found the agencies to be unnecessary. He recommended dismissing Nisqually Agent Milroy, still residing at Olympia and ''clumsy and unmethodical in his accounts,'' and S'Kokomish Agent Eells. The government schools should then be closed and replaced with contract schools.[37]

In his 1882 report on Standing Rock, Inspector Robert S. Gardner similarly included data on the Indian population, the number of acres under cultivation, and the condition of the schools. Gardner also investigated charges by the agency trader that the agency physician was a habitual drinker, evidently the result of ''a hostile feeling'' between the physician and the trader. The new agent, James McLaughlin, requested additional agency buildings for the agency, which Gardner said were needed. However, McLaughlin had failed to account properly for existing agency buildings. Gardner ''invited his attention'' to the appropriate sections of the 1880 *Instructions to Indian Agents*.[38]

Inspector B.N. Benedict's similarly comprehensive reports on Quapaw and Standing Rock Agencies, completed in 1882 and 1883, included alphabetical subject indexes and separate summaries of recommendations, which concerned agency water supplies, agricultural, and school matters.[39] Henry Ward's 1883 inspection report of the Quapaw Agency was more brief, dwelling on the water supply and the need for fencing to protect Modoc farms from cattle grazed by whites under leases negotiated by the agent. His report, like most submitted after 1882, also included a subject index and a list of recommendations.[40] Inspector Gardner attached a form describing government buildings and a list of employees to his report on the Quapaw Agency of December, 1883. R.V. Belt, Chief of the Indian Division of the Secretary's office under Teller and Lamar, wrote a synopsis of Gardner's report for use within the Secretary's Office and by the Indian Office.[41] Belt wrote synopses for most reports submitted after 1883.

The changes in the inspection reports prior to 1883 were the result of formalization. The inspectors responded to the instructions of Secretaries Kirkwood and Teller, described in the previous chapter.[42] The inspection reports of 1884 and 1885 reflected the instruction in the 1883 pamphlet that inspectors prepare subject indexes and summaries of recommendations. Henry Ward included these in his 1884 inspection report on the consolidated Nisqually and S'Kokomish Agency, as did M.R. Barr and Ward in their reports on Standing Rock Agency.[43]

Before Teller issued the pamphlet of instructions in 1883, inspectors were not required to report on the condition of the schools at the agencies they visited. However, most did so. "While not under instructions to visit the schools upon the different reservations, I have invariably done so," wrote B.N. Benedict in 1882. "Believing that the hope of the Indian race lies in the education of the young and their complete separation from Indian associations I take a deep interest in watching the progress made by the schools."[44]

With expenditures for schools accounting for an increasing proportion of Indian Office expenditures in the early 1880s, the publications detailing the *Duties of Inspectors* directed the inspectors' attention to the school programs at the agencies. The 1883 pamphlet required that

> careful examination. . . . be made into the condition of the schools, the attendance thereupon, the disposition of the Indians in the matter of the education of their children, the character and efficiency of the teachers and other school employés, and whether their number and cost are greater or less than the work of the schools justify.[45]

The 1885 edition of the pamphlet required a more extensive examination of school matters. The inspection of agency schools "should be brought, as near as possible, under one general head in each report." The pamphlet specified the matters to be investigated in greater detail. The inspection reports should contain information on the number and sufficiency of school buildings, the adequacy of their furniture, the number of pupils in attendance and their progress, the character and efficiency of school personnel, the textbooks used, and the methods used to encourage attendance.[46] Most inspectors responded to this instruction by submitting a separate school report covering the required areas.[47]

The revised instructions directed inspectors to devote more attention to personnel, as well as school matters. The 1885 pamphlet required inspectors to "examine and report as to the character, fitness, and qualification of the employees at each agency," including school and non-school personnel.[48] Discharging this responsibility within a narrative report proved to be difficult, and in 1887 some inspectors began to submit lists of employees along with their reports.[49] Beginning in 1888, inspectors began using two forms, one for agency employees and one for school employees, on which position titles were printed.

The inspector filled in the name of the employee holding the position and a brief assessment of his or her competence.[50] Clerks in the Education Division copied this information for school employees into rating books, making it possible to locate an inspector's evaluation of a given employee quickly.[51]

Both the 1883 and 1885 pamphlets required inspectors to communicate directly with the Secretary of the Interior regarding their official duties; they were not to make public the contents of their reports, which were to be considered "strictly confidential." Both documents also required Inspectors to report on "the extent to which farming, grazing or other industrial pursuit is carried on at each agency."[52] Education and agriculture thus became the dual foci of inspection reports in the 1880s and '90s, although reports on allotment problems and white intrusions also were significant at Quapaw and the Puget Sound agencies.

From 1882 to the end of the nineteenth century, the inspection reports of Quapaw Agency tended to focus increasingly on education, land use, and individual employee ratings. Complications arising from the leasing of grazing rights on reservation land occupied much of the inspectors' attention prior to the allotment of most of the reservation in 1892. In 1882, B.N. Benedict reported that the grazing fund, made up of receipts from leasing grazing rights to white ranchers, was used by the agent to subsist needy Indians.[53] In 1883, Inspector Henry Ward encouraged an expansion of leasing activity, but urged greater expenditures for fencing, particularly for the Modocs who were bringing more land under cultivation.[54] Robert S. Gardner and B.N. Benedict, in the mid-1880s, suggested that leasing of grazing rights to whites had gone too far; whites were even renting Indian farms on the reservation. The agent, William M. Ridpath, had appointed a white man, Wayland C. Lykins, chief of the Peorias; E. D. Bannister found Peoria resentment of Lykins, and the resentment of other tribes against their "chiefs" appointed by the agent, to be major factors in the tribes' resistence to allotment of the Quapaw Reservation.[55]

In 1887, T. D. Marcum found most of the Indians opposed to allotment, but suggested "to some extent I think they are influenced by white men who want cheap grazing land for their stock."[56] Gardner, who visited Quapaw a month after Marcum, reported the attitudes of the eight Quapaw Agency tribes toward allotment in some detail; most were opposed.[57] However, M. A. Thomas, who visited the agency in the summer of 1888 while allotment was underway, reported that the opposition "seems to have faded away" because of the efficiency of the allotment agent.[58] Yet Frank C. Armstrong found more resistance on his visits in 1888 and 1889.[59] William W. Junkin found little opposition to allotment in 1890; by 1892, all tribes except the Quapaws were allotted, with the allotments in most cases leased to whites.[60] The Quapaws had asked for special legislation to allot two hundred acres to each tribal member; Gardner endorsed this request in 1892.[61]

The Quapaw National Council authorized the allotment of the reservation in 1893. While Congress did not confirm the tribe's action until 1895, the Indian Office allotted the reservation in accordance with the provisions of the council's act.[62] With the allotment of all of the tribes at Quapaw Agency accomplished, the inspectors who visited the Quapaw Agency after 1892 focused on concerns which earlier inspectors had mentioned: the condition of government buildings, the consolidation of the schools, the disposal of surplus lands.[63] Thomas P. Smith observed in 1894 that at the Quapaw Agency "the Indian condition has ceased to exist. . . . they [the Indians] should be declared self-supporting and compelled in every other manner to be independent citizens of the United States."[64] Paul F. Faison found that most of the allotments were leased by whites in 1895, but he found the Indians "more advanced and better qualified for citizenship than any I have yet seen" and suggested that many Indian owners exploited their white tenants.[65] Yet C. F. Nesler three years later thought the full-bloods were exploited by white and mixed-blood lessees.[66] Congress, in the 1897 Indian Appropriations Act, provided that members of Peoria and Miami tribes could sell up to one hundred acres of their two hundred acre allotments without governmental approval.[67] The result had been widespread fraud, Nesler charged in a separate report to the Secretary.[68]

The shift in local administrative leadership, from agents to superintendents, apparently affected the likelihood of a visit by an Indian Inspector. A separate corps of inspectors, the Indian School Supervisors, inspected the schools and evaluated superintendents. After the death of Agent Edward Goldberg in 1900, the Secretary of the Interior placed Quapaw Agency under the control of the Superintendent of the Seneca Boarding School. No inspectors visited the agency after that date. However, excepting Nesler's report on land sale frauds, the reports of the late 1890s tended to focus on school matters, which were the province of the Indian School Supervisors. The last reports on Quapaw Agency, by Cyrus Beede in 1898, consisted of the employee report forms, with a note on the agency water supply and a separate report on the "dictatorial ways" of the reservation Superintendent of Schools.[69] Commissioner W. A. Jones defended his Superintendent's "austerity," citing a need for discipline in the school.[70]

As at Quapaw, inspectors visiting the Puget Sound agencies after 1883 emphasized land problems, education, and evaluations of the efficiency of individual employees in their reports. Because of his long tenure, many inspection reports focused on the character of the agent, Edwin Eells. The Indian Office removed Eells in 1895, after Inspector Province McCormick charged him with discrimination against a Democratic clerk appointed by the Indian Office.[71] Prior to Eells' removal inspectors had a mixed reaction to the agent. William A. Newell in 1884, M. A. Thomas in 1887, and Robert S. Gardner in 1887, praised his administration; Frank C. Armstrong, who was Assistant Commissioner of Indian Affairs when Eells was removed in 1895, criticized the Indian Office in

1884 for removing a Republican appointee of Eells.[72] Commissioner J.D.C. Atkins defended the Indian Office appointment, claiming Eells' appointee was a native of Canada and not a citizen.[73] James H. Cisney described Eells as a "model agent" in 1889.[74]

However, E.D. Bannister found Eells to be "a thoroughly selfish and vindictive partisan" in 1886.[75] T.D. Marcum found that Eells required agency employees to contribute $10.00 a quarter to his brother, a Methodist missionary, in 1889.[76] Gardner's 1890 reports did not mention Eells except in a brief summary of employee qualifications.[77] Benjamin H. Miller noted in 1892 that the Indians were largely self-supporting; two years later, McCormick contended that the Indians recognized no agent. Nine tenths of Eells' work involved supervising the four boarding and two day schools attached to the agency. McCormick recommended abolishing the agency.[78]

Perhaps McCormick succeeded in having Eells removed because he included affidavits from Democrats who claimed that Eells had appointed Republican election judges in the "reservation precincts" and openly campaigned for Republican candidates.[79] Eells was removed from office on January 31, 1895, and the superintendent of the Puyallup Boarding School took charge of the agency. McCormick's two subsequent inspection reports concerned school matters. He recommended consolidating the boarding schools at Quinaielt, Chehalis, and S'Kokomish at Puyallup, removing mixed-bloods, "blue-eyed, blond, flaxen-haired Indians," from the schools, and criticized Eells' brother, who had a position at the S'Kokomish Boarding School "which pays him a good salary for doing nothing."[80] The Indian Office abolished the three schools to which McCormick objected.[81]

John Lam's 1896 reports were similarly restricted to school matters.[82] W.J. McConnell inspected the schools in 1897 and 1899; his 1897 report also discussed the activities of the Puyallup Land Commission, which Congress created in 1893 to buy up Puyallup allotments and school lands for the expanding city of Tacoma. McConnell's major concern was that the Commission's activities would endanger the water supply for the Puyallup Boarding School. McConnell confined himself to school matters in his 1899 report. In particular, he recommended against reopening the Chehallis Boarding School.[83]

The focus on school and employee matters in the Puget Sound inspection reports is understandable, since the Indians at most of the reservations had little contact with the government. The agent and other officials devoted most of their attention to school matters; in addition employee ratings became increasingly important for the organization in the 1890s with the expansion of the civil service classification system. At Standing Rock, where the Hunkpapa Sioux did not agree to allotment until 1905, the reports for the period between 1883 and 1900 included information on agriculture and farming in addition to detailed information on school programs and employees.[84]

Earlier reports emphasized the Indians' progress in bringing land under cultivation. M.R. Barr found nineteen hundred acres being farmed in 1883; three years later, E.D. Bannister claimed that all families farmed and that thirty-five hundred acres were under cultivation.[85] In 1888, Edmond Mallet reported that nearly all Indian families had a few acres of land under cultivation. However, Mallet found the land to be poorly suited for agriculture.[86] Arthur W. Tinker in 1889 found the land to be better for grazing than for farming; in 1890, James H. Cisney recommended that the agent place emphasis on stock-raising.[87] Despite a good crop in 1892, inspectors in 1892, 1894 and 1896, recommended an emphasis on cattle-raising; by 1896, former agent James McLaughlin, whom President Cleveland appointed Indian Inspector in 1895, reported that stock raising was the chief industry at Standing Rock.[88]

The issuing of subsistence rations continued at Standing Rock through the period. Most inspectors evaluated the quality of issue goods in their reports. Cisney in 1890 and Benjamin H. Miller in 1892 complained that beef cattle were issued "in the good old way," on the hoof, to be captured and slaughtered by the Indians. Both recommended employing a butcher and issuing beef from the block.[89] In 1894, McLaughlin introduced the practice of making issues at substations scattered over the reservation. Thomas P. Smith pronounced the idea "very beneficial in many ways, most especially in avoiding larger congregations of Indians at frequent periods."[90]

Only one inspection report of the period responded to a specific complaint regarding agency administration. In 1886, George R. Pearsons investigated charges that McLaughlin had used improper influence in acquiring land on the townsite of Winona, Dakota Territory. Pearsons found McLaughlin's judgment in acquiring land so near the reservation to have been poor. However, he dismissed the charges against McLaughlin as false; "he is an honest man." Pearsons disposed of the charges in a paragraph and devoted the bulk of his report to agency affairs and employees. He added a separate report on the schools.[91]

Two other reports resulted from unusual circumstances. Robert S. Gardner submitted a report on the Ghost Dance at Standing Rock in December, 1890. While the bulk of the report was taken up with a discussion of the potential for unrest which the messianic religion presented, Gardner found time to inspect and report on the two agency boarding schools and reported on the condition of government buildings at the agency.[92] In 1899, Arthur W. Tinker investigated the reported outbreak of glanders, a bacillus, among the Indians' horses at the agency. He found some evidence of infection and recommended that two veterinary surgeons be employed to inspect the herds.[93]

While the inspection reports for Standing Rock Agency covered a greater range of topics than those of either Quapaw or the Puget Sound Agencies, every report, except Tinker's 1889 report on glanders, included data on school enrollment and curriculum, agency employees, and the condition of public buildings. Beginning with Inspector Pearsons' 1886 report, each inspector included a separate school report; earlier reports included separate sections on the reservation schools.[94] Beginning in 1894, inspectors submitted the printed employees reports for all inspections.[95] The Indian Division prepared synopses for all of the reports submitted after 1884.

The development of a specialized school inspection program is discussed in the next chapter. By the late 1890s, the Superintendent of Indian Schools and five Supervisors of Indian Education spent most of their time inspecting independent and agency schools. The development of this specialized inspection corps left the Indian Inspectors free to emphasize other concerns. After 1900, inspection reports on the Puget Sound and Standing Rock Agencies focused on land questions, particularly those arising from the encroachment of whites on Indian lands.

In his 1901 report on the Puyallup Consolidated Agency, W. J. McConnell complained that delays in compensating the Puyallup Indians for lands sold to the Puyallup Land Commission made it difficult for the Commission to induce the Puyallups to dispose of their allotments. At the Squaxin Reservation, an island in the sound, the State of Washington claimed the oyster beds, which Edwin Eells had not included in the allotments made to the Squaxin Indians.[96] Similarly, James E. Jenkins in the same year recommended the leasing of grazing rights on the Standing Rock Reservation to provide the Standing Rock Sioux with a cash income. The Indians now owned thirteen thousand head of cattle; Jenkins recommended a reduction of rations and fencing the western boundary of the reservation to prevent the intrusion of unauthorized cattle.[97]

Two inspectors investigated charges against Standing Rock Agent George H. Bingenheimer in 1901 and 1902. The Washington Agent of the Indian Rights Association, S.M. Brosius, charged the agent with inducing Indians to buy buggies from a Mandan, North Dakota, firm in which he had an interest.[98] Jenkins found no truth in the charges, which he thought originated from traders who had unsuccessfully sought Bingenheimer's complicity in similar schemes.[99] The leasing of grazing lands on the Standing Rock reservation began in 1901. Some area ranchers accused Bingenheimer of favoritism in awarding the leases and the secretary's office sent Inspector C. F. Nesler to the reservation to investigate the charges. Nesler cleared Bingenheimer, saying that the agent's political enemies were behind the charges.[100]

Levi Chubbuck, a special inspector who specialized in agricultural matters, visited Standing Rock in 1902 and 1903. In 1903 Chubbuck recommended the allotment of the reservation, with the surplus to be held by the Indians in common for grazing large herds. His 1903 reports also included a report on fencing and reports on an additional farmer and a livestock supervisor employed at the agency.[101] McLaughlin visited the agency in 1905 to persuade the Indians to accept allotment and to continue leasing unoccupied tribal lands.[102] Chubbuck confined his 1906 report on the Puyallup Agency to a discussion of agriculture, fishing, and the exploitation of the clam beds on the Puget Sound Reservations.[103]

The shifts in the content of the inspector's reports between 1873 and 1900 were in part the result of formalization. As the review of the content of the reports on the Standing Rock Agency suggests, however, the changes were in part the result of changes in the activity going on at the reservations. At Quapaw and the Puget Sound Agencies, where allotment was completed early, and where the Indians posed no great military threat to neighboring whites, the inspection reports came to focus rather quickly on questions of education and land. At Standing Rock, reports covered a broader range of concerns, because the reservation was allotted rather late and the Indians were less "progressive" from the Indian Office perspective. In addition, Standing Rock was one of the last agencies in which the agent was replaced by a reservation superintendent. Agent William L. Belden became Standing Rock Superintendent in 1908.[104] Consequently, political controversy was a significant factor at Standing Rock as late as the investigations of Jenkins and Nesler in 1901 and 1902.

Even with the varying patterns found in the inspection reports of the three agencies, there was a clear narrowing of focus during the first three decades of the inspection program. The content of reports became more predictable, and perhaps with standardization the reports became more reliable. With the maturation of the Education Division, the reports became even more focused. Land and the exploitation of land by whites and Indians were the topics which inspectors emphasized after 1900.

The narrowing of focus reflected the development of characterizing technologies for dealing with the Indian problem. The growth of these technologies, education and land allotment, and their effect on the Indian Office, will be discussed in the next chapter.

CHAPTER IX

ORGANIZATIONAL GOALS AND CHARACTERIZING TECHNOLOGIES: INDIAN EDUCATION AND ALLOTMENT

In the preceding chapters, I reviewed the changing procedures for selecting Indian agents and agency personnel and the changing control structure of the Indian Office. The changes in the method of selecting field personnel resulted in an organization which was better bounded by 1900 than it had been a quarter-century earlier; changes in the control system used by the Washington Office also resulted in a better-bounded organization and one with the ability to elicit coordinated action from organization members. These changes, then, increased the institutionalization of the Indian Office.

While boundedness and the ability to elicit coordinated action from organization members are important indicators of institutionalization, the most significant, in Philip Selznick's conceptualization, involve organizational goals. An institution's goals, he suggested, are specific enough to prevent organizational drift; the defense of institutional goals, or mission, provides the rationale for clear organizational boundaries and for organizational coordination.[1] Further, the formal and informal organizational structure should reflect the organization's goals. "The institutional embodiment of purpose" is a key indicator of institutionalization. Selznick suggested that the organization's division of labor, its stratification system, and the beliefs and interests of its members would reflect organizational goals in an institution.[2]

The specification of organizational goals and their incorporation into the structure of the Indian Office was an important part of the institutionalization of the organization in the last quarter of the nineteenth century. Civilization was always a stated goal of the Indian Office, but the goal had little impact on organizational structure until reformers, Washington Office officials, and the Congress specified the means for accomplishing the goal. Subsequently, the means defined the characteristic ways in which organizational members interacted with Indians, and an organizational structure based on the new methods of work evolved.

While Indian reform organizations campaigned for administrative reforms, particularly the removal of political influence from the administration of the Indian Office, they attempted primarily to influence the government's Indian policy. Most reformers advocated allotment, citizenship, and education as the appropriate means of civilizing the Indians. Government officials increasingly agreed on these means in the years following 1878.[3] The allotment of Indian lands would provide the tribesmen with the instructive experience of private property ownership, while at the same time reducing the amount of land in Indian hands. On his reduced, individually owned allotment, the Indian would learn individualism and the desire to "get ahead" which powered economic interaction in the late nineteenth century.[4] Citizenship would subject the tribesman to law, federal and state or territorial, providing protection for the land he acquired through allotment. Voting in elections would provide him with practical experience in American democracy, while providing a new segment of the electorate for Western politicians to manipulate.[5] Indian education would provide tribesmen with the English language, practical skills, and, most importantly, cultural attitudes thought to be essential for integration into American society.[6] The underlying model of the three reforms was pedagogical: Indians were to learn a new culture. After 1865, with the stabilization of Indian populations on reservations, the Indian Office specified and perfected the means for accomplishing this instruction.

Washington officials specified organizational goals and developed methods of work designed to achieve those goals at the same time as they attempted to reform the procedures for selecting employees and for monitoring the behavior of those employees. As the officials increasingly promoted education and allotment as the processes which would assimilate the Indians, they influenced the structure of the developing organization, the power of its subdivisions, and its character. If the processes which typify the methods employed by members of an organization are called its technology, one may conclude that education became the characterizing technology of the Indian Office and influenced it pervasively.

None of the processes which typified Indian work after the Civil War was new. Allotment of Indian lands had been practiced extensively before the Civil War. The goal of civilization, long a stated objective of the Indian Office, implied the eventual citizenship of the Indians. Both literary and practical education for Indians had been provided since colonial times. What was new was the extent to which these processes were employed, their coordination with each other, and the centralized control of the processes which the Indian Office exerted.

Allotment was always a means for "breaking up" Indian lands into small tracts which would be more manageable than the large reserves. Although allotment meant the distribution of lands held in common by a tribe to individual Indian owners, its purpose, as Mary Young and Paul W. Gates have shown, had been to divest Indians from the control of their lands. Individual owners were more easily dealt with than tribes; speculators could induce them to sell their allotments. In the removal period, before the Civil War, allotment was often employed as a means of hastening the removal of Indian tribes from the route of white settlement. By alloting Indian lands the process of transfer from Indian into white hands could be speeded up and removed from governmental control.[7]

With the gradual abandonment of the removal and concentration policies after the Civil War, the meaning of allotment began to change. While lingering efforts at removal and concentration of the tribes continued for at least a decade and a half after 1865, some suggested the allotment of land to the Indians as a means of forestalling government efforts at removal. The case of the Santee Sioux provides an instructive case in point.[8]

Following the Sioux Uprising of 1862, the Army removed the Santees and Winnebagoes from their reservations in Minnesota to a barren location on the Missouri River below Fort Pierre in Dakota Territory. The reservation, at the mouth of Crow Creek, presented the government with formidable problems of supply: the new reservation was distant from contractors and the Missouri River froze in the winter, making navigation impossible. Overland transportation of goods was expensive and difficult. Further, the development of agricultural self-sufficiency seemed impossible at the new location.

In 1865, The Winnebagoes left Crow Creek without authorization. Traveling south, they joined the Omahas in northeastern Nebraska. Prodded by missionaries of the Episcopal Church and the American Board of Commissioners for Foreign Missions, the Indian Office moved the Santees to a new reservation at the mouth of the Niobrara River, across the Missouri from Yankton. The removal was controversial. Dakota Territory contractors were reluctant to part with a lucrative source of trade, and whites in northeastern Nebraska balked at the removal of the warlike Sioux to their vicinity. In 1868, the Peace Commission attempted to induce the Santees to locate upriver. The sites visited seemed no better than Crow Creek to the delegation of Santee Chiefs who sailed up the Missouri with the Commissioners and removal was deferred temporarily.

Quaker Agent Asa M. Janney arrived in April, 1869, to find the Santees in an uncertain mood. Many of the most progressive of the tribesmen had left to found a new colony at Flandreau, Dakota Territory, on the Big Sioux River near the Minnesota state line. Whites reported seeing other groups of Santees throughout the Big Sioux River Valley and in southwestern Minnesota. Faced with probable removal to the inhospitable lands up river, the Santees were moving northeast, perhaps aware of the provision of the 1868 treaty which allowed them to take up homesteads outside of the great Sioux Reservation.[9]

Believing that the Indians would be exploited by whites in Dakota Territory and reluctant to preside over a diminished number of tribesmen, Janney promoted allotment as a means of maintaining the Santees' tenure on the Niobrara reservation. He drew up a petition, calling for immediate allotment, which most of the remaining Santee chiefs signed. Having secured the approval of the Indian Office, Janney alloted the reservation in 1870. Rather than a means for speeding removal, allotment was now a means for preventing it by giving the Indians individual possession of the lands in question.

Similarly, sympathetic whites proposed allotment to prevent the threatened removal of the Omaha Tribe from their Nebraska reservation to Indian Territory in 1882. Alice C. Fletcher, the pioneer ethnologist, was beginning her studies of the Omaha tribe when she was asked to use her influence to stop the planned removal. Miss Fletcher went to Washington with a petition requesting allotment of the reservation; she returned to supervise its allotment.[10]

The General Allotment Act of 1887 made the allotment of Indian lands national policy.[11] Both Commissioners of Indian Affairs and reformers had been calling for a general allotment law since the late 1860s. While allotment was a program on which both reformers and administrators could agree, the objective of diminishing the size of Indian land holdings was not abandoned. While Indian allotments were inalienable for twenty-five years, the act anticipated that allotment would create a "surplus" of land remaining after all tribesmen had received allotments. The surplus was to be opened to settlement by whites. Section ten of the law reserved to Congress the power to grant rights of way for railroads and other highways across the reservations.

The reduction of the reservations was expected to aid acculturation, as most expected that Indians would resist farming as long as large tracts of reservation land remained available. Opening the reservation lands to whites made the act popular with Westerners and doubtless helped to secure its passage. In addition, the provision for railroad rights of way may have induced railroads to support the act.[12]

While the adoption of the allotment policy was a significant step in the development of federal Indian policy, its immediate administrative consequences for the Indian Office were minor. Allotment was, by its nature, a short-term, transitory activity. Special allotment agents, employed on a per diem basis to conduct specific allotments, did the work of distributing the allotments to Indians; the Indian Office sometimes employed surveyors to locate the boundaries of reservations and allotments. The number of such temporary employees, whose work was directed by the Washington office, was never large, and allotment workers did not continue in other Indian Office positions after completing their work. The number of such specialized workers ranged from eight to twenty-five in the decade following passage of the Allotment Act.[13] The expectation that Indians would farm on their allotments perhaps resulted in some expansion of the agency farmer positions. However, on the larger reservations, as the Indian population became more geographically dispersed, farmers tended to perform administrative functions, representing the agent within a "district."[14]

In 1891, Congress amended the General Allotment Act to enable Indians to lease their allotments to whites.[15] The Burke Act of 1906 provided that, upon a determination of "competence," an Indian allottee could sell his property.[16] Thus, after 1887, the role of Indian Office employees in regard to Indian land use tended to become increasingly passive. Monitoring leasing arrangements and determining Indian competence became more important than instructing Indians in the methods of land use.

With regard to the second objective, citizenship, the Indian Office was similarly passive. The Dawes Act provided that, upon allotment, the Indian became a citizen. The Burke Act of 1906 modified this provision; allottees now became citizens when declared competent or at the end of the twenty-five year period during which title to the allotment was held in trust. The Indian Office made no special organizational efforts to accomplish "citizenship." Both allotment and citizenship were changes in the status of the Indians. The Indian Office expected that such status changes, by themselves, would accomplish changes in the behavior of the former tribesmen. The Burke Act, an Indian Office official observed, embodied the expectation that the control of an allotment would prepare the allotee for citizenship.[17]

While status changes, such as allotment and citizenship, were expected to have automatic consequences for Indian behavior, Indian education was a long-term, resource-consuming activity. Indeed, education, by teaching Indians the English language, practical skills, and the use of cultural artifacts such as beds and machinery, plows and cooking stoves, would prepare Indians for the status changes which were being accomplished by legislation and executive order. Indian education became a major organizational activity, whether measured in terms of budgets, the deployment of staff, or the changing internal structure of the organization.

In the Indian Appropriations Act of March 3, 1875, Congress required the Indian Office to furnish an annual statement of appropriations and expenditures.[18] These statements, for the fiscal years ending on June 30, 1874 to 1893, were printed in the *Executive Documents* of the House of Representatives, and provide a convenient source of information regarding the shifts in budgetary emphasis in the Indian Office over a twenty-year period.[19] Loring Benson Priest used these data in his examination of budget shifts between 1874 and 1887; however, Priest reported expenditures as a percentage of total appropriations, rather than of total expenditures.[20] Since the Indian Office frequently reported expenditures much lower than appropriations during this period, I chose to examine expenditures for schools and "civilization" in relation to total expenditures, rather than in relation to total appropriations. (See Table II.)

Interpretation of these data is complicated by the fact that prices declined relatively steadily in the thirty-odd years after 1865.[21] Initially, prices declined as part of the economic adjustment to the end of the Civil War; the sustained, thirty-year decline in prices reflected technological advances in manufacturing which made "economies of scale" possible.[22] Using the monthly index numbers of the wholesale prices of all commodities, 1797 to 1932, developed by G. F. Warren and F. A. Pearson, I constructed a wholesale price index for the fiscal years (July 1-July 30) 1873-74 to 1894-95 and converted the index to an 1873-74 base. The decline in prices was fairly constant; the index, 100 in 1873-74, reached 74 in 1883-84, and 57 in 1893-94.[23] (See Table III.) I then converted the dollar values of total expenditures, school expenditures, and expenditures for "civilization," from current dollars into constant (1873-74) dollars, by dividing the amounts expended in a fiscal year by the index number for that year. The effect of this conversion was to increase the magnitude of increases in the budget, since the fall in prices, and hence the increase in the buying power of a dollar, was relatively constant. (See Tables IV, V, and VI.)

Expenditures for schools accounted for less than 5% of the organization's total expenditures through the fiscal year ending on June 30, 1882. Expenditures nearly doubled in the following year, however, from $244,209 to $482,336, or over nine per cent of the organization's budget for the 1882-1883 fiscal year. In constant dollars, school expenditures doubled, from $293,051 in 1881-82 to $588,450 in 1882-83. In the next fiscal year, school expenditures increased again, by over fifty per cent when measured in constant dollars. Increases continued throughout the 1880s. By the end of the decade, school expenditures accounted for a quarter of total expenditures, a proportion which was exceeded in the 1890s.

When the rates of increase of total expenditures and school expenditures are compared, the increasing importance of education in the organization's budget is revealed. While total expenditures grew during the period, school expenditures grew faster. In seventeen out of the twenty fiscal years between 1874-75 and 1894-95, the percentage change in expenditures for schools was higher than the percentage change in total expenditures. Expenditures for schools never exceeded $150,000 in current dollars during the 1870s, although the total expenditures of the Indian Service were in one year over five million dollars. After 1890, expenditures for schools approached and exceeded two million dollars in current dollars, out of total expenditures of six million dollars and more. While total expenditures more than doubled, when measured in constant dollars, school expenditures increased nearly ten times between 1873-74 and 1894-95.

The "schools" category in the Statements of Expenditures did not capture all expenditures of an educational nature. In particular, the Indian Office frequently used the "civilization" fund to pay for contract schools as well as for other objects thought to have a civilizing influence on the Indians, such as the employment of tribesmen to do manual labor. Expenditures reported for "civilization" were always less than school expenditures. After the increase in expenditures for schools in fiscal year 1882-83, expenditures for "civilization" were always less than half of school expenditures. Adding school and civilization expenditures together, consequently, does not alter the conclusion that the organization's budget reflected the increasing importance of education.

Table II
Total Expenditures, Expenditures for Schools and Civilization
Indian Office, 1873-1895 (Current Dollars)

Fiscal Year	Total Expenditures	Schools Amount	%	Civilization Amount	%
1873-1874	$4,676,222.90	$ 37,597.31	.804	$ 1,796.12	.038
1874-1875	5,280,122.02	94,320.28	1.786	40,453.99	.766
1875-1876	4,858,653.12	122,920.19	2.530	12,821.77	.264
1876-1877	3,781.948.79	105,172.18	2.781	22,036.60	.583
1877-1878	3,969,749.25	127,649.41	3.216	17,101.75	.431
1878-1879	3,958,373.96	118,928.10	3.004	4,974.87	.126
1879-1880	4,204,271.73	152,411.76	3.625	73,647.88	1.752
1880-1881	4,287,323.74	208,996.47	4.875	117,574.44[3]	2.742
1881-1882	4,897,165.83	244,209.18[2]	4.987	233,364.48[3]	4.765
1882-1883	5,196,218.84	482,336.44	9.282	145,160.25[3]	2.794
1883-1884	5,006,661.49	669,974.21	13.382	92,130.67[3]	1.840
1884-1885	5,192,331.85	887,690.67	17.096	89,215.95[3]	1.718
1885-1886	4,912,736.44	979,716.32	19.942	69,115.76[3]	1.407
1886-1887	5,021,610.13	1,146,773.84	22.837	59,531.68[3]	1.186
1887-1888	4,728,020.01	1,086,259.99	22.975	17,048.89[3]	.361
1888-1889	4,624,817.75	1,149,077.90	24.846	16,143.88[3]	.349
1889-1890	5,188,619.70	1,317,426.35	25.391	16,751.89[3]	.323
1890-1891	5,817,138.11	1,882,471.37	32.361	99,971.93[3]	1.719
1891-1892	8,914,644.28	2,323,284.71	26.061	113,307.20[3]	1.271
1892-1893	6,128,510.64	2,277,557.15	37.163	119,578.78[3]	1.951
1893-1894[1]	--	--	--	--	--
1894-1895	6,364,494.25	1,961,415.80	30.818	84,373.57	1.326

Source: See Note 15.

Notes to Table I:
[1] Data not published.
[2] Does not include amounts paid Indian School employees or subsistence and clothing furnished Indians.
[3] Includes Indian labor.

Table III
Index Numbers of the Wholesale Prices of All Commodities, Fiscal Years, 1873-74 to 1894-95

Fiscal Year	Index Number
1873-74	100
1874-75	95
1875-76	88
1876-77	85
1877-78	76
1878-79	68
1879-80	76
1880-81	77
1881-82	83
1882-83	82
1883-84	74
1884-85	68
1885-86	64
1886-87	64
1887-88	66
1888-89	65
1889-90	63
1890-91	64
1891-92	60
1892-93	62
1893-94	57
1894-95	55

Source: Index numbers computed from data in G. F. Warren and F. A. Pearson, "Wholesale Prices in the United States for 135 Years, 1797-1932," in *Wholesale Prices
for 213 Years, 1720 to 1932* (Ithaca, N.Y., 1932), 6-10.

Table IV
Total Expenditures, Expenditures for Schools and Civilization,
Indian Office, 1873-1895 (Constant Dollars)

Fiscal Year	Total Expenditures	Schools	Civilization
1873-74	$ 4,676,222.60	$ 37,597.31	$ 1,796.12
1874-75	5,544,122.10	99,036.29	42,476.69
1875-76	5,538,864.50	140,129.01	14,673.82
1876-77	4,462,699.40	124,103.17	26,003.18
1877-78	5,240,068.90	168,497.22	22,574.31
1878-79	5,818,809.60	174,824.30	7,313.06
1879-80	5,549,638.60	201,183.52	97,215.20
1880-81	5,573,520.80	271,695.41	152,856.77[3]
1881-82	5,876,598.90	293,051.01[2]	280,037.37[3]
1882-83	6,339,386.90	588,450.45	177,095.50[3]
1883-84	6,758,992.80	904,465.18	124,376.40[3]
1884-85	7,632,727.70	1,304,905.20	131,147.44[3]
1885-86	7,663,868.70	1,528,357.40	107,820.58[3]
1886-87	7,833,711.70	1,788,967.10	92,869.42[3]
1887-88	7,186,590.40	1,651,115.00	25,914.31[3]
1888-89	7,122,219.20	1,769,579.90	24,861.58[3]
1889-90	8,249,905.30	2,097,707.80	26,635.51[3]
1890-91	9,074,735.40	2,936.655.20	155,956.21[3]
1891-92	14,887,455.00	3,879,885.40	189,223.02[3]
1892-93	9,866,902.00	3,666,866.90	192,521.83[3]
1893-94[1]	--	--	--
1894-95	11,583,379.00	3,569,776.70	153,559.89

Source: Tables II and III.

Notes to Table IV:
[1] Data Not published.
[2] Does not include amounts paid Indian school employees or subsistence and clothing furnished Indians.
[3] Includes Indian labor.

Table V
Per Cent Change from Preceding Fiscal Year,
Total Expenditures, Expenditures for Schools, and
Expenditures for Schools and Civilization (Combined),
Indian Office, 1874-1895
(Based on Current Dollar Amounts)

Fiscal Year	Total Expenditures	Schools	Schools and Civilization
1874-1875	12.914	150.870	242.358
1875-1876	- 7.982	30.322	0.718
1876-1877	- 22.161	- 14.439	- 6.286
1877-1878	4.966	21.372	13.790
1878-1879	- 0.287	- 6.832	- 14.403
1879-1880	6.212	28.155	82.449
1880-1881	1.975	37.126	44.462
1881-1882	14.224	7.279	46.239
1882-1883	6.107	97.510	31.393
1883-1884	- 3.648	38.902	21.452
1884-1885	3.708	32.496	28.185
1885-1886	- 5.385	10.367	7.363
1886-1887	2.216	17.052	8.538
1887-1888	- 5.847	- 5.277	- 8.538
1888-1889	- 2.183	5.783	5.612
1889-1890	12.191	14.651	14.500
1890-1891	12.113	42.890	48.589
1891-1892	53.248	23.417	22.909
1892-1893	- 31.253	- 1.968	- 1.619
1893-1894[1]			
1894-1895	3.851[2]	- 13.881[2]	- 14.657[2]

Source:　Table I

Notes to Table II:
[1] Data not published.
[2] Per cent change from 1892-1893 fiscal year.

Table VI
Per Cent Change from Preceding Fiscal Year,
Total Expenditures, Expenditures for Schools, and
Expenditures for Schools and Civilization (Combined),
Indian Office, 1874-1895
(Based on Constant Dollar Amounts)

Fiscal Year	Total Expenditures	Schools	Schools and Civilization
1874-75	18.560	163.413	259.230
1875-76	- .095	41.488	9.391
1876-77	- 19.429	- 11.436	- 3.034
1877-78	17.419	35.772	27.291
1878-79	11.045	3.755	- 4.676
1879-80	- 4.626	15.078	63.832
1880-81	.430	35.049	42.273
1881-82	5.438	7.860	34.990
1882-83	7.875	100.801	33.825
1883-84	6.619	53.703	34.393
1884-85	12.927	44.274	39.580
1885-86	.408	17.124	13.936
1886-87	2.216	17.052	15.014
1887-88	- 8.261	- 7.706	- 10.883
1888-89	- .896	7.175	7.001
1889-90	15.833	18.543	18.385
1890-91	9.998	39.994	45.580
1891-92	64.054	32.119	31.575
1892-93	- 33.723	- 5.490	- 5.154
1893-94[1]	--	--	--
1894-95	17.396[2]	- 2.648[2]	- 3.525[2]

Source: Table IV

Notes to Table VI:
[1] Data not published.
[2] Per cent change from 1892-93 fiscal year.

Table VII
Number of Employees in Field (Agency and School) Service, Indian Office, 1865-1897

Year	Agents and Clerks	Education	Law and Order	Medical	Other	Total
1865[1]	42	71	0	12	208	333
1867[2]	44	32	0	13	210	299
1869[3]	71	53	0	26	389	539
1871[4]	71	71	12	32	647	833
1873[5]	82	91	22	42	799	1036
1875	99	117	4	46	438	704
1877	98	114	9	41	461	723
1879	115	139	295	54	854	1457
1881	128	238	824	60	852[6]	2102
1883	121	267	633	53	569	1643
1885	111	403	639	59	680	1892
1887	117	708	695	66	641	2227
1889	117	708	795	65	654	2339
1891	126	1088	930	77	696	2917
1893	128	1326	937	78	650	3119
1895	139	1736	958	79	734	3646
1897	141	1936	954	86	800	3917

Source: *Official Register of the United States,* 1865-1897.

Notes to Table IV:

[1] Data incomplete; 41 agencies reported, 18 agency reports missing.

[2] Data incomplete; 40 agencies reported, 27 agency reports missing.

[3] Data incomplete; 68 agencies reported, 2 agency reports missing.

[4] Data incomplete; 61 agencies reported, 15 agency reports missing.

[5] Data incomplete; 63 agencies reported, 14 agency reports missing.

[6] Excludes 349 Indian freighters at Pine Ridge Agency and 35 "irregular employees" at Rosebud Agency. These personnel performed work which was usually contracted for, and were paid on a piecework basis.

Table VIII
Percentage of Employees in Various Categories,
Field Service, Indian Office, 1865-1897

Year	Agents and Clerks	Education	Law and Order	Medical	Other
1865	12.6	21.3	0	3.6	62.5
1867	14.7	10.7	0	4.3	70.2
1869	13.2	9.8	0	4.8	72.2
1871	8.5	8.5	1.4	3.8	77.7
1873	7.9	8.8	2.1	4.1	77.1
1875	14.1	16.6	0.6	6.5	62.2
1877	13.6	15.8	1.2	5.7	63.8
1879	7.9	9.5	20.2	3.7	58.6
1881	6.1	11.3	39.2	2.9	40.5
1883	7.4	16.3	38.5	3.2	34.6
1885	5.9	21.3	33.8	3.1	35.9
1887	5.3	31.8	31.2	3.0	28.8
1889	5.0	30.3	34.0	2.8	28.0
1891	4.3	37.3	31.9	2.6	23.9
1893	4.1	42.5	30.0	2.5	20.8
1895	3.8	47.6	26.3	2.2	20.1
1897	3.6	49.4	24.4	2.2	20.4

Source: Table VII

Changes in the deployment of staff provides another means of measuring the organization's changing emphasis. During the nineteenth century, the *Official Registers* of the United States, published biennially, listed all employees of the federal government. Using the *Registers* published between 1865 and 1897, I classified all Indian Office field (agency and school) employees into five categories based on the job title listed for the individual employee.[24] The five categories and job titles are: administration (agent and clerks), education (teachers, matrons, and other school helpers), law and order (police, detectives, and judges), medical (physicians, nurses, and physician's assistants), and other (principally farmers and skilled and unskilled laborers). Prior to 1875, the returns in the *Official Registers* were incomplete: a varying number of agencies failed to report employees in time for inclusion. The *Registers* published after 1875 included returns from all agencies and other field units.

A tabulation of the total number of employees in each of the five categories for the years 1865-1897 shows that the work of the Indian Service became more labor-intensive between the 1870s and 1890s. (See Table VII.) In 1875, the first year for which complete data are available, the Indian Office employed 704 individuals in the field service, while the expenditures for the Indian Service were over five million dollars. By 1895, expenditures had increased twenty per cent to over six million dollars, while the total number of field employees had increased more than five-fold, to 3,646. Even when expenditures are put into constant dollars, the Indian Office spent only slightly more than twice as much during the 1894-95 fiscal year as it had in 1874-75 and 1875-76. The dramatic increase in employment, while reflected in each of the five categories, was due primarily to increases in the numbers of employees in the education and law and order categories. In 1875, education accounted for 16.6% of total field service employees; by 1895, it approached one-half of all field service employment. Similarly, law and order employment rose from less than one per cent of the total in 1875 to more than one-third in the early 1880s. By 1895, despite a decline in proportional importance after 1885, law and order personnel accounted for over one-fourth of all field employees. (See Table VIII.) These gains were at the expense, in proportional importance if not in absolute numbers, of the administrative, medical and "other" categories. Further, the expansion of personnel was much less costly in the law and order category than elsewhere. Indian police and judges, who made up the vast majority of these positions, were paid much less than other employees. Usually these employees received from five to ten dollars per week and rations.[25]

These changes in the allocation of funds and the deployment of personnel reflected the increasing importance of education in the Indian Service program. Education emerged during the last quarter of the nineteenth century as the dominant, and characterizing, technology of Indian work. Education dominated budgets and personnel lists. Indian Office officials viewed schooling as the key to the success of the allotment and citizenship policies. School training, not subsistence, became the essential activity of Indian Service workers. The change reflected an increasing emphasis on regarding the Indian as a client, an individual who would learn a new social role as a result of government action. Indians were to be assimilated into American society.

In the decade after the Civil War, most expenditures for education were from appropriations for fulfilling treaties with the tribes. Many of the treaties concluded prior to 1871 committed the government to provide educational services to Indians. For example, the 1868 Navajo Treaty obligated the government to provide a teacher and school house for every thirty Navajo children. The Indian Office rarely met such stipulations; indeed, as late as the 1930s, the Navajos complained of the failure of the government to live up to its obligation.[26]

In addition to the educational services provided by the Indian Service in the fulfillment of treaty obligations, some missionary organizations provided some schooling under contract with the Indian Office. Patterned after the famous Choctaw Academy operated by the Baptists in Kentucky in the 1830s, such contract institutions at first operated mostly for the benefit of tribes east of the Mississippi River. However, the removal of some tribes westward and the expansion of church activity in the Grant administration resulted in the creation of denominational contract schools on many reservations west of the Mississippi. The American Board of Commissioners for Foreign Missions established the Santee Normal Training School, which served Sioux from many reservations, in 1869.[27] The Catholic Church was perhaps the most active of the denominations in establishing contract schools during the Grant administration.[28] The Indian Office provided for such schools through treaty funds or through the Civilization fund.

A third pattern for the provision of educational services was that of the Five Civilized Tribes of the Indian Territory, where the tribes ran their own schools. The Indian Office held the funds of these tribes in trust and paid funds directly to the tribes for the support of schools. Often missionary societies operated these schools for the tribes.

The government usually reimbursed mission schools on a capitation basis; the schools received funds according to the number of Indian students taught. Agents controlled the non-contract government schools, located at the agencies. School teachers reported directly to the agents who hired and fired them. With the increases in funds and personnel in the 1880s, however, autonomous organizational units devoted to education emerged at both the local and national office levels. At the local level, the agency educational divisions eventually grew to such an extent that their directors, the Superintendents of Schools, replaced the agents as the chief executive officers on the reservations. At the national level, the Superintendent of Indian Schools for a time seemed likely to become equal in status and power to the Commissioner of Indian Affairs. At the middle level, the inspection of schools in the field became the responsibility of a specialized inspection corps devoted solely to education, the Supervisors of Indian Education who supervised schools in five education districts. This proliferation of structure reflected the increasing importance of Indian education. It illustrates, in a dramatic way, the effect of changing goals and changing technology upon the organization. (See Chart VIII.)

The structural changes outlined above followed the changes in the organization's budget and staff composition between 1875 and 1890. As officials came to view education as the key to Indian assimilation, they urged Congress to increase school appropriations. As the budget grew, the number of persons employed in schools grew as did the number of educational institutions. Such growth gave rise to appeals for administrative coordination, particularly on the part of reformers dismayed by the abandonment of the religious appointments policy, but also on the part of Commissioners of Indian Affairs concerned with managing an increasingly complex organization.

The first proposal for a specialized educational functionary within the Office of Indian Affairs structure came in 1874, when Commissioner E. P. Smith asked for authorization to appoint a superintendent of education for the Indian Territory. The superintendent would supervise the expenditures of funds for education by the Five Civilized Tribes, a function which neither the Indian Office nor the local agents then performed. "The government expends annually according to treaty large sums of money for this purpose," wrote Smith; said "monies being disbursed through the Treasurers of the government[s] of these tribes. . . . The [federal] government [has] no supervision over this expenditure in any way." Smith believed a full-time superintendent would promote efficiency and recommended that the Secretary of the Interior be authorized to hire a superintendent from the educational funds of the tribes of Indian Territory.[29] Congress never created the position, however, and, despite periodic complaints of inefficiency, the government exercised no supervision over the educational activities of the five tribes until the creation of the Dawes Commission in the 1890s.[30]

In 1877, Commissioner E. A. Hayt called for the compulsory education of all Indian youth between six and fourteen years of age in the English language. Recommending an appropriation of fifty thousand dollars as a special fund for establishing Indian schools, Hayt declared that the chief hope for the civilization of the Indians lay in the education of the young.[31] He advocated a common school system, consisting of a network of day schools on the reservations and a system of industrial boarding schools where graduates of the common schools could be sent for advanced training.[32] However, the existing school system was far from adequate to make compulsory schooling practicable. In his next annual report, Hayt estimated that there were thirty-three thousand Indians of school age on the reservations. However, only 2,589 were in boarding schools, with an

Chart VIII

Structural Changes

Indian Office, 1873-1892

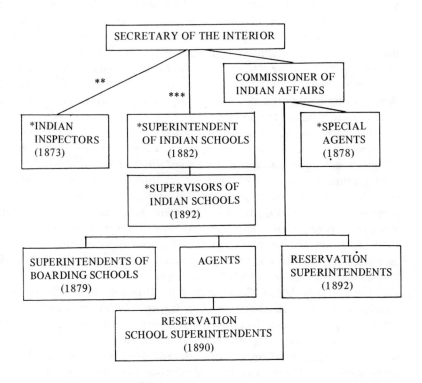

Key: * Inspection positions.

   ** Reported to Commissioner of
      Indian Affairs before 1880.

  *** Reported to Commissioner of
      Indian Affairs after 1890.

   (1873) Years indicate first creation of position.

additional 5,082 in day schools, "those expensive makeshifts for educational appliances among Indians." Inspired, perhaps, by the success of Indian education at Hampton Institute in Virginia, Hayt was now prepared to support boarding schools as the essential element in Indian education. He requested a $200,000 appropriation for schools in the next fiscal year.[33]

While Congress did not appropriate funds in the amount Hayt requested, the year 1879 brought the establishment of the first of the off-reservation boarding schools, at Carlisle, Pennsylvania. Headed by Richard Henry Pratt, an Army officer who had previously supervised Indian captives in Florida and directed the Indian program at Hampton Institute, Carlisle became a model for the many off-reservation boarding schools which the Indian Office established in the late nineteenth century. Carl Schurz supported Pratt's efforts to establish the Carlisle School; Congress appropriated funds to begin the program based on the success of the Indian program at Hampton.[34]

The year 1880 saw a modest expansion in the number of Indian schools. However, the expansion left many agencies still without educational facilities. Congressional appropriation practice limited the flexibility of the Indian Office in responding to the needs of agencies; for tribes with treaties providing for education, Congress made separate appropriations. In most cases, these appropriations were inadequate. To supplement these funds, the Indian Office administrators could tap a general appropriation "for support of schools" at any location. However, seventeen agencies supervised tribes having no treaty provisions for schools, and the small general appropriation, $75,000 in 1880, was insufficient even to provide for these tribes.[35]

The Eleventh Annual Conference of the Board of Indian Commissioners with Representatives of Missionary Boards met in Washington on January 12, 1882. The previous year had seen the inauguration of James A. Garfield as President. Hopes that Garfield would support the Board in its efforts to secure adequate funding from Congress and return to denominational appointment of agents were dashed by the shooting of the President in July and his death two and a half months later. Reformers hoped that the new President, Chester A. Arthur, could be persuaded to promote a return to the principles of the Peace Policy. After hearing reports of missionary activity on the reservations, which emphasized the need for an expansion in educational activity, the conferees appointed a committee, composed of representatives of three of the mission boards, to prepare resolutions for submission to President Arthur.

The resolutions, as adopted, called for a continuation of the religious appointments policy, but only denominations willing to engage in educational work should be allowed to participate. To encourage the churches to invest in schools, the conference asked Congress to guarantee continuance of support for Indian education for "a term of years." The resolutions called for a reallocation of agencies to the denominations, based on their willingness to engage in educational work, and for "an equitable division" of educational appropriations "between all Indians in the country." A superintendent of Indian education would supervise the expenditure of the increased appropriations contemplated under the law.[36]

In part, the resolutions of 1882 reflected the frustrations of the operators of contract schools with an unsympathetic and secular bureaucracy. While President Hayes frequently appointed agents over the objections of the denominations, contract school personnel remained at the agencies; conflicts were frequently the result. Indian Inspectors often "did not understand education." John Eaton, U.S. Commissioner of Education, complained that inspectors reported against contract schools which were doing good work.[37] While some delegates were fearful that a superintendent would interfere with the operation of the contract schools, Eaton and others seemingly assumed that the superintendent would be more sympathetic to denominational problems than other officials.

The Indian Appropriations Act of May 17, 1882, authorized the President to appoint a person to inspect all Indian Schools and to develop a plan for providing educational services both to tribes whose treaties required schooling and to tribes for which there was no such obligation.[38] The act provided the inspector with a salary of $3,000 a year, equivalent to the salary of other Indian Inspectors and also equivalent to the salary of the Commissioner of Indian Affairs, with travel expenses of $1,500 per year. President Arthur appointed James M. Haworth, an Indian Inspector, as the first Inspector of Indian Schools on July 18, 1882.[39] Haworth had been called to Washington a month earlier, presumably to discuss the appointment with the President and the new Secretary of the Interior, Henry M. Teller.[40] Haworth spent most of 1882 investigating sites for off-reservation boarding schools to be modeled after Hampton and Carlisle. He inspected Chillocco in the Indian Territory, Genoa, Nebraska, and Fort Riley and Lawrence, Kansas.[41]

In his first annual report, Haworth estimated that there were forty thousand Indians of school age. The modest expansion of educational services during the past four years had led to the provision of schooling for less than ten thousand of them.[42] However, six new boarding schools had been opened during 1882. Progress seemed likely in Indian education. In his annual report, Commissioner of Indian Affairs Hiram Price commented that the creation of the Inspector of Indian Schools position made possible the development of a "*system* in Indian education."[43] Price favored the development of a system of district day schools to make compulsory education possible. In addition, such day schools would provide employment opportunities for the female graduates of Hampton Institute and the Carlisle Indian School.[44]

Secretary Teller condemned previous efforts in Indian education, writing in his annual report that a "literary and religious education" for the Indians had proved a failure. What the Indians needed was a more practical, vocational education.[45] By the 1881-1882 fiscal year, expenditures for schools and education approached ten per cent of total Indian Office spending. Indeed, since 1877, the Congress had doubled appropriations for Indian education, and these increases reflected increases in the general appropriations for schooling, rather than increases in appropriations for specific tribes.[46] Still, the Commissioner urged the need for continued expansion of the Indian schools. He warned that the cost of such an expansion would be great. For the 1883-1884 fiscal year the Indian Office requested over $900,000 for education.[47]

In the 1883 Indian Appropriations Act, Congress provided $640,200 for education, in addition to the funds provided individual tribes under treaty stipulations.[48] This was nearly a fifty-percent increase over the 1882 appropriation of $487,200.[49] However, Congress made no further provision for the development of a "system" in Indian education. The 1883 act changed Haworth's title to Superintendent of Indian Schools but made no change in his responsibilities. The Superintendent, who engaged primarily in the inspection of Indian Schools, had no administrative authority or responsibility.[50]

Congress initiated two programs in 1882 and 1883 which Haworth attempted to implement. His efforts to place Indian students in industrial schools in the states were hampered because, as the schools contended, the $167 per pupil which Congress authorized for the program was not sufficient to cover the costs of instruction, room, and board. Only a limited number of schools were willing to participate in the program under these terms, but Congress refused to increase the per-pupil expenditure.[51] Similarly unsuccessful was an attempt to extend the "placing out" system begun at Carlisle. In 1883, Congress authorized the placement of Indian children in white homes for a term of three years. However, no families could be found to take the children, since the legislation authorized no payments to the foster parents, the Congressmen expecting that the labor of the Indian children would compensate the families for the costs of caring for them.[52]

Despite the increases in unrestricted appropriations for Indian education, Commissioner Price continued to urge more administrative flexibility in allocating funds. The War Department's appropriations of twenty-five million dollars were made under less than sixty different headings, "leaving, very properly as I believe, a large discretion with the Secretary of War as to their disposal." The Indian Service appropriations, about one-fourth of the War Department's, were made under two hundred and sixty headings.[53] The consequent inflexibility resulted in waste. Because the appropriation for the construction of school buildings was insufficient to replace burned buildings, some of the reservation school programs were curtailed, resulting in the return of unexpended funds for education to the Treasury. In the case of the Indian Office, Price concluded, "Law knows no necessity."[54] An increase in administrative discretion, the Commissioner argued, would enable the Indian Office to increase off-reservation placement of Indian children in white boarding schools and with white families, to provide educational services to Alaskan natives, and to distribute funds to existing reservation schools more rationally.

Still, the increasing amount appropriated and expended for education had produced a change in the Indian school system which explains in part the concern of the representatives of the mission boards. As government expenditures increased, the domination of the churches in Indian education declined. By 1883, out of eighty-two boarding schools supported in whole or in part by the government, only fifteen were contract schools, operated by the churches. (Religious societies operated an additional seven boarding schools without government assistance and fourteen boarding schools among the Five Civilized Tribes, supported by tribal funds.) Of the 5,182 students in all boarding schools except those for the Five Civilized Tribes, only 1,093 were in the twenty-two contract and non-contract schools operated by religious societies.[55]

The declining influence of the churches, then, was the result of the rapid expansion in appropriations for Indian education, rather than of a deliberately anti-church policy. While the government could have encouraged the churches to expand their educational operations, rapid expansion of contract schools was unlikely in the absence of the government's commitment to support the schools for a period of more than a year at a time. Further, Congress provided no funds for the construction of contract schools, while the appropriations acts of the 1880s routinely included funds for the construction of government schools.[56]

Yet a growth in "system" did not at first accompany the expansion of the government's Indian school system. Indian School Superintendent James Haworth, a Quaker and former Kiowa Agent, apparently was not aggressive in defining his duties. His successor complained that he made no attempt to determine the functions of his office.[57] Still, Haworth maintained close ties to reformers. He represented the Indian Office at the meetings of the Board of Indian Commissioners with the representatives of missionary societies. Sometimes Eliphant Whittlesey, Secretary of the Board, accompanied him in his inspections of Indian schools.[58] The Mission Boards blamed their declining influence on the administrative system, specifically on Congress's failure to provide Haworth with administrative authority.

At the thirteenth annual Conference of the Board of Indian Commissioners with representatives of mission boards, in January, 1884, the conferees acknowledged that they had failed in their intent to reform Indian education by creating the position of Superintendent of Indian Education. C. C. Painter of the Boston Branch of the Indian Rights Association introduced a resolution, which the body passed, calling for the establishment of a Bureau of Indian Education as an autonomous division within the Indian Office. He complained of a lack of "system" in Indian Education. "Any success we have achieved in Indian Education," he said, "must be a happy accident, not the outcome of a wise system, for there is none, wise or otherwise. . . . We had great hopes from the appointment of a Superintendent of Education, but he has not been able to do the work that we want done." While not criticizing Haworth directly, Painter complained that Haworth had no administrative responsibilities. The appointment of teachers by agents meant that Indian education was decentralized and under political control.[59] At the 1885 conference, Richard Henry Pratt, the Carlisle Superintendent, called for a man to "direct" Indian education "and everybody work under him." However, Pratt's motion was connected with a resolution favoring independent departmental status for the Indian Office, which many opposed on the grounds of administrative expense.[60]

Haworth died in March, 1885, while inspecting the Indian Boarding School at Albuquerque. President Cleveland named John H. Oberly, an Illinois politician, as Haworth's successor on May 9, 1885. Oberly moved quickly to establish some authority for the Superintendent of Indian Schools. In July, J. D. C. Atkins, the newly appointed Commissioner of Indian Affairs, ordered that all correspondence coming to the Indian Office which was related to schools be directed to Oberly or his representative. Further, Atkins gave Oberly the authority to determine whether the Indian agents' requests for school funds were adequate.[61]

In his first annual report, Oberly complained of his lack of administrative authority. "The Indian schools are supervised and the school system is managed by the Indian Bureau," he wrote, "which in its supervision and management, is subjected by the Secretary of the Interior to only occasional modifying negatives of its suggestions and requests for authority."[62] Atkins' order of July 17, routing school correspondence to the Superintendent, had helped in some ways. The effect of the order was to place the superintendent in charge of all school matters and to establish an educational division under him. However, the Indian School system had not been planned, it had evolved. Indian agents who were not particularly interested in education appointed school personnel, although in theory these personnel were the appointees of the commissioner. Oberly recommended that reservation schools be made independent of agents and placed under bonded superintendents of education.[63] He also recommended that the expanded powers of the superintendent resulting from Atkins' order be made official through legislation. He requested an assistant superintendent to supervise the Indian schools while he was out of Washington. He also recommended an annual conference of reservation superintendents of Indian schools.[64]

Oberly's service as Indian School Superintendent was brief, despite his vigorous start. He left the Indian Service in April, 1886, when Cleveland appointed him to the Civil Service Commission as part of a general reorganization. An undistinguished Civil Service Commissioner, Oberly returned to the Indian Office as Commissioner in June, 1888, after Atkins resigned to campaign for the Senate.[65] Oberly's tenure as Indian Commissioner was similarly brief; Benjamin

Harrison, who became President in March, 1889, replaced him with a Republican, Thomas J. Morgan, late in the year.[66]

Some reformers, including Herbert Welsh of the Indian Rights Association, had lobbied for Oberly's retention as Commissioner under Harrison.[67] In part, Oberly was popular because the Tennessee politicians, Atkins and Assistant Commissioner A. B. Upshaw, were detested by reform groups.[68] Yet his vigorous promotion of educational reform, combined with a pleasant personality, suggests that Oberly's popularity was not attributable to negative virtues alone. At the 1885 Lake Mohonk Conference, he delivered a spirited defense of Democratic policies to that largely Republican gathering. Oberly pledged that no removals would be made from the Indian school service for political reasons, despite an insatiable Democratic hunger for patronage.[69]

Atkins' decision to require applicants for Indian Service positions to demonstrate their competence prior to appointment was probably instigated by Oberly. In addition, the Superintendent promoted the separation of boarding schools from agencies. These schools were placed under bonded superintendents, who were responsible for the selection of personnel. Agents and bonded superintendents could make no removals of school personnel without first stating the reasons for the removals and obtaining Indian Office authorization. Reformers "should thank the Lord that the Democratic party has come into power, and is determined to make merit and competency. . . . paramount tests" for office holders, Oberly told the Lake Mohonk conferees.[70]

Oberly's successor as Indian School Superintendent, John B. Riley, attempted to continue his predecessor's program of increasing the authority of the superintendent. Riley, who took office in June, 1886, noted in his first annual report that Atkins' order of June 17, 1885, gave the Indian School superintendent access to correspondence, but "no executive authority."[71] In an undated communication to the Secretary of the Interior, received on April 6, 1887, Riley asked that "such authority as is now exercised by the Commissioner of Indian Affairs over the Indian schools. . . . be vested in the Superintendent," who would have "the control and direction" of all school employees.[72] Secretary Lamar solicited Commissioner Atkins' response to the proposal. Atkins claimed that such a bifurcation of responsibility would make the management of Indian affairs difficult if not impossible. Under the law the Commissioner had sole responsibility for "the management of all Indian affairs and of all matters arising out of Indian relations." He suggested that it would be unlawful and unwise to give the Superintendent of Indian Schools further powers. Indeed, the superintendent had enough to do inspecting the Indian schools.[73] Lamar supported Atkins; in a talk with Riley, Lamar "informed him that he would remain as heretofore an officer under immediate direction of the Secretary's Office and be engaged in investigating and reporting on schools."[74]

While attempting to secure increased authority for his position, Riley spent much less time than his predecessor inspecting Indian schools. Oberly, while pressing for an enhanced administrative role, spent a great deal of time in the field. Riley, in contrast, made only fourteen inspection reports during his first year in office. In addition, his personal relationships with both Lamar and Atkins were strained. "I cannot say that he has ever shown a desire to discharge those duties of the position which his predecessor found it possible to perform," Lamar complained. "He seems to have discovered that his office was between two utilities, and to have become impressed with the idea that he can make himself useful to neither of them."[75]

By 1887, education had emerged as a significant component of the Indian Office program. In the 1886-1887 fiscal year, expenditures for the support of schools exceeded one million dollars (in current dollars) for the first time, comprising almost twenty-three percent of all Indian Service spending. By June 30, 1887, almost thirty-two percent of the field employees worked in education, compared to twenty-one percent two years earlier. For the first time in a decade more employees were engaged in education than in law and order. Eleven independent boarding schools, administered by bonded superintendents and not under the supervision of agents, existed in 1887. Most of them had been created during the previous two years.

While the growth of the Indian School system produced some pressure for administrative centralization, another event resulted in increased interest in the administration of the schools. The approval of the Dawes Act on February 8, 1887, released the energies of many reformers who had devoted themselves to allotment as the fundamental reform in Indian Affairs. The passage of the act made allotment and citizenship imminent for thousands of Indians; the importance of education became, if anything, more clear.

Writing after the passage of the Dawes Act, James E. Rhoads called for increased authority for the superintendent. With land allotment national policy, "our next duty to the Indians" was to provide education for citizenship. The Superintendent should spend more time in Washington to develop a plan for Indian education. The actual inspections of schools, Rhoads thought, should be carried out by assistants responsible for schools in defined educational districts.[76]

In a report on conditions on some of the Western reservations, undertaken for the Indian Rights Association, J. B. Harrison also called for enlarged powers for the Superintendent. Citing the annual reports of Oberly and Riley, Harrison condemned what he considered Indian Office meddling in school affairs.[77] In what may have been an attack on Atkins and Riley, Harrison suggested appointing only men who had proved themselves by serving as Indian Agents or teachers in Indian schools to the Commissioner and Superintendent positions.[78] Like Rhoads, he called for the appointment of specialized school inspectors to supervise the Indian schools. With unspecified expanded duties, the Superintendent should report to the Commissioner and should spend most of his time in Washington.[79]

Riley made a second attempt to expand the scope of his position in the fall of 1887. In a cautiously-worded letter to Secretary Lamar, he stated the "facts" regarding Indian schools. While over fourteen thousand Indian students attended school regularly, twenty-five thousand were still unprovided for. Passage of the Dawes Act made increased appropriations for schools imperative, since the Indians were to be made citizens. No less imperative was "an organized system" of Indian education, which would emphasize industrial boarding schools.[80] With little hope for an increase in his responsibilities, Riley submitted a perfunctory annual report for 1887; in December, he resigned.[81] Seemingly, Lamar was in no great haste to have the position filled. In any event, Cleveland allowed the position to remain vacant for nearly a year, before naming S. H. Albro to the Superintendent of Indian Schools position on October 29, 1888.

The leisurely pace at which the Superintendent's position was filled proved to be embarrassing to the Cleveland administration. In the Indian Appropriations Act of June 29, 1888, Congress redefined the Superintendent's powers. Section eight of the Act provided him with the power to "employ and discharge superintendents, teachers, and other persons connected with schools wholly supported by the government."[82] Thus Congress provided what Riley had requested over a year earlier; but since the Superintendent's position was vacant, the authority for employing all of the employees in the Indian School Service between June and October was in doubt.[83]

The increase in the Superintendent's authority proved to be short-lived. The Indian Appropriations Act of 1889, approved a few days before Benjamin Harrison's inauguration, provided that the duties of the Superintendent were to inspect schools supported in whole or in part by the government, to make reports to the Commissioner, and to perform other duties as ordered by the Secretary of the Interior.[84] With Harrison's Commissioner, Thomas J. Morgan, extremely active in Indian education, Secretary John W. Noble assigned no additional duties to the Superintendent. Daniel Dorchester, Albro's successor, spent most of his time in the field.[85] The Superintendent was in an anomalous position, "an officer both of the Department [of the Interior] and of this [Indian] Office."[86]

The shifting provisions for the duties of the Superintendent reflected confusion regarding the best way to organize the Indian school system. Expenditures had become immense without a corresponding increase in administrative control. Inspection seemed necessary; so did central control. Before Morgan, most Commissioners were neither competent nor did they have the time to approach Indian educational problems systematically. Yet an increase in the powers of the Superintendent seemed likely to result in administrative chaos as a result of divided responsibilities. The appointment of Morgan, with his great interest in education, resolved the problem for a time as the Commissioner played an active role in Indian education.

The contract schools provided Morgan with his first major challenge. The Indian educational system by 1890 included schools controlled entirely by the government, contract schools supported but not controlled by the government, and a few religious schools supported only in part or not at all by the government. The contract system was difficult to administer. The contract schools were nominally independent of the government although most of them depended on government funds for their support. Commissioner Morgan attempted to organize the system under Indian Office control. He devoted large sections of his four annual reports to problems of Indian education. Morgan, perhaps prompted by R. V. Belt, his Assistant Commissioner and previously chief clerk of the Indian Division under Secretaries Teller and Lamar, wanted to end the contract system. Belt believed that public support of sectarian schools was a bad principle.[87] Contractors were difficult to deal with. Protestant denominations, for example, frequently wanted the government to construct school buildings for them, not merely to depend on the payments for services provided after the buildings had been built.[88] The Catholics resisted Morgan's efforts to expand federal supervision of the contract schools. They believed he was a bigot.[89] Morgan denied the accusation, saying that he intended to administer the contract system impartially, although he favored a "national," secular system of Indian education, modeled on the public schools. Catholic schools received more than half of all funds paid to contract schools, but they resisted efforts to monitor their activities.[90] Morgan admitted removing Catholics from school positions, as his detractors claimed, but asserted that the dismissals were for cause, not religion, and included Protestants as well as Catholics.[91]

Some support for Catholic complaints may be found in Morgan's remark that he was against allowing foreign priests and nuns to teach, since the function of the schools was to prepare Indians for citizenship. Foreign priests and nuns, who staffed many of the Catholic contract schools, were suspect on grounds of loyalty to the United States as well as because of presumed difficulties with the English language.[92] Morgan had determined that there would be "no extension of the contract system" during his administration. Indeed, he hoped to discontinue existing contracts gradually.[93]

The success of the Catholic schools in securing contract funds was due in part to the efforts of the Bureau of Catholic Indian Missions. Organized in 1873 to press for a more equitable division of agencies to the Catholics under Grant's church appointments policy, the Bureau contracted directly with the Indian Office for all Catholic contract schools. Contract funds were then distributed to the schools by the Catholic Bureau. In 1884, the Archbishop of Baltimore, James Cardinal Gibbons, appointed Father Joseph Stephan, former agent at Standing

Rock, Dakota Territory, director of the Bureau. During the Cleveland administration, Stephan was able to increase the Catholic share of contract school funds from $65,220 in 1884 to $347,672 in 1889, seventy-five percent of the total appropriation.[94]

In July, 1891, Morgan announced that the Indian Office would no longer contract through the Catholic Bureau. Rather, contracts would be made with each Catholic contract school on an individual basis. Many of the schools welcomed the change, Morgan claimed. He said that the Bureau had failed to keep its promises to the schools. One Catholic superintendent had requested direct contracting. Direct contracting would make it easier to supervise the conduct of education and would bring all contract schools into "a closer sympathy" with the government.[95] While the Catholic Bureau protested, Cardinal Gibbons ultimately acquiesced and the decision was not reversed.[96]

While Dorchester spent most of his time in the field, Morgan gave his Superintendent of Indian Schools some assistance. He appointed the Superintendent's wife, Merial A. Dorchester, Special Agent in the Indian School Service. Appointed to assist her husband by looking into the "conduct, habits, condition, treatment, and training of the female pupils" in the boarding schools, Mrs. Dorchester campaigned for the appointment of field matrons "to visit the Indian families and teach the mothers to cook, to make and mend garments [and] to elevate the homes."[97] Congress authorized the appointment of field matrons, who usually worked under the direction of the reservation school superintendents, in 1891.[98]

Morgan also appointed Elaine Goodale, a graduate of Smith College with ties to Indian reform organizations, Superintendent of Sioux Education. Miss Goodale carved out an active role for herself. While Morgan at times attempted to restrain her from interfering with the prerogatives of the agents, he made use of her reports in expanding the powers of the central office over Indian education. The President removed Pine Ridge Agent Hugh D. Gallagher, a holdover Democratic appointee, in 1890, partly because of Miss Goodale's complaints of his interference with her attempts to improve the day schools on the reservation.[99]

Underlying charges of agent "interference" with Indian schools was the question of the autonomy of these units within the agencies. Morgan recommended that agents be required to give orders to school employees only through the reservation school superintendents, thus creating a semiautonomous organizational unit within the agencies. In support of this recommendation he cited a report of Superintendent Dorchester. According to the Superintendent,

In numerous instances bad agents have used their power to the detriment of the schools, interposing directly between the Superintendent and the teachers and other employés in matters pertaining *solely to school exercises and discipline*. It will be perceived that no school in which the officials are so hampered can succeed. The power of the agent thus to do should be limited.[100]

Morgan ordered that school superintendents at the Reservation level, not agents, should nominate their subordinates. However, he reserved the right to suggest who those subordinates should be. As he wrote to the superintendent of a new boarding school in Arizona,

> I will send you from time to time, the papers of application of such persons as seem to be especially worthy of your consideration. I desire, however, in as much as you are responsible to the school, that you shall select your own subordinates, and you are to regard the papers which I send you merely as suggestions and not at all as indicating my wish to have anybody appointed to any position unless I shall specifically say so.[101]

The 1890 Indian Appropriations Act gave the Commissioner of Indian Affairs, rather than the Secretary of the Interior, the power to prescribe the duties of the Superintendent of Indian Schools.[102] While this change probably resulted from Morgan's activist approach to Indian education, it seemingly ended what had been a difficult administrative problem during the first Cleveland administration. Morgan gave Dorchester no administrative duties. He asked the Superintendent "to look more carefully than ever into the moral condition of the agencies you visit."[103]

Since Morgan himself appointed the reservation school superintendents and now supervised the work of the Indian School Superintendent, the growing autonomy of the schools within the agencies increased the Commissioner's control over reservation education. Morgan and his Assistant, R. V. Belt, made most of the decisions on the appointment of the reservation superintendents, even in some cases checking Superintendent Dorchester's recommendations.[104] While reservation superintendents were in theory subordinate to the agents, Morgan encouraged them to write him "unofficially" on developments at the agencies. His letters to superintendents revealed a familiarity with the details of local conditions, including even the health of subordinate employees.[105]

In 1891 Harrison placed the school service under civil service regulations. The positions of superintendent, matron, teacher, and physician were now in the classified service. However, other positions at the agencies, including other school positions, while regarded officially as non-partisan positions, were in effect partisan, since preference was given "to those who were in sympathy with the present administration."[106] In 1892, Morgan created five education districts, each with a supervisor of Indian education, whose duties primarily involved inspection.[107] Dorchester continued to devote himself to inspection also.[108] By the last year of the Harrison administration, schools were planned for all but about ten thousand Indian children; expenditures for Indian education had increased by over one million dollars in four years.[109]

When Morgan left office in 1893, the educational system was an integral part of the Indian Office at the national level. At the local level, however, because of the extension of civil service regulations and because of the centralization of school functions under the reservation superintendents, educational work had been partially segregated from other aspects of administration. Between these two levels, an inspection force, composed of the national superintendent and the district supervisors, reported on local developments to the Commissioner. The effect of Morgan's administration, then, was to centralize educational work, while increasing its importance, both in terms of the absolute amount expended for schooling and in terms of the proportion of funds and personnel devoted to education.

Morgan's successor, Daniel M. Browning, continued the policy of allowing reservation superintendents the privilege of nominating school employees not covered by the civil service regulations. He permitted agents to nominate their clerks and other non-classified agency personnel.[110] However, Browning and his Assistant Commissioner, Frank Armstrong, occasionally rejected the superintendents' choices for political reasons.[111]

Charges of political interference in the schools led Indian School Superintendent William H. Hailmann to attempt to gain increased administrative responsibility. Cleveland's Secretary of the Interior, Hoke Smith, declared that the Indian School Superintendent, not the Commissioner, should have administrative responsibility for Indian schools.[112] However, Hailmann was not successful in his efforts to have himself made appointing officer for classified positions in the Indian school service or *ex officio* chief of the Indian Office's Education Division.[113]

While an attempt to abolish Hailmann's position failed, Browning and Armstrong were successful in their efforts to restrict the Superintendent's duties to inspection.[114] Even Hailmann's attempt to employ his son as an administrative assistant was rebuffed; under the laws creating his office, he was allowed assistance only for the inspection of schools.[115] The appropriation acts of the 1890s continued to give the commissioner the power to define the superintendent's duties.[116] Hailmann spent most of his time visiting schools, as did his successor, Estelle Reel.[117]

Between 1893 and 1908, as noted above, the position of agent was abolished at all reservations. The reservation school superintendents replaced the agents as chief executive officer at the local level throughout the Indian Service. Thus, the expansion of the Indian education program led first to the development of semi-autonomous organizational units on the reservations, with the reservation superintendent of schools supervising the operations of the schools. Administrative regulation in the early 1890s protected the superintendent from interference by the agent. During the '90s and the first decade of the twentieth century the superintendents gained administrative control of the Indian agencies. On the national office level, The Superintendents of Indian Education attempted to expand their responsibilities and powers. They were unsuccessful in achieving a clear statement of administrative responsibility and after 1889 the Indian Appropriations Acts clearly subordinated the Superintendent to the Commissioner of Indian Affairs. On the middle level, the district supervisors of Indian education had positions which were analogous to those of the inspectors. In summary, the development of an education program changed the Indian Office by creating autonomous units of power at the local level. At the national level, the Commissioner's powers over Indian education increased as the Commissioner came to control local appointments, the making of rules, and the duties of the school superintendent.

The increasing importance of education in the Indian Service program resulted in an organization which was much more centralized than it had been earlier. Ironically, the initial impetus for the creation of an independent educational unit at the national level came from reformers who felt excluded from Indian administration in the early 1880s. The Indian Rights Association was always a major defender of the Superintendent of Indian Schools. Before the administration of Thomas J. Morgan, the School Superintendent seemed likely to become an independent force in Indian administration. Such a result might well have weakened the Indian Office, as Commissioner Atkins predicted, by creating an autonomous center of power within the organization.

In Philip Selznick's conceptualization, the leadership of administrators is a condition of successful institutionalization. By making critical decisions, particularly those concerned with the definition of the organization's purpose, its embodiment in the organization's social structure, the defense of the organization's integrity, and the ordering of internal conflict, the institutional leader can "transform a neutral body of men into a committed polity."[118] Thomas J. Morgan would appear to fit Selznick's description of an institutional leader. By devoting himself to educational questions at a crucial period of organizational evolution, he was able to centralize the Indian Service's school program by bringing the Indian School Superintendent under his direction and by reducing the autonomy of the contract schools.

Another student of formal organization, Alfred D. Chandler, Jr., suggested that organizational structure followed market strategy in the development of the American business corporation. Improved transportation and industrial processes made possible the expansion of production and of the market potential of industrial enterprises. Expanded production and markets resulted in expanded resources for the firms, which had to be rationalized through the development of new organizational structures.[119] A similar process took place in the Indian Office. Congress created the Inspector of Indian Schools position in the year in which appropriations for the schools doubled; similarly, Commisioner Morgan took charge of the Indian schools during a period of rapid expansion of the Indian Office's educational budget. In current dollars, school expenditures increased by nearly one million dollars between the 1889-90 fiscal year and the 1892-93 fiscal year. When the effect of deflation is taken into account, the increase was more than 50%. In Indian administration, as in big business, structure followed strategy.

Boundary problems, the problem of central control, and the differentiation of local units according to function were all important elements of the emergence of schooling as the central organizational activity of the Indian Office. The increased importance of education was a significant component in the Indian Office's institutionalization. Education provided a focus for efforts to centralize the organization; as school budgets and personnel increased, uniformity and coordinated action could be achieved through a national personnel system, uniform job titles and descriptions, and the development of a standard curriculum for the Indian schools. The curriculum exemplified the cultural values of white society at the end of the century, and the educational emphasis of the organization provided organizational members with a specific set of goals to which they could devote themselves.

By identifying a specific means for accomplishing organizational goals. Indian education made the institutionalization of the Indian Office possible. Education became both the major function of the organization and its major goal. For nearly three-quarters of a century after 1900, Indian workers, whether they worked in schools or not, would conceive of their task as primarily educational, and of their clients as pupils.[120]

CHAPTER X

THE EMERGING INSTITUTION

In Chapter I, I listed the three indicators of institutionalization which are used in this study. The strengthening of organizational integrity and boundedness, as measured by the organization's ability to control the entry of personnel, the development of internal procedures to achieve coordination, and the definition of an organizational mission on which internal differentiation could be based, are indicators of the institutionalization of the Indian Office. In all three areas, increasing formalization and centralization promoted institutionalization, since the decentralized character of the Indian Office in the first fifteen years after the Civil War made it possible for external organizations to influence personnel selection, to control subordinates, and to define organizational goals. Thus centralization, with its concomitant formalization and routinization of official functions, made possible the institutionalization of the Indian Office.

Chapters III-IX traced the development of the emerging institution. By the 1890s, the central office dominated the selection of subordinate agency personnel. The subsequent abolition of the position of agent, and its replacement with the bonded reservation superintendent, resulted in the centralized selection of the local executive officer by the first decade of the twentieth century. These changes increased organizational integrity since the control of the Washington office over entry into the organization at the local level increased; formerly, when agents, themselves appointed through religious or political patronage systems, named their own subordinates, the Washington office had only a passive role in personnel selection.

Control of the field service of the Indian Office was a formidable problem. Reservations were scattered over a large expanse of territory. Efforts to concentrate Indians on a few large reservations were not successful. The earliest efforts to achieve coordinated effort were imposed from outside. The Peace Commission in the late 1860s bypassed the Indian Office; the Board of Indian Commissioners attempted to exert external control during the 1870s. The organization's own internal control system in the 1860s and early '70s involved superintendents, whose allegiance was often to external structures, the political system or the denominations. The development of an inspection service brought control functions into the organization's structure. Ultimately, inspectors functioned as organizational representatives, rather than as agents of external organizations or movements. The inspection system was flexible enough to permit modifications in line with the organization's emerging educational focus, as exemplified in the evolution of the Indian School Inspector's position and the development of the supervisors of Indian education in the 1890s. Significantly, the development of inspection accompanied the increasing formalization of the organization after the Grant administration.

The education of Indian youth became the organization's primary mission in the 1880s and '90s. Educational activities accounted for an increasing proportion of the organization's budget after 1880, and an increasing proportion of the field staff worked in the Indian schools. Most significantly, education provided the basis for the internal structural differentiation of the emerging organization. After 1885, independent schools proliferated. For those schools still under the direction of agents, the central office endeavored to insulate them from "interference" by the agent through the creation of the reservation superintendent position. At the middle and upper levels of the administrative hierarchy, specialized school inspection positions reflected the increasing importance of schooling in the Indian Service program. Significantly, the Superintendent of Indian Schools was made subordinate to the Commissioner of Indian Affairs during T. J. Morgan's tenure as Commissioner in the early 1890s.

At the beginning of the period, the Office of Indian Affairs could hardly be described as an organization, let alone an institution. The Commissioner and his clerks in the Washington Office monitored reports from the superintendents and agents in the field and conveyed these reports to the Secretary of the Interior and the Congress. The Indian Office did not participate in the appointment of superintendents and agents; both of these positions were Presidential appointments, subject to Senate confirmation. While Commissioners could recommend legislation, they had no reliable sources of information about developments on the reservations other than the reports of these nominal subordinates. The Congress and, during periods of Indian warfare, the Army dominated the making of Indian policy.

During the 1870s, the Indian inspectors provided, for the first time, an internal control and information mechanism. The demise of the transfer movement, the development of the Indian police forces, and the decline of the Board of Indian Commissioners reduced the intrusion of external organizations into the Indian Service. Indian Office appointment of subordinate agency employees and the development of semi-autonomous educational subdivisions within the agencies circumscribed the powers of the politically appointed agents, who were ultimately replaced by bonded superintendents. The classification of an increasing number of civil service positions in the 1890s made the new, centralized personnel system permanent and stable.

Thirty-five years after the end of the Civil War, the Indian Office was a very different kind of organization than it had been in 1865. Better-bounded, centralized, and internally differentiated, the organization was imbued with a mission, the education and acculturation of the Indians, which guided organizational activity. It could be described as an emerging institution.

The growth of the education program was an essential element in the institutionalization of the Office of Indian Affairs. Indian education provided the organization with specific means to achieve the assimilation of the American Indians; administrators viewed even such seemingly unrelated policies as citizenship and land allotment as educational in their impact on the Indians. An educational focus fit well with the widespread belief that the Indian cultures represented a lower level of evolutionary development than white American culture; the task of education was to speed up an evolutionary process of cultural development.[1]

The development of the educational emphasis resulted in increased internal differentiation, exemplified in the growth of specialized educational units at all levels of the organization. The adaptation of universalistic criteria for selecting personnel, along with the development of formal rules and a means to check on whether rules were followed, resulted in an organization which was more centralized and better-bounded than it had been in the decade after the Civil War.

In part, institutionalization also resulted simply from increases in the number of Indian Office employees and in the size of the budget. More employees necessitated the development of new methods of coordination; the expenditure of an increased amount of money made such coordination seem essential. Total federal civilian employment and total government expenditures mirrored the trends in Indian Service employment and expenditures reported in Chapter IX. The number of paid civilian federal employees increased nearly sevenfold between 1861 and 1901, from 36,106 to 231,056; civilian employment increased three-fold in the twenty years between 1871 and 1891, from 50,155 to 150,844.[2]

Federal expenditures increased less rapidly during the late nineteenth century. In 1871, budget expenditures, excluding debt repayment and funds expended from trust accounts, were $292 million. After declines in the late 1870s and '80s, expenditures reached $365 million in 1891, an increase of less than twenty-four percent in current dollars.[3] In constant (1873-74) dollars, however, federal expenditures doubled between 1870-71 and 1890-91, from $286,333,460 in 1870-71 to $570,607,440 in 1890-91.[4]

The two series, federal civilian employment and total federal budget expenditures, are not strictly comparable. For example, federal budget expenditures included the payment of the salaries of military personnel. However, the number of military personnel remained relatively stable between 1871 and 1891, reaching a high of 43,609 in 1874 and a low of 34,094 in 1877. A substantial increase in the size of military establishment occurred only with the outbreak of the Spanish-American War, in 1898.[5]

In general terms, what happened to the Indian Office also happened to the federal government as a whole between the 1870s and the 1890s. Both the number of employees and the amount of expenditures increased during the period with the number of employees increasing at a higher rate than the amount of expenditures. Such an expansion in federal employment led to pressures for reform in administration. In 1881, federal civilian employment exceeded one hundred thousand; two years later, Congress passed the Pendleton Act. Between 1883 and 1891, the number of classified employees rose from 13,780 to 33,873. Total federal employment exceeded 157,000 in the latter year. By 1901, the classified civil service numbered 106,205, nearly half of the civilian employees of the federal government.[6]

The increases in budgets and personnel reflected increases in the responsibilities of the Indian Office and of the federal government. The Indian Office increased the scope of its education program; the attainment of universal schooling for Indian children required increased expenditures for education and the employment of more teachers, matrons, and school administrators. The emphasis on education was in part the result of the rapid settlement of the American west after the completion of the transcontinental railroad, which made the gradual acculturation envisioned in the removal and concentration policies unworkable.

The expansion of federal employment in the forty years after the Civil War also reflected increased government responsibilities. Jonathan R. T. Hughes concluded that the closing of the frontier, the growth of business corporations, and a cyclical pattern of business activity resulted in "an elaborate system of government control" of the economy by the early twentieth century.[7] Even those agencies which did not have direct responsibility for regulating segments of the economy or providing services expanded in their functions during the late nineteenth century. In 1908, Theodore Roosevelt wrote to a union official,

> Already our Bureau of Labor, for the past twenty years of necessity largely a statistical bureau, is practically a Department of Sociology, aiming not only to secure exact information about industrial conditions but to discover remedies for industrial evils.[8]

Under the leadership of Carroll Wright, the Bureau conducted a broad variety of studies of industrial conditions after its establishment in 1885.[9]

One indicator of expanding governmental responsibilities is the creation of new agencies. Carl Grafton, in a study of the creation of federal agencies between 1933 and 1972, concluded that social, economic, or technological change was "a major stimulus of federal agency creation."[10] Such changes, labelled "SET novelties," included scientific and technical developments, such as atomic energy, radio, and rockets, and social and economic developments, such as the growth of labor unions and corporations, and the development of Keynesian economic theory.[11] Of the fifty-one new agencies studied by Grafton, twenty-six (51%) "were created as a direct result" of one of the eleven "SET novelties" identified by him. The budgets of these agencies represented over

90% of the current budgets of the fifty-one agencies.[12] An additional eight agencies (16%) were created in response to "perceived SET novelties." These were agencies created in the 1950s, '60s, and '70s to deal with problems of civil rights and poverty.[13]

Herbert Kaufman, in a study of the creation of federal agencies since 1789, found that the Grant and Harrison administrations were periods of sharp increases in the numbers of government agencies.[14] Kaufman's data were admittedly incomplete; his sample included only organizations still in existence by 1923. However, his data suggest a pattern of federal agency creation after the Civil War which was unprecedented. Between 1865 and 1900, the number of government agencies in his sample doubled, from forty-five at the close of Lincoln's first term to ninety at the turn of the century.[15]

In his study of the U. S. House of Representatives, Nelson Polsby suggested that increasing "density," the growth of the federal government's size and workload, resulted in institutionalization. In his words, "As the responsibilities of the national government grew, as a larger proportion of the national economy was affected by decisions taken at the center, the agencies of the national government institutionalized."[16] Increased boundedness, the development of mechanisms designed to achieve coordination, the regularization of procedures, and increased internal differentiation resulted from increases in the size and responsibilities of federal agencies.

The impetus for institutionalization was, in part, external. The historian of the civil service reform movement, Ari A. Hoogenboom, suggested that the civil service reformers of the 1870s and '80s were members of an eastern, Protestant elite "who wished to return to the good old days before Jacksonian democracy and the industrial revolution, when men with their background, status, and education were the unquestioned leaders of society."[17] A similar motivation might be ascribed to the churchmen and members of the Board of Indian Commissioners who lost their influence over the Indian Office program after the Grant administration. In the joint meetings of the Board and the missionary societies, at the Lake Mohonk Conferences, and through the Indian Rights Association, these "displaced elites" campaigned for an independent education division, for the extension of civil service rules to Indian agency and school positions, and for the allotment of Indian lands during the 1880s.

Such an interpretation would be incomplete, however. The effect of civil service reform was to strengthen organizational integrity and to increase the powers of Washington administrators, whether they were reformers or politicians. Further, the earlier administrative reforms, the central selection of agency personnel, the departure from religious patronage, and the development of an inspection service, were attempts to reduce the power of the churchmen and reformers who wielded influence during the Grant administration. The reformers attacked Carl Schurz and E. A. Hayt for their appointments policy as well as for the Ponca removal. Five years later, they attacked Commissioner J. D. C. Atkins' use of job descriptions and his examination of the qualifications of the applicants for Indian Service positions because they viewed these as a smokescreen for political interference and spoils.

Philip Selznick suggested that the institutionalization of a complex organization results from the leadership available to the organization. Leaders further institutionalization by making decisions regarding the recruitment and socialization of personnel, by developing ways in which internal interest groups can represent themselves, and by determining the organization's approach to other organizations and outside interest groups.[18] The decisions made will determine organizational goals and their embodiment in the organization's internal social structure, the way in which internal conflicts are resolved, and the boundedness of the organization.[19] A review of the organizational development of the Indian Office in the decades after the Civil War suggests that institutional leadership was significant in the institutionalization of the Indian Office.

During the Hayes administration, Carl Schurz played a central role in defending the organization from external attack and in creating the conditions for internal development. The results of the Galpin investigation, initiated and guided by Schurz, enabled him to dissolve the remaining superintendencies, replace the nominal leadership of the Indian Office, and begin a gradual disengagement from the religious appointment policy of the Grant administration. His decision to have the Indian inspectors report to the Secretary of the Interior, rather than to the Commissioner of Indian Affairs, resulted in the subsequent formalization of the inspectors' activities under Secretaries Kirkwood and Teller. Schurz's vigorous defense of Indian Office policy probably ended the transfer movement.[20] His advocacy of education and allotment anticipated programs which dominated Indian Office activity for the next fifty years. His Commissioner of Indian Affairs, E. A. Hayt, initiated the policy of having the Washington Office appoint some of the agency personnel, a development which decreased the autonomy of the Indian agents and anticipated the civil service system of the 1890s.

John Oberly, Cleveland's first Superintendent of Indian Schools, had an influence much greater than his brief tenure in the organization would suggest. With ties both to the Democratic Party and to reform groups, Oberly argued for increased administrative authority for the School Superintendent. While his successors attempted unsuccessfully to build on Oberly's accomplishments in this area, another cause advocated by the Illinois Democrat ultimately succeeded. Oberly advocated the independence of schools at the local level and the development of a personnel system for the Indian Service organized along civil service principles. Both of these objectives were realized during the 1890s.

Benjamin Harrison's Commissioner of Indian Affairs, Thomas J. Morgan, was a third institutional leader. During Morgan's tenure, spending for Indian schools increased, the number of school employees increased, and agency school systems became semi-autonomous organizational units under the reservation superintendents. Morgan reduced the influence of the churches in Indian education as a result of his conflict with the Catholic Indian Bureau. He suggested turning over the functions of the agents to the reservation school superintendents, a policy which eventually resulted in the centralization of all agency appointments. During Morgan's tenure, Congress settled the question of ultimate administrative authority for Indian education, by making the Superintendent of Indian Schools responsible to the Commissioner of Indian Affairs.

Schurz, Oberly, and Morgan functioned as institutional leaders, in Selznick's sense. All three made decisions or successfully advocated policies which governed the entry of personnel into the Indian Service, shaped the internal social structure of the organization, and determined the relationship of the Indian Office to its clients and its reformist and religious constituencies. The organizational position of these leaders may have been significant for the way in which the organization institutionalized. In a little more than a decade, leadership shifted from the Secretary of the Interior to the Superintendent of Indian Schools and finally to the Commissioner of Indian Affairs. By the end of Morgan's administration, the conditions for a centralized bureaucratic organization, directed by the Commissioner of Indian Affairs and devoted to the assimilation of its wards, had been established.

Eighty years later, American Indians were the nation's most deprived minority group, whether deprivation was indicated by nutritional level, educational accomplishment, median income, or morbidity and mortality rates.[21] A study conducted for the Joint Economic Committee in 1969 concluded that "the American Indian population is rural, poor, and essentially outside of the mainstream of the larger society," echoing the findings of the Meriam Report forty years earlier.[22] Another contributor blamed the failure to achieve assimilation on the paternalistic nature of federal programs, which created and maintained "an attitude of dependence on the part of Indians, with attendant indifference and hostility arising at various places and times toward any throughgoing efforts to induce change."[23]

A decade before the publication of the Meriam Report in 1928, the failure of the assimilation program was evident. Yet the program which the Indian Office developed during the 1880s continued to guide administrators through the 1920s.[24] The way in which the Indian Office institutionalized explains in part the failure to adapt to changing conditions after 1900.

The emerging institutional structure of the Indian Office was well-bounded, routinized, and directed toward accomplishing the goal of Indian assimilation through education, land allotment, and citizenship. Such a focus assumed that economic opportunity for the Indians would result from the substitution of reduced allotments for undivided tribal holdings, from the provision of schooling to Indian youth, and from the grant of citizenship. Such an assumption was not tenable even in the first decade of the twentieth century. Schools trained Indians for jobs which were non-existent, reservations were allotted before Indians were ready for the ownership of private property, and citizenship proved to be little protection against the efforts of whites to control Indian land and resources. Yet the Indian Office was seemingly unable to adjust its program to take these conditions into account. The Meriam Report described an organization which was well-bounded, highly centralized, committed to the goal of Indian assimilation, and unresponsive to the needs of its Indian clientele.[25]

This conclusion should not suggest that the organization was "finished" in 1900 or that all of its administrative problems had been solved. Problems of political interference, lack of central control, corruption, and fraud continued to plague the organization. Few reformers or administrators were satisfied with the state of the organization in the first decade of the twentieth century. Indian Inspectors were still political appointees; they still reported to the Secretary of the Interior, rather than to the Commissioner of Indian Affairs. More seriously, the statutes assigned the making of decisions regarding Indian Affairs to various officials, including the President and the Secretary of War, as well as the Secretary of the Interior and the Commissioner of Indian Affairs. Francis E. Leupp, the Indian Rights Association's Washington lobbyist in the 1890s and Theodore Roosevelt's second Commissioner of Indian Affairs, complained of "the absurd patchwork of law which has been continued in force long after the conditions that called its inconsistencies into being have passed away."[26] Leupp and his successor, Commissioner Robert G. Valentine, called for a recodification of the statutes regulating Indian Affairs.[27] Leupp's major effort was to accomplish the extension of civil service regulations to all positions in the Indian Service, "to remove the Indian service from the domination of partisan politics." By 1914, he claimed that political interference had been "reduced to a minimum."[28] However, developments such as the White Earth scandal of 1909 made such an assertion doubtful. When the Indian Office allotted the White Earth Reservation in 1905, a 1909 investigator concluded, the agent provided mixed bloods with the most valuable allotments; many of the allottees subsequently sold their lands to non-Indians under suspicious circumstances.[29] Warren K. Moorehead, the investigator and a member of the Board of Indian Commissioners, suggested that the inefficiency of the inspection service permitted these and other frauds of the early twentieth century to occur undetected.[30]

Robert Valentine, who served as Commissioner of Indian Affairs during Moorehead's investigation, also called for an improved inspection service. In words reminiscent of the statements of Commissioners in the 1870s and '80s, he observed that

> Repeated experiences have demonstrated that superintendents can practice irregularities which a distant office force cannot detect, and can so color reports . . . that the office is for a

time misled. Both experience and the dictates of sound administration require frequent examination of agency affairs . . .[31]

The inspecting officers of the Indian Office visited 141 of the 152 Indian Service jurisdictions during the 1911-12 fiscal year, submitting over 318 reports.[32] Still, the Commissioner called for a larger inspection staff and for more clerks in his Washington office.[33]

If the institutionalization of the Indian Office was incomplete by 1900, the direction which organizational development would take was not in doubt. Difficulties in administration, confusion in defining the responsibilities of officials, continued corruption and fraud all resulted in demands for more institutionalization—an extension and elaboration of civil service rules, a codification of the statutes, more inspectors, more clerks.[34] The focus of organizational work was set and would prove very difficult to change, even when another reform movement took charge of the Indian Office in the 1930s. In part, the "New Deal for the Indians" failed because of a lingering commitment to assimilation on the part of Indian Office personnel and, significantly, on the part of some of the clients of the Indian Office.[35]

Philip Selznick once observed that too much institutionalization could be pathological.[36] Indeed, the outcome of the institutionalization of the Indian Office in the late nineteenth century appears to be an instance of Selznick's "tragedy of organizations." The development of administrative capacity by 1900, combined with a premature consensus on the means required to achieve the goal of assimilation, resulted in organizational inflexibility and rigidity. Even when the reform movement of the 1920s, led by John Collier, captured the organization in 1933, basic change proved difficult to achieve. After World War II, the Collier program was dead; in 1963, a historian of Indian policy concluded that "the emphasis on the tribal relationship [during the New Deal years] may now be regarded as an interlude in the effort to assimilate the Indians."[37] In our own time, as in the late 1860s, some proponents of administrative reform in Indian affairs advocate the creation of a new federal agency, independent of the Interior Department and perhaps of the past, to serve the first Americans.[38]

NOTES

INTRODUCTION

1. Alfred D. Chandler, Jr., *Strategy and Structure: Chapters in the History of the Industrial Enterprise* (Cambridge, Mass., 1962).

2. Robert M. Wiebe, *The Search for Order, 1877-1920* (New York, 1967).

3. Quoted in U. S., Comptroller General, *Report to the Congress: Federal Management Weaknesses Cry Out for Alternatives to Deliver Programs and Services to Indians to Improve their Quality of Life* (Washington, 1978), 4.

4. *Ibid.*, 8-14. Previous General Accounting Office Reports on federal management of Indian programs are summarized in *Ibid.*, 27-50.

5. William T. Hagan, *American Indians* (Chicago, 1961), 152-153. See below, pp. 5-6.

6. Philip Selznick, *Leadership in Administration: A Sociological Interpretation* (New York, 1957).

7. Samuel P. Huntington, *Political Order in Changing Societies*, (New Haven, Conn., 1968), 12-24.

8. Nelson W. Polsby, "The Institutionalization of the U. S. House of Representatives," *American Political Science Review*, LXII (March, 1968), 145.

9. Allan G. Bogue, Jerome M. Clubb, Carroll R. McKibbin, and Santa A. Traugott, "Members of the House of Representatives and the Process of Modernization, 1789-1960," *Journal of American History*, LXIII (September, 1976), 278; J. Rogers Hollingsworth, "An Approach to the Study of Comparative Historical Politics," in Hollingsworth, ed., *Nation and State Building in America: Comparative Historical Perspectives* (Boston, 1971), 257-260.

10. Max Weber, *The Theory of Social and Economic Organization*, ed. Talcott Parsons (New York, 1947), 328-341; *From Max Weber: Essays in Sociology*, ed. H. H. Gerth and C. Wright Mills (New York, 1946), 196-198.

CHAPTER I

1. W. Lloyd Warner, *et al.*, *The Emergent American Society: Large-Scale Organizations* (New Haven, Conn., 1967), 10.

2. Charles Perrow, *Complex Organizations: A Critical Essay* (Glenview, Ill., 1972), 5-6.

3. *Ibid.*, 6.

4. Robert K. Merton, "Bureaucratic Structure and Personality," *Social Forces*, XVIII (May, 1940), 560-568.

5. Perrow, *Complex Organizations*, 6.

6. *Ibid.*, 6-7.

7. Laurence F. Schemeckebier, *The Office of Indian Affairs: Its History, Activities, and Organization* (Baltimore, 1927), 1, 26-28. The Carter administration replaced the position of Commissioner of Indian Affairs with that of Assistant Secretary of the Interior for Indian Affairs in 1977. See *New York Times*, November 1, 1977, 16.

8. Section 5, Act of March 3, 1849, in U. S., *Statutes at Large*, IX, 395.

9. Institute for Government Research, *The Problem of Indian Administration* (Baltimore, 1928), 8-21.

10. Warren King and Associates, Inc., *Bureau of Indian Affairs Management Study: Report on BIA Management Practices to the American Indian Policy Review Commission* [Committee Print] (Washington, 1976), 6-7. Prior assessments of the management of the Bureau are summarized in *Ibid.*, 59-63.

11. Edgar S. Cahn, *Our Brother's Keeper: The Indian in White America* (New York, 1969), 147-155. See also Vine Deloria, Jr., *Custer Died for Your Sins: An Indian Manifesto* (New York, 1969), 125-145.

12. Philip Selznick, "An Approach to a Theory of Bureaucracy," *American Sociological Review*, VIII (February, 1943), 49.

13. Robert H. Wiebe, *The Search for Order, 1877-1920* (New York, 1967).

14. In addition to Wiebe, see Alfred D. Chandler Jr., *Strategy and Structure: Chapters in the History of the Industrial Enterprise* (Cambridge, Mass., 1962), 24-36; Samuel P. Hays, *The Response to Industrialism: 1885-1914* (Chicago, 1956), esp. Chapter III; Barrington Moore, Jr., *Social Origins of Dictatorship and Democracy* (Boston, 1966), Chapter III.

15. Chandler, *Strategy and Structure*, 24, 29-31.

16. Warner, *et al.*, *The Emergent American Society*, 10.

17. *Ibid.*, 10-13.

18. National growth prior to the developments of the late nineteenth century was based on a multiplicative principle, in which political and religious structures were duplicated in western regions as the nation expanded. See Robert F. Berkhofer, Jr., "Space, Time, Culture, and the New Frontier," *Agricultural History*, XXXVIII (January, 1964), 21-30.

19. For a theoretical statement regarding the differentiation of political institutions from other institutions, see J. Rogers Hollingsworth's essay, "An Approach to the Study of Comparative Historical Politics," in *Nation and State Building in America: Comparative Historical Perspectives* (Boston, 1971), 257-260. Political parties served in nineteenth century America

to define and articulate cultural, particularly ethnic-religious, values. See Lee Benson, *The Concept of Jacksonian Democracy: New York as a Test Case* (Princeton, N. J., 1961). Political parties, in the absence of a differentiation of the executive branch from partisan politics, dominated governmental administration for much of the nineteenth century. See Leonard D. White, *The Republican Era: 1869-1901, A Study in Administrative History* (New York, 1963), 10-14.

20. Max Weber, *The Theory of Social and Economic Organization*, edited by Talcott Parsons (New York, 1946), 196-198.

21. *Ibid.*, 333-334; From Max Weber: *Essays in Sociology*, edited by H. H. Gerth and C. Wright Mills (New York, 1946), 196-198.

22. Weber, *The Theory of Social and Economic Organization*, 337-339.

23. *Ibid.*, 340; *From Max Weber*, 221-224.

24. White, *The Republican Era*, 19.

25. *Ibid.*, 18-19.

26. Tenure of Office Act, approved March 2, 1867, in U.S., *Statutes at Large*, XIV, 430.

27. Act of April 5, 1869, in U.S., *Statutes at Large*, XIV, 6; White, *The Republican Era*, 28-30; Grover Cleveland, "The Independence of the Executive," in *Presidential Problems* (New York, 1904), 30-37.

28. Act of March 3, 1887, in U.S., *Statutes at Large*, XXIV, 500; White, *The Republican Era*, 30-31; Cleveland commented, "The President, freed from the Senate's claim of tutelage, became again the independent agent of the people, representing a coordinate branch of their government, charged with responsibilities which, under his oath, he ought not to avoid or divide with others, and invested with powers, not to be surrendered, but to be used, under the guidance of patriotic intention and an unclouded conscience." "The Independence of the Executive," 76.

29. White, *The Republican Era*, 392.

30. Act of January 16, 1883, in U.S., *Statutes at Large*, XXII, 403; Ari Hoogenboom, "The Pendleton Act and the Civil Service," *American Historical Review*, LXIV (January, 1957), 301-318.

31. White, *The Republican Era*, 393-394.

32. *Ibid.*, 387-392.

33. *Ibid.*, 19.

34. Samuel P. Huntington, *Political Order in Changing Societies* (New Haven, Conn., 1968), 12.

35. Nelson W. Polsby, "The Institutionalization of the U.S. House of Representatives," *American Political Science Review*, LXII (March, 1968), 145.

36. Harold W. Pfautz, "The Sociology of Secularization: Religious Groups," *American Journal of Sociology*, LXI (September, 1955), 126.

37. See, for example, Talcott Parsons, "The Professions and Social Structure," *Social Forces*, XVII (May, 1939), 457-467.

38. Charles Perrow identified the analysis of the connection between the organization and its environment as the major conceptual contribution of the institutional school in organizational analysis, in *Complex Organizations*, 203.

39. Robert Michels, *Political Parties: A Sociological Study of the Oligarchic Tendencies of Modern Democracy* (Glencoe, Ill., 1949).

40. Selznick, "An Approach to a Theory of Bureaucracy," 47-54.

41. *Ibid.*, 48.

42. *Ibid.* David Mechanic identified such factors as "access to persons, information, and instrumentalities," possession of "expert knowledge," effort and interest, and central organizational position as "Sources of Power of Lower Participants in Complex Organizations," *Administrative Science Quarterly*, VII (December, 1962), 349-362.

43. Philip Selznick, *TVA and the Grass Roots: A Study in the Sociology of Formal Organization* (Berkeley, Calif., 1949), esp. 249-266; see also, Philip Selznick, "Foundations of the Theory of Organization," *American Sociological Review*, XIII (February, 1948), 25-35; James D. Thompson and William J. McEwan, "Organizational Goals and Environment: Goal-Setting as an Interaction Process," *American Sociological Review*, XXIII (February, 1958), 23-31.

44. Selznick, *Leadership in Administration: A Sociological Interpretation* (New York, 1957), 5. Emphasis in original.

45. *Ibid.*, 61-64.

46. See Thompson and McEwan, "Organizational Goals and Environment."

47. Howard Aldrich discusses organizational control of entry to and exit from membership in "Organizational Boundaries and Inter-Organizational Conflict," *Human Relations*, XXIV (August, 1971), 279-293.

48. See Jerald Hage, Michael Aiken, and Cora Bagley Marrett, "Organization Structure and Communications," *American Sociological Review*, XXXVI (October, 1971), 860-871.

49. Selznick, *Leadership in Administration*, 91-99.

50. *Ibid.*, 132-133. Selznick was perhaps unique in emphasizing the identity of interest between professionalism and organizational goals. One student of the professions, Eliot Freidson, has argued that the growth of professions in the mid-twentieth century, with its concomitant emphasis on professional discretion and independence, has the potential for challenging "the administrative principle" of the organizational control of work, in "Professions and the Occupational Principle," *The Professions and Their Prospects* (Beverly Hills, Calif., 1973), 19-38.

51. Quoted in Perrow, *Complex Organizations*, 194.

52. *Ibid.*, 193-197.

53. But see Polsby's conclusions in "The Institutionalization of the U. S. House of Representatives," 164-168.

54. Selznick's student, Charles Perrow, examined the influence of the internal organization and the environment on organizational goals in his case study of a general hospital. See Charles Perrow, "The Analysis of Goals in Complex Organizations," *American Sociological Review*, XXVI (April, 1961), 854-866.

55. Selznick, *Leadership in Administration*, 139.

56. *Ibid.*, 111-112; Aldrich, "Organizational Boundaries."

57. Selznick, *Leadership in Administration*, 16.

58. *Ibid.*, 132.

59. Hage, Aiken, and Marret, "Organization Structure and Communications;" James L. Price summarized recent investigations of organizational control systems in *Organizational Effectiveness: An Inventory of Propositions* (Homewood, Ill. 1968), esp. 181-183.

CHAPTER II

1. Among the many secondary treatments of the United States Indian policy after the Civil War, I have found the following to be most useful: Henry E. Fritz, *The Movement for Indian Assimilation, 1860-1890* (Philadelphia, 1963); Robert Winston Mardock, *The Reformers and the American Indian* (Columbia, Mo., 1971); Loring Benson Priest, *Uncle Sam's Stepchildren: The Reformation of United States Indian Policy, 1865-1887* (New Brunswick, N.J., 1942); Francis Paul Prucha, *American Indian Policy in Crisis: Christian Reformers and the Indian, 1865-1900* (Norman, Okla., 1976); Lawrence F. Schmeckbier, *The Office of Indian Affairs: Its History, Activities, and Organization* (Baltimore, 1927), pp. 42-48. Convenient document collections on policy during the period include Francis Paul Prucha, ed., *Americanizing the American Indians: Writings by "Friends of the Indian," 1880-1900* (Cambridge, Mass., 1973), and Wilcomb E. Washburn, *The Assault on Indian Tribalism: The General Allotment Law (Dawes Act) of 1887* (Philadelphia, 1975).

2. Mary E. Young, "Congress Looks West: Liberal Ideology and Public Land Policy in the Nineteenth Century," in *The Frontier in American Development: Essays in Honor of Paul Wallace Gates*, edited by David M. Ellis (Ithaca, N.Y., 1969), 74-112; Washburn, *The Assault on Indian Tribalism*, 16-18.

3. William T. Hagan, *Indian Police and Judges: Experiments in Acculturation and Control* (New Haven, Conn., 1966); on the growth of the Indian Office's educational system, see pp. 123-133.

4. Most historians have perhaps underestimated the influence of white land hunger on the evolution of Indian policy in the post-Civil war years. D.S. Otis presented a balanced account of the "aims and motives of the allotment movement" in his *The Dawes Act and the Allotment*

of Indian Lands (1934; rev. ed., Norman, Okla., 1973), 8-32. Otis concluded that "Allotment was first of all a method of destroying the reservation and opening up Indian lands," but it was "a humane and progressive movement." *Ibid.*, 32. Paul W. Gates presented considerable evidence of the use of allotment as a technique for white intrusion in his "Indian Allotments Preceeding the Dawes Act," in *The Frontier Challenge: Responses to the Trans-Mississippi West*, edited by John G. Clark (Lawrence, Kansas, 1971), 141-170. William T. Hagan concluded that "The one area in which the reservation system after 1865 was made to perform up to expectations was in the reduction of the Indian's land base." He cited white cupidity as a major contributing factor. See his "The Reservation Policy: Too Little and Too Late," in *Indian-White Relations: A Persistent Paradox*, edited by Jane F. Smith and Robert M. Kvasnicka (Washington, 1976), 164.

5. In 1872, Commissioner of Indian Affairs Francis A. Walker predicted that the completion of the Northern Pacific Railroad "will in itself completely solve the great Sioux problem, and leave the ninety thousand Indians ranging between the two trans-continental lines as incapable of resisting the government as are the Indians of New York or Massachusetts." Commissioner of Indian Affairs, *Annual Report, 1872* in U.S., House of Representatives, *Executive Documents*, 42nd Congress, 3rd Session, No. 1, Part 5 (Serial 1560), 397. Walker added a report on "The Indians and the Railroads," in *Ibid.*, 463-469. For historians' assessments of the importance of the railroad in reducing the Indians' capacity to resist, see Robert M. Utley, *Frontier Regulars: The United States Army and the Indian, 1866-1891* (New York, 1973), 93-94, 110; and S. Lyman Tyler, *A History of Indian Policy* (Washington, 1973), 86. For a case study, see Robert M. Utley, *The Last Days of the Sioux Nation* (New Haven, Conn., 1963).

6. Act of April 10, 1869, U.S., *Statutes at Large*, XVI, 40. For a discussion of the early functions of the Board, see Chapter V. Henry E. Fritz discussed the later evolution of the body in "The Board of Indian Commissioners and Ethnocentric Reform, 1878-1893," in Smith and Kvasnicka, eds., *Indian-White Relations*, 57-78. Robert F. Berkhofer, Jr., provided a valuable "Commentary" to Fritz's paper in *Ibid.*, 79-86.

7. Francis Paul Prucha discussed the origins and activities of the Indian Rights Association, "the most important" of several reform organizations, in his *American Indian Policy in Crisis*, 138-143.

8. Reports of the annual conference of the Board with missionary societies, beginning in 1869, may be found in the *Annual Reports* of the Board of Indian Commissioners. The Lake Mohonk Conference *Proceedings* (1883-1916) were generally also included in the Board's *Annual Reports* and were published separately. See Larry E. Burgess, *The Lake Mohonk Conference of Friends of the Indian: Guide to the Annual Reports* (New York, 1975).

9. See Philip Selznick, *Leadership in Administration: A Sociological Interpretation* (New York, 1957), 66-74.

10. Robert A. Trennert, Jr., *Alternative to Extinction: Federal Indian Policy and the Beginnings of the Reservation System, 1846-51* (Philadelphia, 1975), 194.

11. During the years 1853-1856, fifty-two treaties were negotiated with the tribes. Commissioner of Indian Affairs, *Annual Report, 1856*, in U.S., Senate, *Executive Documents*, 34th Congress, 3rd Session, No. 5 (Serial 875), pp. 571-572, quoted in Edmund J. Danziger, Jr., "The Indian Office During the Civil War: Impotence in Indian Affairs," *South Dakota History*, V (Winter, 1974), 54.

12. Robert M. Utley, *Frontiersmen in Blue: The United States Army and the Indian, 1848-1865* (New York, 1967), 214-215; Danziger, "The Indian Office"; in *Indians and Bureaucrats:*

Administering the Reservation Policy During the Civil War (Urbana, Ill., 1974), Edmund J. Danziger, Jr. presented three case studies of administrative problems during the war years.

13. Utley, *Frontiersmen in Blue*, 217-218, 231-340; Danziger, *Indians and Bureaucrats*; Utley, *Frontier Regulars*, 1-9.

14. "Indian Hostilities," July 13, 1867, U.S., Senate, *Executive Documents*, 40th Congress, 1st Session, No. 13 (Serial 1308), 1-5. See also Fritz, *The Movement for Indian Assimilation*, 33.

15. The Army executed thirty-nine of the 303 Santee Sioux condemned by the tribunal after Lincoln's intercession. Roy W. Meyer, *History of the Santee Sioux: United States Indian Policy on Trial* (Lincoln, Nebr., 1967), 128.

16. Fritz, *The Movement for Indian Assimilation*, 34-38.

17. *Ibid.*, 54-55; Mardock, *The Reformers and the American Indian*, 14-18.

18. Priest, *Uncle Sam's Stepchildren*, 15. Robert M. Utley has stated that "the attitudes and goals represented in the officer corps were essentially those professed by the Indian administrators" after the Civil War. See his "The Frontier Army: John Ford or Arthur Penn?" in Smith and Kvasnicka, eds., *Indian-White Relations*, 133-145, and the "Discussion Note," in *Ibid.*, 152.

19. Joint Resolution of March 3, 1865, in U.S., *Statutes at Large*, XIII, 572.

20. Doolittle submitted the ten-page report, entitled "Condition of the Indian Tribes," on January 26, 1867. It appeared as U.S., Senate, *Reports*, 39th Congress, 2nd Session, No. 156 (Serial 1279). A 527-page appendix consisted of the individual reports of the committee members, together with transcripts of the testimony taken by them. For a discussion of the preparation of the report, see Harry Kelsey, "The Doolittle Report of 1867: Its Preparation and Shortcomings," *Arizona and the West*, XVII (Summer 1975), 107-120.

21. "Condition of the Indian Tribes," 1-10.

22. "Indian Hostilities," 5-6. Taylor's report was dated July 12, 1867.

23. "Report to the President by the Indian Peace Commission, January 7, 1868," in U.S., House of Representatives, *Executive Documents*, 40th Congress, 2nd Session, No. 97 (Serial 1337), esp. 17-22. The Peace Commission's Report was reprinted in the *Annual Report* of the Commissioner of Indian Affairs for 1868, in U.S., House of Representatives, *Executive Documents*, 40th Congress, 3rd Session, No. 1 (Serial 1366), 486-510.

24. U.S., *Statutes at Large*, XII, 793.

25. These removals are summarized in Schmeckebier, *The Office of Indian Affairs*, 107-121.

26. Treaty with the Sioux—Brule, Oglala, Miniconjou, Yanktonai, Hunkpapa, Blackfeet, Cuthead, Two Kettle, Sans Arcs, and Santee—and Arapahoe, April 29, 1868 (U.S., *Statutes at Large*, XV, 635), in Charles J. Kappler, comp., *Indian Affairs, Laws and Treaties*, II (Washington, 1904), 998-1007; "An Act to Ratify an Agreement with Certain Bands of the Sioux

Nation," approved February 28, 1877, in U.S., *Statutes at Large*, XIX, 254; "An Act to Divide a Portion of the Sioux Nation," approved March 2, 1889, in U.S., *Statutes at Large*, XV, 888.

27. Fritz, *The Movement for Indian Assimilation*, 80-81.

28. This policy is well-stated in Commissioner of Indian Affairs E. S. Parker's circular letter to Indian Agents and Superintendents, dated July 12, 1869: "Indians who fail or refuse to come in and locate in permanent abodes, upon reservations, will be subject wholly to the control and supervision of the military authorities, who, as circumstances may justify, will at their discretion treat them as friendly or hostile." The circular letter is reprinted in Commissioner of Indian Affairs, *Annual Report, 1869*, in U.S., House of Representatives, *Executive Documents*, 41st Congress, 2nd Session, No.1, Part 3 (Serial 1414), 894.

29. Indian Appropriations Act, approved March 3, 1871, in U.S., *Statutes at Large*, XVI, 566.

30. Commissioner of Indian Affairs, *Annual Report, 1869*, in U.S., House of Representatives, *Executive Documents*, 41st Congress, 2nd Session, No. 1, Part 3 (Serial 1414), 448. See also Prucha, *American Indian Policy in Crisis*, 63-71.

31. Schemeckebier, *The Office of Indian Affairs*, 65.

32. See, for example, the Fort Laramie Treaty (1868), Article 10, in Kappler, comp., *Indian Affairs*, II, 1001. See also Schemeckebier, *The Office of Indian Affairs*, 69-70.

33. Commissioner of Indian Affairs, *Annual Report, 1872*, in U.S., House of Representatives, *Executive Documents*, 42nd Congress, 3rd Session, No. 1, Part 5 (Serial 1560), 391-398.

34. *Ibid.*, 396; Richard M. Ellis, *General Pope and U.S. Indian Policy* (Albuquerque, N.M., 1970), 38; Hagan, "The Reservation Policy," 162-163.

35. Section 3, Indian Appropriations Act, approved March 3, 1875, in U.S., *Statutes at Large*, XVIII, 420.

36. Robert F. Berkhofer, Jr., *Salvation and the Savage: An Analysis of Protestant Missions and the American Indian Response, 1787-1862* (Lexington, Ky., 1965), Chapter VII.

37. Prucha, *American Indian Policy in Crisis*, 194-196.

38. Priest, *Uncle Sam's Stepchildren*, 18-20.

39. Hagan, *Indian Police and Judges*, 29-30.

40. See p. 110.

41. Gates, "Indian Allotments Preceding the Dawes Act," 141.

42. Mary E. Young, *Redskins, Ruffleshirts, and Rednecks: Indian Allotments in Alabama and Mississippi, 1830-1860* (Norman, Okla., 1961).

43. Tribal History Program, *History of the Flandreau Santee Sioux Tribe* (Flandreau, S.D., 1971), 67.

44. Nancy Oestreich Lurie, "Women in Early American Anthropology," in *Pioneers of American Anthropology: The Uses of Biography*, edited by June Helm (Seattle, 1966), 43-54; Alice C. Fletcher, "Allotment of Land to Indians," *Proceedings of the National Conference of Charities and Correction, 1887* (Boston, 1887), 172-180.

45. Hagan, "The Reservation Policy," 165.

46. Again, see the Fort Laramie Treaty, Article 6, in Kappler, comp., *Indian Affairs*, II, 999-1000. Provision for Indian homesteading was made in Section 16 of the Deficiency Act, approved March 3, 1875, in U.S., *Statutes at Large*, XVIII, 402. The failure of the Indian homestead provisions was discussed in general terms by Priest, *Uncle Sam's Stepchildren*, 180-182; for a description of the operation of the homesteading provisions at Flandreau, Dakota Territory, see Meyer, *History of the Santee Sioux*, 251-252.

47. The phrase was used by James Thayer, "A People Without Law," *Atlantic Monthly*, LXVIII (October, 1891), 540-551.

48. Hagan, *Indian Police and Judges*, 30-37.

49. Quoted in Flora Warren Seymour, *Indian Agents of the Old Frontier* (New York, 1941), 167-168.

50. Quoted in Hagan, *Indian Police and Judges*, 38.

51. Indian Appropriations Act, approved May 27, 1878, U.S., *Statutes at Large*, XX, 86.

52. Hagan, *Indian Police and Judges*, 42-43; Seymour, *Indian Agents of the Old Frontier*, 176.

53. Quoted in Elaine Goodale Eastman, *Pratt, The Red Man's Moses* (Norman, Okla., 1935), 272.

54. Richard Henry Pratt, "The Advantages of Mingling Indians with Whites," *Proceedings of the National Conference of Charities and Corrections, 1892* (Boston, 1892), 45-59.

55. Seymour, *Indian Agents of the Old Frontier*, 269.

56. For a convenient summary, see Kenneth E. Davison, "President Hayes and the Reform of American Indian Policy," *Ohio History*, LXXXII (Summer-Autumn, 1973), 205-214, or Chapter XII in the same author's *The Presidency of Rutherford B. Hayes* (Westport, Conn., 1972).

57. Hagan, *Indian Police and Judges*, 108-110; *Rules Governing the Court of Indian Offenses* (Washington, 1883).

58. Hagan, "The Reservation Policy," 164.

59. Mardock, *The Reformers and the American Indian*, 168-191.

60. See Article 1, "An Act to Ratify an Agreement with Certain bands of the Sioux Nation," approved February 28, 1877, in U.S., *Statutes at Large*, XIX, 254.

61. Mardock, *The Reformers and the American Indian*, 192-197.

62. Hagan, "The Reservation Policy," 165.

63. Washburn, *The Assault on Indian Tribalism*, 21-22.

64. Section 3 of the Act of February 28, 1891, in U.S., *Statutes at Large*, XVI, 794, authorized grazing leases on unalloted lands. For developments on Indian Territory reservations, see Donald J. Berthrong, "Federal Indian Policy and the Southern Cheyennes and Arapahoes, 1887-1907," *Ethnohistory*, III (Spring, 1956), 138-153; Berthrong, "Cattlemen on the Cheyenne-Arapahoe Reservation, 1883-1885," *Arizona and the West*, XIII (Spring, 1971), 5-32; and William T. Hagan, "Kiowas, Commanches, and Cattlemen, 1867-1906: A Case Study of the Failure of U.S. Reservation Policy," *Pacific Historical Review*, XL (August, 1971), 333-355.

65. See below, pp. 123-133. Hagan argued that the commitment to education was half-hearted in "The Reservation Policy," 163-164.

66. General Allotment Act, approved February 8, 1887, in U.S., *Statutes at Large*, XXIV, 388.

67. Act of March 2, 1889, in U.S., *Statutes at Large*, XXV, 888.

68. H. Craig Miner, *The Corporation and the Indian: Tribal Sovereignty and Industrial Civilization in Indian Territory, 1865-1907* (Columbia, Mo., 1976), 116-117; Section II, "An Act for the Protection of the People of Indian Territory," approved June 28, 1898, in U.S., *Statutes at Large*, XXX, 495.

69. The act also modified the size of allotments, providing for the allotment of one-eighth of a section to each eligible individual and for double allotments of lands suited only for grazing. Act of February 28, 1891, in U.S., *Statutes at Large*, XXVI, 794.

70. Indian Appropriations Act, approved August 15, 1894, in U.S., *Statutes at Large*, XXVIII, 305.

71. Sections 13 and 23, "An Act for the Protection of the People of Indian Territory," approved June 28, 1898, in U.S., *Statutes at Large*, XXX, 495.

72. Indian Appropriations Act, approved May 31, 1900, in U.S., *Statutes at Large*, XXXI, 229.

73. Act of May 8, 1906, in U.S., *Statutes at Large*, XXXIV, 182-183; Institute for Government Research, *The Problem of Indian Administration* (Baltimore, 1928), 471-472.

74. See Charles Perrow's discussion of stated and operative goals in "The Analysis of Goals in Complex Organizations," *American Sociological Review*, XXVI (December, 1961), 854-866.

75. See Hazel W. Hertzberg, *The Search for an American Indian Identity: Modern Pan-Indian Movements* (Syracuse, N.Y., 1971), 15-19; Donald Parman, "J.C. Morgan: Navajo Apostle of Assimilation," *Prologue: The Journal of the National Archives*, IV (Summer, 1972), 83-98.

76. Theodore Stern and James P. Boggs, "White and Indian Farmers on the Umatilla Indian Reservation," *Northwest Anthropological Research Notes*, V (Spring, 1971), 37-76.

77. William A. Brophy and Sophie D. Aberle, *The Indian: America's Unfinished Business* (Norman, Okla., 1966), 60-61.

CHAPTER III

1. Howard Aldrich, "Organizational Boundaries and Inter-Organizational Conflict," *Human Relations*, XXIV (August, 1971), 279-293.

2. See Chapter IV for a discussion of the appointment of subordinate agency employees.

3. See Chapter VI, pp. 73-80, for a discussion of superintendents.

4. Commissioner of Indian Affairs, *Annual Report, 1883* in U.S., House of Representatives, *Executive Documents*, 48th Congress, 1st Session, No. 1, Part 5, Vol. II (Serial 2191), 5.

5. Commissioner of Indian Affairs, *Annual Report, 1882*, in U.S., House of Representatives, *Executive Documents*, 47th Congress, 2nd Session, No. 1, Part 5, Vol. II (Serial 2100), 2-3.

6. Emmett Womack, *History and Business Methods of the Department of the Interior, Its Bureaus and Offices* (Washington, 1897), 14.

7. F.E.L. [Francis E. Leupp], "Ring Rule," *City and State*, February 13, 1896. Reprinted as No. 27, 2nd Series, Indian Rights Association Pamphlets (Philadelphia, 1896).

8. Edmund J. Danziger, Jr., *Indians and Bureaucrats: Administering the Reservation Policy During the Civil War* (Urbana, Ill., 1974); Henry E. Fritz, *The Movement for Indian Assimilation, 1860-1890* (Philadelphia, 1962), 15-33.

9. "Report to the President by the Indian Peace Commission, January 7, 1868," in U.S., House of Representatives, *Executive Documents*, 40th Congress, 2nd Session, No. 97 (Serial 1337), 21. Hereafter cited as "Report by Peace Commission, 1868."

10. Harry J. Carman and Reinhard J. Luthin, *Lincoln and the Patronage* (New York, 1943), 331-333.

11. Erick McKitrick, *Andrew Johnson and Reconstruction* (Chicago, 1960), 377-394, suggests that Johnson hurt his own cause because of his indecisiveness in handling the patronage.

12. Act of June 30, 1834, in U.S., *Statutes at Large*, IV, 735.

13. Commissioner of Indian Affairs, *Annual Report, 1869*, in U.S., House of Representatives, *Executive Documents*, 41st Congress, 2nd Session, No. 1, Part 3 (Serial 1414), 447.

14. D.C. Poole, *Among the Sioux of Dakota: Eighteen Months Experience as an Indian Agent* (New York, 1881), 23.

15. Act of July 15, 1870, in U.S., *Statutes at Large*, XVI, 319.

16. William T. Sherman, *Memoirs of General W.T. Sherman* (4th ed., 2 vols., New York, 1891), II, 437. See also Henry G. Waltmann, "Circumstantial Reformer: President Grant and the Indian Problem," *Arizona and the West*, XIII (Winter, 1971), 323-342, esp. 334.

17. Commissioner of Indian Affairs, *Annual Report, 1870*, in U.S., House of Representatives, *Executive Documents*, 41st Congress, 3rd Session, No. 1, Part 4 (Serial 1449), 473-474.

18. *Ibid.*, 474.

19. J. Randolph Bayley, Archbishop of Baltimore, to Columbus Delano, Secretary of the Interior, Baltimore, May 28, 1873; Charles Ewing to Delano, Washington, May 29, 1873; both in NARS, RG 48, Appointments Division, LR, Box 84.

20. Henry W. Bellows, Pastor, First Unitarian Church, New York City, to J.D. Cox, Secretary of the Interior, New York, October 26, 1870; Charles Lowe, Secretary, American Unitarian Association, to Cox, Boston, November 2, 1870; NARS, RG 48, Appointments Division, LR, Box 84.

21. Edward Anthon, Secretary, American Church Missionary Society, to J.D. Cox, Secretary of the Interior, New York, October 10, 1870, NARS, RG 48, Appointments Division, LR, Box 84.

22. J.M. Ferris to Columbus Delano, Secretary of the Interior, New York, November 20, 1872, NARS, RG 48, Appointments Division, LR, Box 84.

23. Martha L. Edwards, "A Problem of Church and State in the 1870s," *Mississippi Valley Historical Review*, XI (June, 1924), 51.

24. For the Northern Superintendency, see B. Rush Roberts to Columbus Delano, Secretary of the Interior, Sandy Spring, Maryland, 5th month, 1st day, 1874, NARS, RG 48, Appointments Division, LR, Box 84.

25. E.S. Parker to H. Dyer, Washington, November 9, 1870, NARS, RG 75, OIA, LS, Land and Civilization Letterbook, Vol. 98, pp. 356-357.

26. A.T. Twing, Secretary and General Agent for Domestic Missions, Protestant Episcopal Church, to Columbus Delano, Secretary of the Interior, New York, August 1, 1871, NARS, RG 48, Appointments Division, LR, Box 84; B.R. Cowen, Acting Secretary of the Interior, to Twing, Washington, August 9, 1871, NARS, RG 48, Special Records Letterbook, Vol. 8, 223.

27. John C. Lowrie, Secretary, Board of Foreign Missions, Presbyterian Church, to Columbus Delano, Secretary of the Interior, New York, May 16, 1872, NARS, RG 48, Appointments Division, LR, Box 84.

28. B.R. Cowen, Acting Secretary of the Interior, to Rev. John C. Lowrie, Washington, May 18, 1872, NARS, RG 48, Appointments Division, Special Records Letterbook, Vol. 9, 42.

29. E.P. Smith, Commissioner of Indian Affairs, to Agent John D. Miles, Washington, July 20, 1874, NARS, RG 75, CIA, LS (Entry 165); Rush R. Shippen to the Secretary of the Interior, Boston, March 11, 1874, NARS, RG 48, Appointments Division, LR, Box 84.

30. E.P. Smith, Commissioner of Indian Affairs, to Rev. J.M. Ferris, Washington, January 25, 1875, NARS, RG 75, CIA, LS (Entry 165).

31. J.M. Ferris to B.R. Cowen, Acting Secretary of the Interior, New York, October 4, 1872; Ferris to Cowen, October 25, 1872, NARS, RG 48, Appointments Division, LR, Box 84.

32. Commissioner of Indian Affairs, *Annual Report, 1865*, in U.S., House of Representatives, *Executive Documents*, 39th Congress, 1st Session, No. 1 (Serial 1248), 170-171. See also Poole, *Among the Sioux of Dakota*, 228-229.

33. See J.M. Ferris to Columbus Delano, Secretary of the Interior, New York, November 20, 1872, NARS, RG 48, Appointments Division, LR, Box 84. Ferris asked that a Reformed Church agent at Camp Grant, Arizona, be made Superintendent of Indian Affairs for Arizona Territory because of the inadequacy of his salary. See also J.Q. Smith, Commissioner of Indian Affairs, to Kiowa Agent J.M. Haworth, Washington, March 14, 1877, NARS, RG 75, CIA, LS (Entry 165), denying his request to be appointed Indian Inspector. Haworth was eventually successful in securing an appointment as Inspector and was subsequently appointed the first Superintendent of Indian Schools in 1882.

34. Commissioner of Indian Affairs, *Annual Report, 1890*, in U.S., House of Representatives, *Executive Documents*, 51st Congress, 2nd Session, No. 1, Part 5, Vol. II (Serial 2841), cxviii-cxx; Indian Appropriations Act, approved May 27, 1878, in U.S., *Statutes at Large*, XX, 64-65.

35. Secretary of the Interior, *Annual Report, 1877*, in U.S., House of Representatives, *Executive Documents*, 45th Congress, 2nd Session, No. 1, Part 5 (serial 1800), xiv.

36. Robert Winston Mardock, *The Reformers and the American Indian* (Columbia, Mo., 1971), 158

37. E.A. Hayt, Commissioner of Indian Affairs, to Rev. S.S. Larson, Washington, June 3, 1878, NARS, RG 75, CIA, LS (Entry 165).

38. Commissioner of Indian Affairs, *Annual Report, 1878*, in U.S., House of Representatives, *Executive Documents*, 45th Congress, 3rd Session, No. 1, Part 5 (Serial 1850), 439.

39. *Report of the Joint Transfer Committee* (Washington, 1879), in U.S., Senate, *Miscellaneous Documents*, 45th Congress, 3rd Session, No. 53 (Serial 1853), 321-325.

40. *Ibid.* See also Hayt's comments before the Board of Indian Commissioner's Ninth Annual Conference with Representatives of Missionary Boards, January 8, 1880, in Board of Indian Commissioners, *Annual Report, 1879* (Washington, 1880), 99-100.

41. John Pope to Carl Schurz, Fort Levenworth, Kansas, April 20, 1877, Schurz Papers, Library of Congress.

42. B. Rush Roberts to Carl Schurz, Sandy Springs, Maryland, February 8, 1880, Carl Schurz Papers, Library of Congress.

43. William Welsh to Carl Schurz, Philadelphia, February 9, 1878, Schurz Papers, Library of Congress; Rush R. Shippen, Secretary American Unitarian Association, to George F. Hoar, Boston, April 25, 1879, Schurz Papers, Library of Congress.

44. Fritz, *The Movement for Indian Assimilation*, 156.

45. Robert L. Whitner, "Grant's Indian Peace Policy on the Yakima Reservation, 1870-82," *Pacific Northwest Quarterly*, L (October, 1959), 135-142.

46. R. Pierce Beaver, *Church, State, and the American Indians* (St. Louis, 1966), 157-161; Schurz's order is reprinted in the "Report of the Bureau of Catholic Indian Missions," in Board of Indian Commissioners, *Annual Report, 1881*, in U.S., House of Representatives, *Executive Documents*, 47th Congress, 1st Session, No. 79 (Serial 2027), 75.

47. *Ibid.*, 84-85.

48. *Ibid.*, 88.

49. *Ibid.*

50. Secretary of the Interior, *Annual Report, 1882*, in House of Representatives, *Executive Documents*, 47th Congress, 2nd Session, No. 1, Part 5 (Serial 2099), xiv.

51. Commissioner of Indian Affairs, *Annual Report, 1882*, in U.S., House of Representatives, *Executive Documents*, 47th Congress, 2nd Session, No. 1, Part 5, Vol. II (Serial 2100), 427.

52. H.M. Teller to J.M. Reid, Washington, August 5, 1882, in Board of Indian Commissioners, *Annual Report, 1882*, in House of Representatives, *Executive Documents*, 47th Congress, 2nd Session, No. 77 (Serial 2110), 53-54.

53. Nathan Bishop to E.S. Parker, Commissioner of Indian Affairs, New York, December 2, 1870, copy in NARS, RG 48, Appointment Division, LR, Box 84.

54. A.M.A. Blanchet, Bishop of Nisqually, to Columbus Delano, Secretary of the Interior, Vancouver, Washington Territory, March 31, 1871, NARS, RG 48, Appointments Division, LR, Box 84.

55. P.J. DeSmet, S.J., to Columbus Delano, St. Louis, June 19, 1872, NARS, RG 48, Appointments Division, LR, Box 84. DeSmet disclaimed any Catholic prentention to control the superintendency: "All that the Catholic Bishops & Missionaries aim at, in this country of religious liberty, is to be allowed to follow out their right. . . . to evangelize the Indians." The affair is discussed at greater length in Peter J. Rahill, *The Catholic Indian Missions and Grant's Peace Policy, 1870-1884* (Washington, 1953), 66-67.

56. See, for example, Rahill, *The Catholic Indian Missions*, 320-321; Loring Benson Priest, *Uncle Sam's Stepchildren: The Reformation of United States Indian Policy, 1865-1887* (New Brunswick, N.J., 1942), 38.

57. Kenneth S. Davison, *The Presidency of Rutherford B. Hayes* (Westport, Conn., 1972), 182-193.

58. Indian Appropriations Act, approved July 13, 1892, in U.S., *Statutes at Large*, XXVII, 120-121.

59. Commissioner of Indian Affairs, *Annual Report, 1892*, in U.S., House of Representatives, *Executive Documents*, 52nd Congress, 2nd Session, No. 1, Part 5, Vol. II (Serial 3088), 10-12. The Commissioner, Thomas J. Morgan, concluded his comment by citing the con-

clusion of the 1868 Indian Peace Commission that teaching "Indian children to read and write, or Indian men to sow and reap. . . . are emphatically civil, and not military, occupations." "Report by Peace Commission, 1868," 21.

60. See, for example, William M. Leeds, Acting Commissioner of Indian Affairs, to the Secretary of the Interior, Washington, May 10, 1878, NARS, RG 75, Chief Clerk, LS (Entry 181).

61. Indian Appropriations Act, approved July 13, 1892, in U.S., *Statutes at Large*, XXVII, 122.

62. Act of March 3, 1893, in U.S., *Statutes at Large*, XXVII, 614.

63. Commissioner of Indian Affairs, *Annual Report, 1892*, in U.S., House of Representatives, *Executive Documents*, 52nd Congress, 2nd Session, No. 1, Part 5, Vol. II (Serial 3088), 9-10.

64. U.S. Civil Service Commission, *Annual Report, 1890-91*, in U.S., House of Representatives, *Executive Documents*, 52nd Congress, 1st Session, No. 1, Part 8 (Serial 2942), 2.

65. Francis E. Leupp, *The Indian and His Problem* (New York, 1910), 97-98.

66. W.A. Jones, Commissioner of Indian Affairs, to President Theodore Roosevelt, Washington, March 20, 1901, NARS, RG 75, CIA, LS (Entry 165).

CHAPTER IV

1. Changes in the composition of Indian Service personnel, by categories, are discussed above, p. 132.

2. E.S. Parker to Rev. Charles Lowe, American Unitarian Association, Washington, November 4, 1870, NARS, RG 75, OIA, LS, LB, Land and Civilization, Vol. 98, p. 32 (Entry 84).

3. Arden R. Smith to E.A. Hayt, Seneca, Missouri, February 10, 1878, NARS, RG 75, Special Files of the Office of Indian Affairs, No. 221 (Entry 98; M575, Reel 63).

4. Commissioner of Indian Affairs, *Annual Report, 1877*, in U.S., House of Representatives, *Executive Documents*, 45th Congress, 2nd Session, No. 1, Part 5 (Serial 1800), 403.

5. E.A. Hayt to W.J. Pollock, Washington, November 17, 1879, NARS, RG 75, CIA, LS (Entry 165).

6. Commissioner of Indian Affairs, *Annual Report, 1865*, in U.S., House of Representatives, *Executive Documents*, 39th Congress, 1st Session, No. 1 (Serial 1248), 170.

7. Section 4, Indian Appropriations Act, approved July 26, 1866 (U.S., *Statutes at Large*, XIV, 280), reprinted in Commissioner of Indian Affairs, *Annual Report, 1866*, in U.S., House of Representatives, *Executive Documents*, 39th Congress, 2nd Session, No. 1 (Serial 1284), 312; D.N. Cooley to James Harlan, Washington, March 16, 1866, in *Ibid.*, 310-311.

8. Acting Commissioner of Indian Affairs, *Annual Report, 1867*, in U.S., House of Representatives, *Executive Documents*, 40th Congress, 2nd Session, No. 1, Part II (Serial 1326), 6.

9. E.S. Parker to U.S. Grant, Washington, January 24, 1867, in "Indian Hostilities," July 13, 1867, U.S., Senate, *Executive Documents*, 40th Congress, 1st Session, No. 13 (Serial 1308), 43-44.

10. Indian Appropriations Act, approved August 15, 1876, in U.S., *Statutes at Large*, XIX, 200.

11. *Report of Board of Inquiry Convened by Authority of Letter of the Secretary of the Interior of June 7, 1877, to Investigate Certain Charges Against S.A. Galpin, Chief Clerk of the Indian Bureau, and Concerning Irregularities in Said Bureau* (Washington, 1878), 1vi. Hereafter cited as *Report of Board of Inquiry* (1878).

12. S. A. Galpin, *Report upon the Condition and Management of Certain Indian Agencies in the Indian Territory, now under the Supervision of the Orthodox Friends* (Washington, 1877), 32-33. Hereafter cited as Galpin, *Report*.

13. *Report of Board of Inquiry* (1878), 1vii.

14. Galpin, *Report*, 32.

15. *Report of Board of Inquiry* (1878), 1viii.

16. Commissioner of Indian Affairs, *Annual Report, 1877*, in U.S., House of Representatives, *Executive Documents*, 45th Congress, 2nd Session, No. 1, Part 5 (Serial 1800), 404-405.

17. Commissioner of Indian Affairs, *Annual Report, 1878*, in U.S., House of Representatives, *Executive Documents*, 45th Congress, 3rd Session, No. 1, Part 5 (Serial 1850), 439-440.

18. Commissioner of Indian Affairs, *Annual Report, 1879*, in U.S., House of Representatives, *Executive Documents*, 46th Congress, 2nd Session, No. 1, Part 5 (Serial 1910), 76.

19. E.A. Hayt to T.E. Berry [trader, Pawnee Agency], Washington, October 7, 1878, (telegram), NARS, RG 75, CIA, LS (Entry 165).

20. *Laws and Regulations Relating to Trade with Indian Tribes* (Washington, 1883), 7-9. The 1883 pamphlet appears to be a revision of the 1879 edition, which is listed in the *Checklist of United States Public Documents, 1789-1909* (Third ed., Washington, 1911), 502. The 1876 edition is not listed in the *Checklist*, and I have been unable to examine a copy.

21. Commissioner of Indian Affairs, *Annual Report, 1877*, in U.S., House of Representatives, *Executive Documents*, 45th Congress, 2nd Session, No. 1, Part 5 (Serial 1800), 403.

22. E. A. Hayt to Pawnee Agent Charles Searing, Washington, October 20, 1877, disapproving the appointment of George L. Howell as agency clerk, and Hayt to Searing, Washington, October 20, 1877, notifying Searing of the appointment of Joseph Hertford as agency clerk, both in NARS, RG 75, CIA, LS (Entry 165); E.A. Hayt to Crow Creek Agent Henry F. Livingston, Washington, March 25, 1878, appointing E.F. Durfee as agency farmer to replace Mr. Russell, the incumbent, NARS, RG 75, Chief Clerk, LS (Entry 181).

23. William M. Leeds to [William E.] Dougherty, Washington, May 3, 1878 (telegram), NARS, RG 75, Chief Clerk, LS (Entry 181); see also, E.A. Hayt to Pawnee Agent Samuel S. Ely, Washington, April 23, 1878, NARS, RG 75, CIA, LS (Entry 165).

24. E.A. Hayt to J.W. Phillips, Washington, August 20, 1878, NARS, RG 75, CIA, LS (Entry 165). Phillips, of Poughkeepsie, N.Y., had been appointed clerk at the Pawnee Agency.

25. Inspector J.H. Hammond to H.L. Henry, Washington, April 25, 1878 (telegram), directing Henry to carry dispatches from Council Bluffs, Iowa, to Crow Creek Agency, Dakota Territory, and then report for duty as Superintendent of Farming at the Yankton Agency; William M. Leeds to James M. Eby, Washington, May 10, 1878, directing Eby to investigate affairs at the Western Shoshone Agency, Nevada, and then report to the Nevada Agency for duty as clerk; both in NARS, RG 75, Chief Clerk, LS (Entry 181).

26. William M. Leeds to the Secretary of the Interior, Washington, May 10, 1878, requesting a $125.00 travel advance for Eby "to defray his expenses while traveling on business for this Department," in NARS, RG 75, Chief Clerk, LS (Entry 181).

27. E.A. Hayt to Rev. W.S. Clapp, Washington, December 18, 1879, NARS, RG 75, CIA, LS (Entry 165).

28. E.A. Hayt to Arden R. Smith, Washington, May 21, 1878, NARS, RG 75, CIA, LS (Entry 165).

29. E.A. Hayt to Pawnee Agent Samuel S. Ely, Washington, April 23, 1878, NARS, RG 75, CIA, LS (Entry 165).

30. T.P. Pendleton to Carl Schurz, Berryville, Virginia, August 5, 1879, NARS, RG 48, Indian Division, LR.

31. William M. Leeds to Yankton Agent [John W.] Douglas, Washington, June 24, 1878 (telegram), NARS, RG 75, Chief Clerk, LS (Entry 181).

32. E.A. Hayt to Rev. W.S. Clapp, Washington, December 18, 1879, NARS, RG 75, CIA, LS (Entry 165).

33. E.A. Hayt to Senator John B. Gordon, Washington, May 31, 1878; Hayt to Gordon, Washington, June 3, 1878; both in NARS, RG 75, CIA, LS (Entry 181).

34. Acting Commissioner E.L. Stevens to Rosebud Agent James G. Wright, Washington, May 3, 1883, NARS, RG 75, Chief Clerk, LS (Entry 181). In recommending an applicant for the position of agency clerk at Rosebud, Stevens stated, "His appointment would be acceptable to the Office, but it must be understood that you are left free to name your own employees, except the physician." See also Hiram Price to Blackfoot Agent John Young, Washington, October 11, 1883, NARS, RG 75, Chief Clerk, LS (Entry 181); Board of Indian Commissioners *Annual Report, 1881*, in U.S., House of Representatives, *Executive Documents*, 47th Congress, 1st Session, No. 79 (Serial 2027), 88.

35. *Ibid.*

36. See, for example, A.B. Upshaw, Chief Clerk, to William L. Wilson, House of Representatives, Washington, January 5, 1886, regarding the appointment of a clerk at Lemhi Agency; Upshaw to Senator Henry B. Payne, Washington, January 12, 1885, regarding an applicant for an agency physician position; Upshaw to James H. Blount, House of Representatives, Washington, January 12, 1886, regarding the appointment of a clerk at the Mescalero Apache Agency; J.D.C. Atkins to Senator P.B. Plumb, Washington, January 19, 1886, regarding the tradership at the Sac and Fox Agency, Indian Territory; and Upshaw to John H. Rogers,

House of Representatives, Washington, February 13, 1886, regarding the appointment of a protégé of Rogers to an agency tradership; all in NARS, RG 75, Chief Clerk, LS (Entry 181).

37. J.D.C. Atkins to John J. O'Neil, House of Representatives, Washington, February 20, 1886, NARS, RG 75, Chief Clerk, LS (Entry 181).

38. J.D.C. Atkins to Senator W.B. Allison, Washington, January 27, 1886, NARS, RG 75, Chief Clerk, LS (Entry 181).

39. Acting Chief Clerk S.M. Yeatman to J.B. Weaver, House of Representatives, Washington, February 26, 1886, NARS, RG 75, Chief Clerk, LS (Entry 181).

40. J.D.C. Atkins to Siletz Agent J.B. Lane, Washington, September 24, 1887; Atkins to J.N. Mitchell, Washington, September 24, 1887; both in NARS, RG 75, Chief Clerk, LS (Entry 181).

41. J.D.C. Atkins to J.E. Clardy, Washington, September 22, 1887, NARS, RG 75, Chief Clerk, LS (Entry 181).

42. J.D.C. Atkins to the Secretary of the Interior, Washington, May 6, 1886, NARS, RG 48, Indian Division, LR. McGullycuddy was suspended on May 16.

43. *Ibid.*

44. Act of January 16, 1883, U.S., *Statutes at Large*, XXII, 403; Ari Hoogenboom, "The Pendleton Act and the Civil Service," *American Historical Review*, LXIV (January, 1959), 301-318; U.S. Civil Service Commission, *Annual Report, 1883*, in U.S., House of Representatives, *Executive Documents*, 48th Congress, 1st Session, No. 105 (Serial 2206), 15-17. Outside Washington, government employees in post offices or customs districts having fifty or more employees were included in the classified service. *Ibid.*, 45-46.

45. Commissioner of Indian Affairs, *Annual Report, 1886*, in U.S., House of Representatives, *Executive Documents*, 49th Congress, 2nd Session, No. 1, Part 5 (serial 2467), 106-107.

46. *Ibid.*, 158-160.

47. "A Good Field for Reform," *The Nation*, March 15, 1888, reprinted as Indian Rights Association Pamphlet No. 31 (Philadelphia, 1888).

48. "Reform in the Indian Service," Indian Rights Association Pamphlet (Philadelphia, 1887).

49. "Extract. Report of the Special Committee of the National Civil Service Reform League upon the Present Condition of the Reform Movement and the Relations to it of the National, State and Municipal Administrations," Indian Rights Association Pamphlet (Philadelphia, 1887). Hereafter cited as "Report of Special Committee" (1887).

50. T.J. Morgan to the Secretary of the Interior, Washington, June 27, 1890, NARS, RG 75, CIA, LS (Entry 165).

51. T.J. Morgan to Herbert Welsh, Washington, July 5, 1890, NARS, RG 75, CIA, LS (Entry 165);

Assistant Commissioner of Indian Affairs R.V. Belt to Osage Agent Laban J. Miles, Washington, July 22, 1889, NARS, RG 75, Chief Clerk, LS (Entry 181).

52. T.J. Morgan to School Superintendent S.M. Abbott, Washington, July 8, 1890, regarding Abbott's conflicts with the agent; T.J. Morgan to the Secretary of the Interior, Washington, July 12, 1889, regarding the removal of the physician at Puyallup Agency upon the recommendation of Agent Edwin Eells; both in NARS, RG 75, CIA, LS (Entry 165).

53. T.J. Morgan to the Secretary of the Interior, Washington, June 27, 1890, NARS, RG 75, CIA, LS (Entry 165).

54. Harry J. Sievers, "The Catholic Indian School Issue and The Presidential Election of 1892," *Catholic Historical Review*, XXXVIII (July, 1952), 129-155.

55. T.J. Morgan to Herbert Welsh, Washington, March 4, 1890. NARS, RG 75, CIA, LS (Entry 165).

56. T.J. Morgan to the Secretary of the Interior, Washington, March 27, 1891, NARS, RG 75, CIA, LS (Entry 165).

57. U.S. Civil Service Commission, *Annual Report, 1890-91*, in U.S., House of Representatives, *Executive Documents*, 52nd Congress, 1st Session, No. 1, Part 8 (Serial 2942), 2, 72.

58. U.S. Civil Service Commission, *Annual Report, 1891-92*, in U.S., House of Representatives, *Executive Documents*, 52nd Congress, 2nd Session, No. 1, Part 8 (Serial 3097), 118. The Indian Rules are in *Ibid.*, 41-44.

59. "Report of Hon. Theodore Roosevelt made to the United States Civil Service Commission upon a visit to Certain Indian Reservations and Indian Schools in South Dakota, Nebraska, and Kansas," Indian Rights Association Pamphlet (Philadelphia, 1893).

60. U.S. Civil Service Commissioners (John F. Winter, Charles Lyman, Theodore Roosevelt) to the President, Washington, April 21, 1894, NARS, RG 146, USCSC, LS, vol. [2], April 23-August 2, 1894, pp. 8-14; U.S. Civil Service Commission, *Annual Report, 1893-94*, in U.S., House of Representatives, *Miscellaneous Documents*, 53rd Congress, 3rd Session, No. 79 (Serial 3336), 67-68.

61. U.S. Civil Service Commission, *Annual Report, 1891-92*, in U.S., House of Representatives, *Executive Documents*, 52nd Congress, 2nd Session, No. 1, Part 8 (Serial 3097), 308-309.

62. Hoogenboom, "Pendleton Act and the Civil Service," 304.

63. Herbert Welsh, "A Dangerous Assault Upon the Integrity of the Civil Service Law in the Indian Service," Indian Rights Association Pamphlets, 2nd Series, No. 9 (Philadelphia, 1893).

64. D.M. Browning to Frank W. Beane, Washington, July 1, 1893, NARS, RG 75, CIA, LS (Entry 165); Francis E. Leupp, "Civil Service Reform Essential to a Successful Indian Administration," Indian Rights Association Pamphlets, 2nd Series, No. 23 (Philadelphia, 1892).

65. U.S. Civil Service Commission, *Annual Report, 1895-96*, in U.S., House of Representatives, *Executive Documents*, 54th Congress, 2nd Session, No. 321 (Serial 3539), 15, 82-83.

66. John R. Proctor, President, U.S.C.S.C., to the Secretary of the Interior, Washington, April 25, 1894; W.S. Noblitt, M.D., to Theodore Roosevelt, Lewiston, Idaho, April 12, 1894 (copy); both in NARS, RG 146, USCSC, LS, vol. [2], April 23-August 2, 1894, pp. 26-27, 36.

67. W.A. Jones to J.M. Greene, Washington, September 26, 1900; Jones to Dr. Howard L. Dumble, Washington, October 3, 1900; Jones to Greene, Washington, October 15, 1900; Jones to Dr. Charles A. Eastman, Washington, October 13, 1900; Jones to Eastman, Washington, October 29, 1900; all in NARS, RG 75, CIA, LS (Entry 165).

68. In Cleveland's first administration, of the 377 Presidential offices in the Interior Department, only three were reappointed. "Report of Special Committee" (1887). The average tenure for all Indian agents between 1865 and 1905 was less than thirty-six months. Data compiled from Edward E. Hill, *The Office of Indian Affairs, 1824-1880: Historical Sketches* (New York, 1974), and "Rosters of Field Officials, 1849-1911," NARS, RG 75 (Entry 176).

69. Hoogenboom, "Pendleton Act and the Civil Service," 311.

70. W.A. Jones to R.J. Gamble, Washington, October 12, 1901; Jones to R.M. Bashford, Washington, July 19, 1901; Jones to W.C. Hughes, Washington, November 1, 1901; all in NARS, RG 75, CIA, LS (Entry 165).

71. Hoogenboom, "Pendleton Act and the Civil Service," 311-313. The comment regarding the decreased "missionary spirit" of Indian Workers is that of Civil Service Commissioner John R. Procter, January 27, 1901, cited in *Ibid.*, 315.

CHAPTER V

1. Arnold S. Tannenbaum, *Control In Organizations* (New York, 1968), 310.

2. The elements of organizational control systems are discussed by James L. Price, *Organizational Effectiveness: An Inventory of Propositions* (Homewood, Ill., 1968), 181-183. Price places major emphasis on the sanctions used by the organization and the communications structure. The location of control was particularly important for the Indian Office because of its boundary problems, particularly during the period 1865-1880.

3. For a discussion of the Board's later functions, see Henry E. Fritz, "The Board of Indian Commissioners and Ethocentric Reform, 1878-1893," in Jane F. Smith and Robert M. Kvasnicka, eds., *Indian-White Relations: A Persistent Paradox* (Washington, D. C., 1976), 56-78.

4. Joint Resolution of March 3, 1865, in U. S., *Statutes at Large*, XIII, 572-573.

5. "Condition of the Indian Tribes: Report of the Joint Special Committee, Appointed under Joint Resolution of March 3, 1865, with an Appendix" (Washington, 1867), U.S., Senate, *Reports*, 39th Congress, 2nd Session, No. 156 (Serial 1279), 6-10.

6. "Indian Hostilities," July 13, 1867, U.S., Senate, *Executive Documents*, 40th Congress, 1st Session, No. 13 (Serial 1308), 55-74.

7. Eli S. Parker to General U. S. Grant, Washington, January 24, 1867, in *Ibid.*, 42-49.

8. N. G. Taylor to W. T. Otto, Acting Secretary of the Interior, Washington, July 12, 1867, in *Ibid.*, 1-6.

9. Donald J. D'Elia, "The Argument over Civilian or Military Indian Control, 1865-1880," *The Historian*, XXIV (February, 1962), 207-225.

10. Act of July 20, 1867, in U. S., *Statutes at Large*, XV, 17-18.

11. "Report to the President by the Indian Peace Commission, January 7, 1868," U.S., House of Representatives, *Executive Documents*, 40th Congress, 2nd Session, No. 97 (Serial 1337), 20-22.

12. For the Medicine Lodge treaties, see Charles J. Kappler, comp., *Indian Affairs: Laws and Treaties* (5 vols., Washington, 1904-1941), II, 977-989; for the Fort Laramie treaties, see *Ibid.*, II, 998-1007.

13. Robert M. Utley, *Frontier Regulars: The United States Army and the Indian, 1866-1891* (New York, 1973), 133.

14. Indian Appropriations Act, approved March 3, 1871, in U.S., *Statutes at Large*, XVI, 566.

15. N. G. Taylor to the President, Chicago, October 9, 1868, in Commissioner of Indian Affairs, *Annual Report, 1868*, in U.S., House of Representatives, *Executive Documents*, 40th Congress, 3rd Session, No. 1 (Serial 1366), 831-832.

16. S. F. Tappan to N. G. Taylor, Washington, December 4, 1868, in *Ibid.*, 832-836; E. W. Wynkoop to S. F. Tappan, Washington, October 5, 1868, in *Ibid.*, 836.

17. Act of July 27, 1868, in U.S., *Statutes at Large*, XIV, 222.

18. Secretary of War, *Annual Report, 1868*, in U. S., House of Representatives, *Executive Documents*, 40th Congress, 3rd Session, No. 1 (Serial 1367), 8-9.

19. William T. Sherman to U. S. Grant, Fort Laramie, May 8, 1868, in "Subsistence of Indian Tribes," May 26, 1868, U.S., House of Representatives, *Executive Documents*, 40th Congress, 2nd Session, No. 239 (Serial 1341), 1-3.

20. Loring Benson Priest, *Uncle Sam's Stepchildren: The Reformation of United States Indian Policy, 1865-1887* (New Brunswick, N. J., 1942), 42.

21. Indian Appropriations Act, approved April 10, 1869, in U.S., *Statutes at Large*, XVI, 40.

22. *Congressional Globe*, 41st Congress, 1st Session, April 2, 1869, 448.

23. *Ibid.*, 451.

24. *Ibid.*

25. Nathan Bishop to J. D. Cox, New York, July 2, 1869, NARS, RG 48, Appointments Division, LR, Box 77, "Board of Indian Commissioners." Emphasis in original.

26. J. D. Cox to Felix R. Brunot, Acting Chairman, Board of Indian Commissioners, Washington, July 5, 1869, copy in NARS, RG 48, Appointments Division, LR, Box 77.

27. *Ibid.*

28. Priest, *Uncle Sam's Stepchildren*, 44.

29. Indian Appropriations Act, approved July 15, 1870, in U.S., *Statutes at Large*, XVI, 360.

30. Indian Appropriations Act, approved March 3, 1871, in U.S., *Statutes at Large*, XVI, 568.

31. *Congressional Globe*, 41st Congress, 3rd Session, February 22, 1871, 1480.

32. Indian Appropriations Act, approved May 29, 1872, in U.S., *Statutes at Large*, XVII, 186.

33. Board of Indian Commissioners, *Annual Report, 1873* (Washington, 1874), 9-11. The total amount of the accounts rejected by the Board was $426,909.96; payment was withheld on accounts totalling $5,679.00.

34. Priest, *Uncle Sam's Stepchildren*, 46-62.

35. Board of Indian Commissioners, *Annual Report, 1871*, in U.S., House of Representatives, *Executive Documents*, 42nd Congress, 2nd Session, No. 1, Part 5 (Serial 1505), 579-580.

36. "Affairs in the Indian Department," February 25, 1871, in House of Representatives, *Reports*, 41st Congress, 3rd Session, No. 39 (Serial 1464), ii, 126-127; Acting Commissioner of Indian Affairs, *Annual Report, 1871*, in U.S., House of Representatives, *Executive Documents*, 42nd Congress, 2nd Session, No. 1, Part 5 (Serial 1505), 417; *Report of Hon. E. S. Parker, Commissioner of Indian Affairs, to the Hon, Secretary of the Interior, on the Communication of William Welsh, Esq., Relative to the Management of Indian Affairs* (Washington, 1870).

37. Columbus Delano to Felix R. Brunot, Chairman, Board of Indian Commissioners, Washington, January 12, 1872 (copy); Vincent Colyer to the President, Washington, February 17, 1872; and Colyer to Delano, Washington, February 19, 1872; all in NARS, RG 48, Appointments Division, LR, Box 77.

38. Samuel Walker, Clerk, Board of Indian Commissioners, to Felix R. Brunot, Chairman, Board of Indian Commissioners, Washington, December 6, 1873, in *Report of the Special Commission Appointed to Investigate the Affairs of the Red Cloud Indian Agency, July, 1875; Together with the Testimony and Accompanying Documents* (Washington, 1875), 801-806. Hereafter cited as *Report of Special Commission* (1875).

39. William H. Hare to C. Delano, Secretary of the Interior, Washington, April 22, 1874, in *Ibid.*, 807-818. The commission was appointed by the Secretary of the Interior and included, in addition to Bishop Hare, Samuel D. Hinman, an Episcopal missionary, J. D. Bevier, an Indian Inspector, and F. H. Smith, Collyer's successor as Secretary of the Board of Indian Commissioners. Agents Saville and Howard had been nominated by the Episcopal Church. See C. Delano to T. C. Fletcher, Washington, August 2, 1875, in *Ibid.*, XII-XIV.

40. Felix R. Brunot, Robert Campbell, Nathan Bishop, W. E. Dodge, John V. Farwell, and George

H. Stuart to the President, Washington, May 27, 1874, NARS, RG 48, Appointments Division, LR, Box 77.

41. D. Stuart Dodge, *Memorials of William E. Dodge* (New York, 1887), 177-178; Charles Lewis Slattery, *Felix Reville Brunot* (New York, 1901), 219-224.

42. Act of June 22, 1874, in U.S., *Statutes at Large*, XVIII, part III, 141.

43. Indian Appropriations Act, approved June 22, 1874, in U.S., *Statutes at Large*, XVIII, part III, 176.

44. Priest, *Uncle Sam's Stepchildren*, 51.

45. B. Rush Roberts to Columbus Delano, Sandy Springs, Maryland, Sixth month, eleventh day, 1874; John C. Lowrie to Delano, New York, February 8, 1875, J. M. Ferris to Delano, New York, August 5, 1874, E. A. Hayt to B. R. Cowan, Assistant Secretary of the Interior, New York, August 20, 1874, all in NARS, RG 48, Appointments Division, LR, Box 77.

46. Priest, *Uncle Sam's Stepchildren*, 47.

47. C. Delano to Clinton B. Fisk, Washington, May 10, 1875, in *Report of Special Commission* (1875), III.

48. *Ibid.*, LXXIV-LXXV.

49. E. P. Smith to F. H. Smith, Washington, September 22, 1874, NARS, RG 75, CIA, LS (Entry 165).

50. J. Q. Smith to E. A. Hayt, Washington, May 4, 1876, NARS, RG 75, CIA, LS (Entry 165).

51. Commissioner of Indian Affairs, *Annual Report, 1876*, in U.S., House of Representatives, *Executive Documents*, 44th Congress, 2nd Session, No. 1, Part 5 (Serial 1749), 383-384.

52. J. Q. Smith to A. C. Barstow, Washington, August 22, 1876, NARS, RG 75, CIA, LS (Entry 165). Smith attempted to persuade Hayt of the wisdom of receiving bids at St. Louis as well as at New York. See Smith to Hayt, Washington, August 23, 1876, NARS, RG 75, CIA, LS (Entry 165).

53. J. Q. Smith to E. A. Hayt, Washington, September 29, 1876, NARS, RG 75, CIA, LS (Entry 165).

54. J. Q. Smith to E. A. Hayt, Washington, October 26, 1876, NARS, RG 75, CIA, LS (Entry 165).

55. J. Q. Smith to William J. Morris, Washington, October 27, 1876, NARS, RG 75, CIA, LS (Entry 165).

56. J. Q. Smith to William J. Morris, Washington, October 30, 1876, NARS, RG 75, CIA, LS (Entry 165).

57. J. Q. Smith to E. A. Hayt, Washington, December 18, 1876, NARS, RG 75, CIA, LS (Entry 165).

58. S. A. Galpin to Commissioner of Indian Affairs, Lawrence, Kansas, January 4, 1877 (copy), NARS, RG 48, Appointment Division, LR, Box 77.

59. William Stickney to E. A. Hayt, Washington, January 9, 1877 (copy), NARS, RG 48, Appointments Division, LR, Box 77.

60. Hayt to Stickney, New York, January 10, 1877 (telegram, copy), NARS, RG 48, Appointments Division, LR, Box 77.

61. Hayt to Zachariah Chandler, New York, January 12, 1877 (copy), NARS, RG 48, Appointments Division, LR, Box 77.

62. Chandler to Hayt, Washington, January 12, 1877 (copy), NARS, RG 48, Appointments Division, LR, Box 77.

63. E. A. Hayt to the President, New York, January 20, 1877, NARS, RG 48, Appointments Division, Box 77.

64. John M. Ferris to Zachariah Chandler, New York, February 7, 1877, NARS, RG 48, Appointments Division, LR, Box 77.

65. J. Q. Smith to E. M. Kinglsey, Washington, March 21, 1877, and Smith to Kingsley, Washington, March 21, 1877 (Marked "Personal"), both in NARS, RG 75, CIA, LS (Entry 165).

66. J. Q. Smith to Dr. Josiah Curtis, Washington, February 14, 1877; Smith to E. J. Brooks, Washington, February 16, 1877; Smith to E. L. Stevens, February 16, 1877; all in NARS, RG 75, CIA, LS (Entry 165).

67. J. Q. Smith to the Secretary of the Interior, Washington, April 21, 1877, NARS, RG 75, CIA, LS (Entry 165).

68. J. Q. Smith to the Secretary of the Interior, Washington, March 26, 1877, NARS, RG 75, CIA, LS (Entry 165).

69. A. Bell to Carl Schurz, New York, May 9, 1877, Carl Schurz Papers, Library of Congress.

70. J. Q. Smith to E. M. Kingsley, Washington, May 22, 1877, NARS, RG 75, CIA, LS (Entry 165).

71. J. Q. Smith to the Secretary of the Interior, Washington, March 26, 1877, NARS, RG 75, CIA, LS (Entry 165).

72. Joseph K. McCammon, President, Board of Inquiry, to C. Schurz, Washington, June 9, 1877, NARS, RG 48, Appointments Division, Box 153, "Board[s] of Inquiry, 1877-78." The Board of Inquiry which investigated the charges against Galpin was the most celebrated of a number of Boards organized by Schurz during his first year as Secretary of the Interior. Some Boards investigated charges against specific Department employees, while others rated the performance of clerks in the various bureaus and others studied methods employed to conduct business.

73. Schurz's endorsement, on McCammon to Schurz, Washington, June 9, 1877, NARS, RG 48, Appointments Division, Box 153.

74. J. Q. Smith to members of the Board of Inquiry, Washington, June 27, 1877, NARS, RG 75, CIA,⁀LS (Entry 165).

75. J. D. Cox to Carl Schurz, Toledo, July 11, 1877, Carl Schurz Papers, Library of Congress.

76. E. A. Hayt to C. Schurz, New York, September 10, 1877. Carl Schurz Papers, Library of Congress.

77. *Report of Board of Inquiry convened by Authority of Letter of the Secretary of the Interior of June 7, 1877, to Investigate Certain Charges Against S. A. Galpin, Chief Clerk of the Indian Bureau, and Concerning Irregularities in Said Bureau* (Washington, 1878), iii-vii.

78. "The Indian Ring," *Harper's Weekly*, February 2, 1878, clipping in Scrapbooks, Vol. V, Carl Schurz Papers, Library of Congress.

79. Commissioner of Indian Affairs, *Annual Report, 1878*, in U.S., House of Representatives, *Executive Documents*, 45th Congress, 3rd Session, No. 1, Part 5 (Serial 1850), 474.

80. E. A. Hayt to Central Superintendent William Nicholson, Washington, October 24, 1877, NARS, RG 75, CIA, LS (Entry 165).

81. The abolition of the Central Superintendency is discussed above, pp. 78-80.

82. Indian Appropriations Act, approved May 11, 1880, in U.S., *Statutes at Large*, XXI, 131.

83. An Act Making Appropriations for the Sundry Civil Expenses of the Government, approved June 16, 1880, in U.S., *Statutes at Large*, XXI, 277.

84. Indian Appropriations Act, approved May 17, 1882, in U.S., *Statutes at Large*, XXII, 70.

85. Indian Appropriations Act, approved March 1, 1883, in U.S., *Statutes at Large*, XXII, 434.

86. Priest, *Uncle Sam's Stepchildren*, 50.

87. *Ibid.*, 84-85; Larry E. Burgess, *The Lake Mohonk Conference of Friends of the Indians: Guide to the Annual Reports* (New York, 1975), 1-23.

88. Priest, *Uncle Sam's Stepchildren*, 49-50.

89. *Congressional Globe*, 41st Congress, 3rd Session, February 22, 1871, 1480.

90. Fritz, "The Board of Indian Commissioners."

91. Board of Indian Commissioners, *Annual Report, 1890*, in U.S., House of Representatives, *Executive Documents*, 51st Congress, 2nd Session, No. 1, Part 5, Vol. II (Serial 2841), 780-781.

CHAPTER VI

1. Like large retail organizations in the twentieth century, the Indian Office in the nineteenth century faced a continuing problem of how much decentralization was appropriate. See Alfred D. Chandler, Jr., *Strategy and Structure: Chapters in the History of the Industrial Enterprise* (Cambridge, Mass., 1962), 241-282, for a discussion of the Sears, Roebuck and Company's problems with decentralization after 1929.

2. See Jack M. Sosin, *Whitehall and the Wilderness: The Middle West in British Colonial Policy, 1760-1775* (Lincoln, Nebr., 1961), 99.

3. Felix S. Cohen, *Handbook of Federal Indian Law* (Washington, 1942), 9-10.

4. For a description of Harrison's activities, see George Dangerfield, *The Era of Good Feelings* (New York, 1952), 26-32. Another historian argued that Harrison and some other early governors "considered their civil responsibilities to be secondary to the administration of Indian and military affairs" because they believed "white settlement depended on Indian removal." Jack Ericson Eblen, *The First and Second United States Empires: Governors and Territorial Government, 1784-1912* (Pittsburgh, 1968), 242.

5. Act of June 30, 1834, in U.S., *Statutes at Large*, IV, 35.

6. "Indian Affairs in the Territories of Oregon and Washington. Report of J. Ross Browne, Special Agent, November 17, 1857," U.S., House of Representatives, *Executive Documents*, 35th Congress, 1st Session, No. 39 (Serial 955), 19-20.

7. Eblen, *The First and Second United States Empires*, 268-269.

8. William M. Neil, "The Territorial Governor as Indian Superintendent in the Trans-Mississippi West," *Mississippi Valley Historical Review*, XLII (September, 1956), 213-237.

9. Dale L. Morgan, "The Administration of Indian Affairs in Utah, 1851-1858," *Pacific Historical Review*, XVII (November, 1948), 383-409.

10. Acting Commissioner of Indian Affairs, *Annual Report, 1867*, in U.S., House of Representatives, *Executive Documents*, 40th Congress, 2nd Session, No. 1, Part II (Serial 1326), 6.

11. "Indian Affairs in the Territories of Oregon and Washington," 18-20; W. Turrentine Jackson, "Indian Affairs and Politics in Idaho Territory, 1863-1870," *Pacific Historical Review*, XIV (September, 1945), 311-325; Commissioner of Indian Affairs, *Annual Report, 1865*, in U.S., House of Representatives, *Executive Documents*, 39th Congress, 1st Session, No. 1 (Serial 1248), 170-171; George B. Wright to Carl Schurz, Washington, February 6, 1879, Schurz Papers, Library of Congress.

12. Eblen, *The First and Second United States Empires*, 256-257; D.C. Poole, *Among the Sioux of Dakota: Eighteen Months Experience as an Indian Agent* (New York, 1881), 228-229.

13. Indian Appropriations Act, approved July 15, 1870, in U.S., *Statutes at Large*, XVI, 360-361; Indian Appropriations Act, approved March 3, 1871, in *Ibid.*, XVI, 545; Indian Appropriations Act, approved February 14, 1873, in *Ibid*, XVII, 438.

14. For a differing interpretation, see Robert A. Trennert, Jr., *Alternative to Extinction: Federal Indian Policy and the Beginnings of the Reservation System, 1846-51* (Philadelphia, 1975).

15. Acting Commissioner of Indian Affairs, *Annual Report, 1871*, in U.S., House of Representatives, *Executive Documents*, 42nd Congress, 2nd Session, No. 1, Part 5 (Serial 1505), 421-422.

16. Indian Appropriations Act, approved February 14, 1873, in U.S., *Statutes at Large*, XVII, 463.

17. Indian Appropriations Act, approved March 3, 1875, in *Ibid.*, XVIII, 430; Indian Appropriations Act, Approved May 11, 1880, in *Ibid.*, XXI, 116.

18. E.A. Hayt to Carl Schurz, Washington, January 2, 1878; Hayt to Schurz, Washington, January 30, 1878; Hayt to Schurz, February 1, 1878, all in NARS, RG 75, CIA, LS (Entry 165). Central Superintendent William Nicholson was relieved by Inspector J.H. Hammond on February 8, 1878.

19. See, for example, Charles F. Coffin and William Nicholson to E.P. Smith, Richmond, Ind., Eleventh month, 13th, 1873, in "Indians in the Central Superintendency," December 18, 1873, U.S., House of Representatives, *Executive Documents*, 43rd Congress, 1st Session, No. 24 (Serial 1606), 2, and *Minutes of Associated Executive Committee of Friends on Indian Affairs, Philadelphia, Pennsylvania, 4th month, 1874* (Richmond, Indiana, 1874), 8-9.

20. J.Q. Smith to Bishop Hare, telegram, Washington, no date (sent on March 14 or 15, 1877), NARS, RG 75, CIA, LS (Entry 165).

21. William M. Leeds, Acting Commissioner of Indian Affairs, to William J. Pollock, telegram, Washington, May 3, 1878, NARS, RG 75, Chief Clerk, LS (Entry 181).

22. E.A. Hayt to William J. Pollock, May 23, 1878, and Hayt to Pollock, May 23, 1878, both in NARS, RG 75, Chief Clerk, LS (Entry 181).

23. "Rosters of Field Officials, 1849-1911," NARS, RG 75 (Entry 976).

24. *Report of Board of Inquiry Convened by Authority of Letter of the Secretary of the Interior of June 7, 1877, to Investigate Certain Charges Against S.A. Galpin, Chief Clerk of the Indian Bureau, and Concerning Irregularities in Said Bureau* (Washington, 1878), xxxii. Hereafter cited as *Report of Board* (1878).

25. S.A. Galpin, *Report upon the Condition and Management of Certain Indian Agencies in the Indian Territory, Now Under the Supervision of the Orthodox Friends* (Washington, 1877), 36-41.

26. *Report of Board* (1878), xxxii.

27. S.A. Galpin to William Nicholson, Washington, February 13, 1877, in *Report of Board* (1878), xxv.

28. J.Q. Smith to E.A. Hayt, Washington, December 18, 1876, NARS, RG 75, CIA, LS (Entry 165).

29. *Report of Board* (1878), xxv-xxvi.

30. E.P. Smith to the Rev. T.M. Eddy, "informal," Washington, March 13, 1873, NARS, RG 75, CIA, LS (Entry 165).

31. J.Q. Smith to James M. Haworth, Washington, March 14, 1877, NARS, RG 75, CIA, LS (Entry 165).

32. Commissioner of Indian Affairs, *Annual Report, 1878*, in U.S., House of Representatives, *Executive Documents*, 45th Congress, 3rd Session, No. 1, Part 5 (Serial 1850), 440.

33. See "Journal of the Twelfth Annual Conference with Representatives of Missionary Boards, January 16, 1882 [sic]," in Board of Indian Commissioners, *Annual Report, 1882*, in U.S., House of Representatives, *Executive Documents*, 47th Congress, 2nd Session, No. 77 (Serial 2110), 56-58. The Conference date was January 16, 1883, not 1882.

34. William A. Howard to Carl Schurz, Yankton, D.T., February 14, 1879, Carl Schurz Papers, Library of Congress.

35. J.H. Hammond to Carl Schurz, San Carlos Agency, Arizona, July 12, 1879, Schurz Papers, Library of Congress.

36. E.A. Hayt to Arden R. Smith, Washington, May 21, 1878, NARS, RG 75, Chief Clerk, LS (Entry 181).

37. E.A. Hayt to Arden R. Smith, Washington, May 21, 1878, NARS, RG 75, Chief Clerk, LS (Entry 181).

38. Commissioner of Indian Affairs, *Annual Report, 1875*, in U.S., House of Representatives, *Executive Documents*, 44th Congress, 1st Session, No. 1, Part 5 (Serial 1680), 517.

39. "Report of Board Appointed by the Secretary of the Interior June 7, 1877, to Examine into the Methods Now in Force in the Transaction of Business in the Indian Office," August 20, 1877, 80-82, NARS, RG 75, Report on Methods (Entry 169); Indian Appropriations Act, approved May 27, 1878, in U.S., *Statutes at Large*, XX, 66; Indian Appropriations Act, approved May 11, 1880, in *Ibid.*, XXI, 116.

40. Carl Schurz to Commissioner of Indian Affairs, Washington, March 25, 1880, NARS, RG 75, OIA, LR, Letter Books, Vol. I, No. 182-1880 (Entry 79).

41. Acting Commissioner of Indian Affairs E.L. Stevens to U.S. Indian Inspector Charles H. Howard, Washington, April 24, 1883, NARS, RG 75, Chief Clerk, LS (Entry 181).

42. Carl Schurz to Inspector W. J. Pollock, Washington, April 30, 1880; Schurz to J.M. Haworth, Washington, April 30, 1880; Schurz to John McNeil, Washington, May 4, 1880; Schurz to Robert S. Gardner, Washington, July 13, 1880; Acting Secretary of the Interior to Isaac T. Mahon, Washington, July 1880; all in NARS, RG 48, Indian Division, Record of Letters Sent, U.S. Indian Inspectors, April, 1880—December, 1882, LB, 5-6, 18, 22.

43. Acting Secretary of the Interior A. Bell to James M. Haworth, Washington, March 3, 1881, NARS, RG 48, Indian Division, Record of Letters Sent, U.S. Indian Inspectors, April, 1880 - December, 1882, LB, 70.

44. "Medical Inspector for the Indian Service," January 18, 1882, U.S., Senate, *Executive Documents,* 47th Congress, 1st Session, No. 59 (Serial 1987).

45. Indian Appropriations Act, approved May 17, 1882, in U.S., *Statutes at Large*, XXII, 70.

46. H.M. Teller, *Laws and Instructions Relating to the Duties of Inspectors of the United States Indian Service* (Washington, 1883); L.Q.C. Lamar, *Laws and Instructions Relating to the Duties of Inspectors of the United States Indian Service* (Washington, 1885).

47. Hiram Price to the Secretary of the Interior, Washington, April 2, 1883; Price to Secretary of the Interior, Washington, April 5, 1883; both in NARS, RG 75, Chief Clerk, LS (Entry 181).

48. Hiram Price to the Secretary of the Interior, Washington, June 26, 1882, NARS, RG 75, Chief Clerk, LS (Entry 181).

49. Valentine T. McGillycuddy to Carl Schurz, Pine Ridge Agency, D.T., December 12, 1879, Carl Schurz Papers, Library of Congress.

50. "The Condition of the Navajo Indians as an Argument for Making the Indian Service Non-Partisan," Indian Rights Association, Pamphlet No. 21, Second Series (Philadelphia, 1895).

CHAPTER VII

1. Charles Perrow argues that bureaucracies endeavor to purge particularism, the use of "irrelevant critieria" for selecting personnel and making decisions, in *Complex Organizations: A Critical Essay* (Glenview, Ill., 1972), 8-17.

2. M.L. Joslyn, Acting Secretary of the Interior, to Inspector Samuel S. Benedict, Washington, October 31, 1882, NARS, RG 48, Indian Division, LS, Indian Inspectors, Letterbook, 206-209.

3. H.M. Teller, *Laws and Instructions Relating to the Duties of Inspectors of the United States Indian Service* (Washington, 1883). Hereafter cited as *Duties of Inspectors* (1883).

4. The synopses prepared in the Indian Division, together with marginal comments added by clerks in the office of the Commissioner of Indian Affairs, may be found filed with the inspection reports, in NARS, RG 48, Indian Division, LR (Inspectors' Reports).

5. F.A. Walker to General John E. Smith, Washington, January 25, 1872; Walker to Smith, Washington, April 1, 1872; both in NARS, RG 75, Chief Clerk, LS (Entry 181).

6. Commissioner of Indian Affairs, *Annual Report, 1875*, in U.S., House of Representatives, *Executive Documents*, 44th Congress, 1st Session, No. 1, Part 5 (Serial 1680), 517.

7. E.A. Hayt to Bess Brownstone, Washington, October 2, 1877, NARS, RG 75, Chief Clerk, LS (Entry 181).

8. E.A. Hayt to A.N. McSween, Washington, March 21, 1878; Hayt to Inspector E.C. Watkins, Washington, March 23, 1878; Hayt to McSween, Washington, March 25, 1878; William M.

Leeds to Watkins, Washington, March 25, 1878; all in NARS, RG 75, Chief Clerk, LS (Entry 181).

9. William M. Leeds, Acting Commissioner of Indian Affairs, to Horace Austin, Third Auditor of the Treasury, Washington, May 20, 1878, NARS, RG 75, Chief Clerk, LS (Entry 181).

10. William M. Leeds, Acting Commissioner of Indian Affairs, to the Secretary of the Interior, Washington, May 6, 1878; Leeds to Henry Dawes, Teacher, Wichita Agency, Washington, May 10, 1878; Leeds to Fordyce Grinnell, M.D., Physician, Wichita Agency, Washington, May 10, 1878; Leeds to Wichita Agent A.C. Williams, Washington, May 10, 1878; all in NARS, RG 75, Chief Clerk, LS (Entry 181).

11. E. A. Hayt to W. J. Pollock, Washington, November 17, 1879, NARS, RG 75, CIA, LS (Entry 165).

12. William M. Leeds to John McNeil, Washington, July 1, 1878, NARS, RG 75, Chief Clerk, LS (Entry 181); J. H. Hammond to Carl Schurz, Chicago, February 1, 1881, Carl Schurz Papers, Library of Congress.

13. Acting Commissioner of Indian Affairs William M. Leeds to John McNeil, Washington, April 25, 1878, NARS, RG 75, Chief Clerk, LS (Entry 181).

14. J. Q. Smith to E. C. Kemble, Washington, July 30, 1877, NARS, RG 75, CIA, LS (Entry 165).

15. E. A. Hayt to J. H. Hammond, Washington, July 22, 1878 (telegram), NARS, RG 75, Chief Clerk, LS (Entry 181).

16. William M. Leeds, Acting Commissioner of Indian Affairs, to "Hart, Agent," Washington, May 24, 1878 (telegram), NARS, RG 75, Chief Clerk, LS (Entry 181).

17. E.P. Smith to O.L. Brown, Washington, November 10, 1875, NARS, RG 75, CIA, LS (Entry 165). O. L. Brown, of Sandlake, Michigan, was the detective appointed to assist Watkins.

18. J. Q. Smith to William Vandever, "Confidential," Washington, July 4, 1876, NARS, RG 75, CIA, LS (Entry 165).

19. William Leeds to J. H. Hammond, Washington, April 18, 1878, NARS, RG 75, Chief Clerk, LS (Entry 181).

20. William M. Leeds to Lt. William E. Dougherty, Acting Crow Creek Agent, Washington, May 4, 1878; Leeds to William J. Pollock, Dakota Superintendent, Washington, May 4, 1878; Leeds to R.G. Randall, Chief, Accounts Division, Indian Office, Washington, May 4, 1878; Leeds to Randall, Washington, May 4, 1878; all in NARS, RG 75, Chief Clerk, LS (Entry 181).

21. E. A. Hayt to Special Indian Agent R. M. Pratt, Washington, June 8, 1878 (telegram), NARS, RG 75, Chief Clerk, LS (Entry 181).

22. E. A. Hayt to the Secretary of the Interior, Washington, May 29, 1878; Hayt to the Secretary of the Interior, Washington, May 29, 1878; Hayt to John H. Hammond, Washington, May 9, 1878; all in NARS, RG 75, Chief Clerk, LS (Entry 181). Inspector Watkins also sought

the District Attorney's cooperation in his investigation of the Mescalero Apache Agency. See William M. Leeds to District Attorney William B. Catron, Washington, May 18, 1878, NARS, RG 75, Chief Clerk, LS (Entry 181).

23. William M. Leeds to John McNeil, Washington, July 24, 1878, NARS, RG 75, Chief Clerk, LS (Entry 181).

24. William M. Leeds to John McNeil, "Confidential," Washington, July 25, 1878, NARS, RG 75, Chief Clerk, LS (Entry 181).

25. E. A. Hayt to John McNeil, Washington, July 30, 1878, NARS, RG 75, Chief Clerk, LS (Entry 181).

26. E. A. Hayt to John McNeil, Washington, August 5, 1878, NARS, RG 75, Chief Clerk, LS (Entry 181).

27. William M. Leeds to John McNeil, Washington, September 9, 1878, NARS, RG 75, Chief Clerk, LS (Entry 181).

28. E. A. Hayt to Quapaw Agent Hiram W. Jones, Washington, January 16, 1878; Hayt to H. H. Gregg (Seneca, Missouri), Washington, January 16, 1878; Hayt to J. H. Hammond, Washington, January 16, 1878; all in NARS, RG 75, Chief Clerk, LS (Entry 181).

29. Arden R. Smith to E. A. Hayt, Seneca, Missouri, February 10, 1878, NARS, RG 75, OIA, Special Files, 1807-1904, File 221 (Entry 98, M 574, Reel 63).

30. E. A. Hayt to Wichita Agent A. C. Williams, Washington, March 19, 1878; Hayt to Arden R. Smith, Washington, March 19, 1878; both in NARS, RG 75, Chief Clerk, LS (Entry 181).

31. E. A. Hayt to the Secretary of the Interior, Washington, January 16, 1878, NARS, RG 75, Chief Clerk, LS (Entry 181).

32. William M. Leeds to Arden R. Smith, Washington, May 13, 1878, NARS, RG 75, Chief Clerk, LS (Entry 181).

33. Arden R. Smith to Carl Schurz, Malheur Agency, Oregon, February 13, 1881, Carl Schurz Papers, Library of Congress.

34. T. P. Pendleton to the Secretary of the Interior, Berryville, Virginia, August 5, 1879, NARS, RG 48, Indian Division, LR.

35. "Roster of Agency Employees, 1879," NARS, RG 75, Rosters of Agency Employees, 1853-1909 (Entry 978).

36. T. P. Pendleton to Rosebud Agent Cicero Newell, Rosebud, May 23, 1879, enclosed in Newell to Commissioner of Indian Affairs, Rosebud, May 24, 1879; Pendleton to the Secretary of the Interior, Washington, July 21, 1879; both in NARS, RG 75, OIA, LR, 1824-80 (Entry 79; M234, Reel 844); Pendleton to the Secretary of the Interior, Berryville, Virginia, August 5, 1879, NARS, RG 48, Indian Division, LR.

37. E. A. Hayt to William J. Pollock, Washington, November 11, 1879, NARS, RG 75, CIA, LS (Entry 165).

38. Carl Schurz to Robert S. Gardner, Washington, September 25, 1880; Schurz to Gardner, Washington, October 11, 1880; both in NARS, RG 48, Indian Division, Indian Inspectors, LS, Letterbook, 39-40, 46.

39. Carl Schurz to W. J. Pollock, Washington, April 30, 1880; Schurz to J. H. Haworth, Washington, April 30, 1880; Schurz to John McNeil, Washington May 4, 1880; Schurz to Robert S. Gardner, Washington, July 13, 1880; A. Bell to Isaac T. Mahan, Washington, July 16, 1880; all in NARS, RG 48, Indian Division, Indian Inspectors, LS, Letterbook, 5-6, 18, 22.

40. A. Bell to Isaac T. Mahan, Washington, July 26, 1880, NARS, RG 48, Indian Division, Indian Inspectors, LS, Letterbook, 24-25.

41. A. Bell to Isacc T. Mahan, Washington, July 16, 1880, NARS, RG 48, Indian Division, Indian Inspectors, LS, Letterbook, 22.

42. A. Bell to Robert S. Gardner, Washington, May 21, 1881. Identical letters were sent to William J. Pollock, Isaac T. Mahan, J. M. Haworth, and John McNeil on the same date. NARS, RG 48, Indian Division, Indian Inspectors, LS, Letterbook, 88-91.

43. S. J. Kirkwood to J. M. Haworth, Washington, February 25, 1882, NARS, RG 48, Indian Division, Indian Inspectors, LS, Letterbook, 140-141.

44. S. J. Kirkwood to Robert S. Gardner, Washington, March 14, 1882, NARS, RG 48, Indian Division, Indian Inspectors, LS, Letterbook, 154-156.

45. A. Bell to James M. Haworth, Washington, March 31, 1881. Identical letters were sent to John McNeil, Robert S. Gardner, and Isaac T. Mahan on the same date. NARS, RG 48, Indian Division, Inspectors, LS, Letterbook, 76-77.

46. S. J. Kirkwood to J. M. Haworth, Washington, April 28, 1881. Identical letters were sent to Isaac T. Mahan, John McNeil, W. J. Pollock, and Robert S. Gardner on the same date. NARS, RG 48, Indian Division, Indian Inspectors, LS, Letterbook, 81-84.

47. S. J. Kirkwood to C.H. Howard, Washington, July 6, 1881. Identical letters were sent to Robert S. Gardner, W.F. Pollock, J.M. Haworth, and John McNeil. NARS, RG 48, Indian Division, Indian Inspectors, LS, Letterbook, 94-95, 98-104.

48. H.M. Teller to C.H. Howard, Washington, June 5, 1882, NARS, RG 48, Indian Division, Indian Inspectors, LS, Letterbook, 168-169. The following notation appears at the end of the letter: "Copies of the above furnished each of the other inspectors."

49. *Duties of Inspectors* (1883), 7-8.

50. L.Q.C. Lamar, *Laws and Instructions Relating to the Duties of Inspectors of the United States Indian Service* (Washington, 1885).

51. See, for example, R.V. Belt, Memorandum in Reference to James E. Jenkins, Washington, June 12, 1889; Belt, Memorandum in Regard to H.C. Fields, Washington, June 17, 1889; Belt, Memorandum Regarding Services of S.E. Snider, Washington, June 20, 1889; Belt, Memorandum in Regard to Leverett M. Kelly, Washington, July 19, 1889; all in NARS, RG 75, Chief Clerk, LS (Entry 181).

52. Thomas J. Morgan to Rev. William S. Owens, Washington, August 8, 1890, NARS, RG 75, CIA, LS (Entry 165).

53. D.C. Poole, *Among the Sioux of Dakota: Eighteen Months Experience As an Indian Agent* (New York, 1881), 228.

54. *Ibid.*, 228-229.

55. "Report on Methods, 1877," NARS, RG 75 (Entry 169), 68; *Instructions to Indian Agents* (Washington, 1877, 1880); *Instructions to Superintendents and Indian Agents* (Washington, 1876, 1877).

56. *Regulations of the Indian Department* (Washington, 1884); *Regulations of the Indian Office* (Washington, 1894, 1904).

57. See pp. 44-45. The Indian Office first issued the pamphlet, *Laws and Regulations Relating to Trade with Indian Tribes* in 1876. Revised editions were issued in 1879, 1883, and 1904.

58. Office of Indian Affairs, *Rules Governing the Court of Indian Offenses* (Washington, 1883).

59. *Rules for Indian Schools* (Washington, 1890). Revised editions were published in 1892 (with Civil Service rules), 1894, 1898, 1900, and 1904.

CHAPTER VIII

1. See Nelson W. Polsby, "The Institutionalization of the U. S. House of Representatives," *American Political Science Review*, LXII (March, 1968), 144-145, for a discussion of predictability of procedures as an indicator of institutionalization.

2. H. M. Teller, *Laws and Instructions Relating to the Duties of Inspectors of the United States Indian Service* (Washington, 1883), 4-7. Hereafter cited as *Duties of Inspectors* (1883).

3. L. Q. C. Lamar, *Laws and Instructions Relating to the Duties of Inspectors of the United States Indian Service* (Washington, 1885), 4-5. Hereafter cited as *Duties of Inspectors* (1885).

4. Edward E. Hill, *The Office of Indian Affairs, 1824-1834: Historical Sketches* (New York, 1974), 145-146; W. David Baird, *The Quapaw People* (Phoenix, 1975), 58-72.

5. Hill, *The Office of Indian Affairs*, 177.

6. Hill, *The Office of Indian Affairs*, 195-196; James R. Masterson, "Research Suggestions: The Records of the Washington Superintendency of Indian Affairs," *Pacific Northwest Quarterly* XXXVII (January, 1946), 31-57; Marian W. Smith, *The Puyallup-Nisqually* (New York, 1940), 1-55.

7. The register is entitled "Abstracts of Inspectors' Reports: 1873-1880," 1 Vol., NARS, RG 75 (Entry 950). The reports for 1873-1880 are to be found in NARS, RG 75, "Inspectors' Reports, 1873-1880" (Entry 951). Prior to the creation of the National Archives, many of the reports were removed from this series and placed with the general incoming correspondence (Entry 79); while I was at the National Archives and Records Service, these reports

were being removed from Entry 79 and placed with the reports remaining in Entry 951 in preparation for a microfilming project. By using the register, it was possible to locate all of the relevant Inspector's Reports. I wish to acknowledge the assistance of the archivist in charge of the project, Michael Goldman, in helping to track down stray items.

8. The registers are to be found in NARS, RG 48, Indian Division; the inspectors' reports in NARS, RG 48, Indian Division, LR (Inspectors' Reports). Again, as with the pre-1880 reports, the staff of the National Archives was preparing these records for microfilming. I wish to acknowledge the assistance of archivists Michael Goldman and Renee Joussaud in helping me to understand the mysteries of Record Group 48.

9. E. C. Kemble to E. P. Smith, Olympia, Washington Territory, November 8, 1873 (Report of Inspection of Puyallup Agency), NARS, RG 75, Inspectors' Reports (Entry 951).

10. E. C. Kemble to R. H. Milroy, Puyallup Agency, October 28, 1873, copy enclosed in Kemble to Smith, Puyallup Agency, October 29, 1873; Kemble to Smith, Olympia, November 7, 1873; Kemble to Smith, Olympia, November 7, 1873; Kemble to Smith, Olympia, November 8, 1873; all in NARS, RG 75, Inspectors' Reports (Entry 951).

11. Kemble to Smith, Olympia, November 7, 1873, NARS, RG 75, Inspectors' Reports (Entry 951).

12. Kemble to the Commissioner of Indian Affairs, Olympia, November, 12, 1873 (telegram); Kemble to Smith, Olympia, November 7, 1873; both in NARS, RG 75, Inspectors' Reports (Entry 951).

13. Columbus Delano to the President, Washington, February 12, 1874, NARS, RG 75, Inspectors' Reports (Entry 951).

14. "Open Letter to Hon. E. C. Kemble, Inspector of Indian Affairs," *Puget Sound Daily Courier*, November 11, 1873, clipping enclosed in Kemble to Smith, Olympia, November 15, 1873, NARS, RG 75, Inspectors' Reports (Entry 951). Kemble charged that the author of the open letter was G. F. Whitworth, Milroy's Chief Clerk and "a thoroughly untrustworthy man" whose "sole endeavor has been to cover up and excuse the frauds and abuses of this Office."

15. [E. C. Kemble,] "The Indian Ring Triumphant," *The Weekly Bulletin of San Francisco*, February 20, 1874, clipping enclosed in R. H. Milroy to E. P. Smith, Olympia, March 16, 1874, NARS, RG 75, Inspectors' Reports (Entry 951).

16. U. S. Grant, endorsement, February 12, 1874, on C. Delano to the President, Washington, February 12, 1874, NARS, RG 75, Inspectors' Reports (Entry 951).

17. R. H. Milroy to E. P. Smith, Olympia, September 25, 1874, reprinted in Masterson, "The Records of the Washington Superintendency of Indian Affairs," 33-34.

18. E. C. Kemble to E. P. Smith, Olympia, November 14, 1873 (Report of Inspection of S'Kokomish Agency), NARS, RG 75, Inspectors' Reports (Entry 951).

19. W. Hadley to Enoch Hoag, Lawrence, Kansas, April 8, 1874, enclosed in E. C. Kemble to E. P. Smith, Quapaw Agency, Indian Territory, November 27, 1874, NARS, RG 75, Inspectors' Reports (Entry 951).

20. E. C. Kemble to E. P. Smith, Quapaw Agency, November 27, 1874, NARS, RG 75, Inspectors' Reports (Entry 951); on the Modoc War and the removal of the Modocs to the Quapaw Reservation, see Robert M. Utley, *Frontier Regulars: The United States Army and the Indian, 1866-1891* (New York, 1973), 198-207.

21. E.C. Kemble to E.P. Smith, Baxter Springs, Kansas, November 27, 1874, "Reports of Inspection of Quapaw Agency," NARS, RG 75, Inspectors' Reports (Entry 951).

22. See J.D. Lang and F. H. Smith to C.B. Fisk, Washington, D.C., November 20, 1874, in Board of Indian Commissioners, *Annual Report, 1874* (Washington, 1875), 76-79. See also William Vandever to Commissioner of Indian Affairs, Portland, Oregon, October 30, 1874, and Vandever to Commissioner of Indian Affairs, San Francisco, November 9, 1874, both in NARS, RG 75, Inspectors' Reports (Entry 951). Smith had previously recommended a consolidation of the scattered tribes in the Puget Sound region. See F.H. Smith to E.P. Smith, Washington, D.C., May 25, 1874, in Board of Indian Commissioners, *Annual Report, 1874*, 74-75. See also Commissioner of Indian Affairs, *Annual Report, 1874*, in U.S., House of Representatives, *Executive Documents*, 43rd Congress, 2nd Session, No. 1, Part 5 (Serial 1639), 386-391.

23. William Vandever to Commissioner of Indian Affairs, San Francisco, November 9, 1874, NARS, RG 75, Inspectors' Reports (Entry 951).

24. William Vandever to Commissioner of Indian Affairs, S'Kokomish, Washington Territory, October 24, 1874, NARS, RG 75, Inspectors' Reports (Entry 951). Treaty with the S'Kallam (Point-No-Point), January 26, 1855, ratified March 8, 1859 (U.S., *Statutes at Large*, XII, 933), in Charles J. Kappler, comp., *Indian Affairs: Laws and Treaties*, II (Washington, 1904), 674-677. See Article 5.

25. William Vandever to Commissioner of Indian Affairs, Portland, Oregon, October 30, 1874, NARS, RG 75, Inspectors' Reports (Entry 951). Treaty with the Nisqualli, Puyallup, etc. (Medicine Creek), December 26, 1854, ratified March 3, 1855 (U.S., *Statutes at Large*, X, 1132), in Kappler, *Indian Affairs*, II, 661-664. See Article 4.

26. J.D. Bevier to E.P. Smith, Grand River Agency, Standing Rock, Dakota Territory, August 22, 1874, NARS, RG 75, Inspectors' Reports (Entry 951).

27. William Vandever to Commissioner of Indian Affairs, Bismark, Dakota Territory, September 17, 1875; Vandever to Commissioner of Indian Affairs, Dubuque, Iowa, September 25, 1875; both in NARS, RG 75, Inspectors' Reports (Entry 951).

28. See pp. 94-95; Smith's many reports on Quapaw may be found in "Investigation of Charges against Agent Hiram W. Jones, Quapaw Agency, 1874-78," NARS, RG 75, Special Files of the Office of Indian Affairs, 1807-1904, No. 211 (Entry 98; M574, Reel 6).

29. John McNeil to E. A. Hayt, St. Louis, April 24, 1879, NARS, RG 75, Inspectors' Reports (Entry 951).

30. J. H. Hammond to Commissioner of Indian Affairs, Standing Rock, July 27, 1878 (telegram), RG 75, Inspectors' Reports (Entry 951).

31. Francis Paul Prucha, *A Guide to the Military Posts of the United States, 1789-1895* (Madison, 1964), 118.

32. John McNeil to the Secretary of the Interior, St. Louis, September 27, 1880, NARS, RG 48, Indian Division, LR (Inspector's Reports).

33. John McNeil to Carl Schurz, St. Louis, September 28, 1880, NARS, RG 48, Indian Division, LR (Inspector's Reports).

34. E. C. Watkins to the Commissioner of Indian Affairs, Portland, Oregon, October 2, 1877, NARS, RG 75, Inspectors' Reports (Entry 951); "The funds. . . . Bender says have been sent to him [Milroy]." "Voorhees," undated note attached to Watkins to Commissioner of Indian Affairs, October 2, 1877. Joseph T. Bender and John H. Voorhees were clerks in the Indian Office. U. S., *Register of Officers and Agents. . . . 1877* (Washington, 1878).

35. E. C. Watkins to the Commissioner of Indian Affairs, Portland, Oregon, September 28, 1877, NARS, RG 75, Inspectors' Reports (Entry 951).

36. *Duties of Inspectors* (1883), 7. This instruction was repeated in the 1885 pamphlet. See *Duties of Inspectors* (1885), 7-8.

37. William J. Pollock to Samuel J. Kirkwood, S'Kokomish Agency, Washington Territory, March 28, 1881; Pollock to [Kirkwood], San Francisco, April 18, 1881; both in NARS, RG 48, Indian Division, LR (Inspectors' Reports).

38. Robert S. Gardner to H. M. Teller, Standing Rock Agency, May 29, 1882, NARS, RG 48, Indian Division, LR (Inspectors' Reports).

39. B. N. Benedict to H. M. Teller, Quapaw Agency, Indian Territory, December 29, 1882; Benedict to Teller, Crow Agency, Montana, June 14, 1883; both in NARS, RG 48, Indian Division, LR (Inspectors' Reports).

40. Henry Ward to H. M. Teller, Muskogee, Indian Territory, July 4, 1883, NARS, RG 48, Indian Division, LR (Inspectors' Reports).

41. Robert S. Gardner to H. M. Teller, Osage Agency, Paw-hus-ka, Indian Territory, December 17, 1883; R. V. Belt, Synopsis of Inspector Gardner's Report on Quapaw Agency, December 21, 1883: both in NARS, RG 48, Indian Division, LR (Inspectors' Reports).

42. See pp. 96-97.

43. *Duties of Inspectors* (1883), 5; Henry Ward to H. M. Teller, Portland, Oregon, April 24, 1884; M. R. Barr to Teller, Devil's Lake Indian Agency, Fort Totten, Dakota Territory, July 5, 1884; Ward to Teller, Standing Rock Agency, January 10, 1885; all in NARS, RG 48, Indian Division, LR (Inspectors' Reports).

44. B. N. Benedict to H. M. Teller, Quapaw Agency, Indian Territory, December 29, 1882, NARS, RG 48, Indian Division, LR (Inspectors' Reports).

45. *Duties of Inspectors* (1883), 6.

46. *Ibid*. (1885), 4-5.

47. See Robert S. Gardner to the Secretary of the Interior, Muskogee, Indian Territory, March 18, 1886; E. D. Bannister to Secretary of the Interior, Quapaw Agency. Indian Territory, November 30, 1886; Bannister to Secretary of the Interior, Seattle, Washington Territory, February 19, 1886; George R. Pearsons to L. Q. C. Lamar, Devils Lake, Dakota Territory, September 17, 1886; all in NARS, RG 48, Indian Division, LR (Inspectors' Reports).

48. *Duties of Inspectors* (1885), 5.

49. See Robert S. Gardner to the Secretary of the Interior, Quapaw Agency, Indian Territory, July 30, 1887; Frank C. Armstrong to L. Q. C. Lamar, Centralia, Washington Territory, August 5, 1887; Gardner to the Secretary of the Interior, Tacoma, Washington Territory, November 22, 1887 (two reports); all in NARS, RG 48, Indian Division, LR (Inspectors' Reports).

50. The forms were first used by Inspector Edmond Mallet in his inspection of Standing Rock Agency. See Edmond Mallet to the Secretary of the Interior, East Pierre, Dakota Territory, December 29, 1888 (two reports), NARS, RG 48, Indian Division, LR (Inspectors' Reports). See also Robert S. Gardner to the Secretary of the Interior, Standing Rock Agency, North Dakota, December 8, 1890; Gardner to the Secretary of the Interior, December 9, 1890; F. C. Armstrong to Secretary of the Interior, Quapaw Agency, December 21, 1889; T.D. Marcum to Secretary of the Interior, Tacoma, Washington Territory, May 4, 1889; James H. Cisney to Secretary of the Interior, Tacoma, December 21, 1889; all in NARS, RG 48, Indian Division, LR (Inspectors' Reports).

51. The volumes are in NARS, RG 75, School Personnel Rating Books, 1889-95, 4 Vols. (Entry 990). The volumes are indexed by name of employee and by name of the agency at which the school was located. See also NARS, RG 75, School Employee Efficiency Ratings, 1895-1906, 6 Vols. (Entry 992), and NARS, RG 75, Index for School Employee Efficiency Ratings, 1895-1906, 1 Vol. (Entry 991).

52. *Duties of Inspectors* (1883), 4-6; *Ibid.* (1885), 4.

53. B.N. Benedict to H.M. Teller, Quapaw Agency, Indian Territory, December 29, 1882, NARS, RG 48, Indian Division, LR (Inspectors' Reports). The use of such grazing funds as a relief measure on Indian Territory reservations was not uncommon; see William T. Hagan, "Kiowas, Commanches, and Cattlemen, 1867-1906: A Cast Study of the Failure of U.S. Reservation Policy," *Pacific Historical Review*, XL (August, 1971), 333-355.

54. Henry Ward to H.M. Teller, Muskogee, Indian Territory, July 4, 1883, NARS, RG 48, Indian Division, LR (Inspectors' Reports).

55. Robert S. Gardner to H.M. Teller, Osage Agency, Paw-hus-ka, Indian Territory, December 17, 1883; B.L. Benedict to the Secretary of the Interior, Cherryvale, Kansas, April 22, 1885; Gardner to the Secretary of the Interior, Muscogee, Indian Territory, March 18, 1886; E.D. Bannister to the Secretary of the Interior, Quapaw Agency, December 1, 1886; all in NARS, RG 48, Indian Division, LR (Inspectors' Reports). Lykins, an adopted Peoria, had eight hundred acres under fence on the Quapaw Reservation. Ridpath, who was suspended on October 31, 1885, had three hundred head of cattle grazing on Lykins' enclosed fields. See Gardner to the Secretary of the Interior, Muscogee, I.T., March 18, 1886, NARS, RG 48, Indian Division, LR (Inspectors' Reports).

56. T. D. Marcum to the Secretary of the Interior, Arkansas City, Kansas, June 9, 1886, NARS, RG, 48, Indian Division, LR (Inspectors' Reports).

57. Robert S. Gardner to the Secretary of the Interior, Quapaw Agency, I.T., July 30, 1887, NARS, RG 48, Indian Division, LR (Inspectors' Reports).

58. M. A. Thomas to the Secretary of the Interior, Quapaw Agency, I. T., June 5, 1888, NARS, RG 48, Indian Division, LR (Inspectors' Reports).

59. Frank C. Armstrong to the Secretary of the Interior, Quapaw Agency, I. T., August 16, 1888; Armstrong to the Secretary of the Interior, Quapaw Agency, I. T., December 21, 1889; NARS, RG 48, Indian Division, LR (Inspectors' Reports).

60. William W. Junkin to the Secretary of the Interior, Quapaw Agency, July, 26, 1890; Arthur W. Tinker to the Secretary of the Interior, Quapaw Agency, March 26, 1892; NARS, RG 48, Indian Division, LR (Inspectors' Reports).

61. Robert S. Gardner to the Secretary of the Interior, Quapaw Agency, I. T., October 1, 1892, NARS, RG 48, Indian Division, LR (Inspectors' Reports).

62. The Quapaw National Council authorized allotment of the reservation in an act passed March 23, 1893. Congress ratified and confirmed the allotments made to the Quapaws under the act in the Indian Appropriations Act, approved March 2, 1895, in U.S., *Statutes at Large*, XXVIII, 907. W. David Baird provides an account on the Quapaw allotments in the *The Quapaw People*, 68-72.

63. C. C. Duncan to the Secretary of the Interior, Quapaw Agency, I. T., August 26, 1893; C. C. Duncan to the Secretary of the Interior, Quapaw Agency, I. T., April 18, 1896; C. F. Nesler to the Secretary of the Interior, Quapaw Agency, I. T., January 6, 1898; Cyrus Beede to the Secretary of the Interior, Quapaw Agency, I. T., October 20, 1898; NARS, RG 48, Indian Division, LR (Inspectors' Reports).

64. Thomas P. Smith to the Secretary of the Interior, Quapaw Agency, I. T., January 7, 1894, NARS, RG 48, Indian Division, LR (Inspectors' Reports).

65. Paul F. Faison to the Secretary of the Interior, Seneca, Missouri, March 11, 1895, NARS, RG 48, Indian Division, LR (Inspectors' Reports).

66. C. F. Nesler to the Secretary of the Interior, Quapaw Agency, I.T., January 6, 1898, NARS, RG 48, Indian Division, LR (Inspectors' Reports).

67. The Peoria and Miami Allotment Act, approved March 2, 1889, provided for allotments for two hundred acres to members of the United Peoria and Miami tribes. The allotments were to be inalienable for a period of twenty-five years. U. S., *Statutes at Large*, XXV, 1013. However, in the Indian Appropriations Act, approved June 7, 1897, in a section also permitting the leasing of allotments on the Quapaw reservation, Congress permitted adult allottees of the Peoria and Miami reservation to sell up to one hundred acres of their allotments. U. S., *Statutes at Large*, XXX, 72.

68. C. F. Nesler to the Secretary of the Interior, Newark, N. J., January 19, 1898, NARS, RG 48, Indian Division, LR (Inspectors' Reports). The Indian Office referred the matter to the Department of Justice for investigation and ordered Agent Edward Goldberg to suspend all land sales. See Acting Commissioner of Indian Affairs A. C. Tonner to the Secretary of the Interior, Washington, March 9, 1898, in NARS, RG 48, Indian Division, LR.

69. Cyrus Beede to the Secretary of the Interior, Quapaw Agency, I. T., October 20, 24, 25, and 28, 1898; NARS, RG 48, Indian Division, LR (Inspectors' Reports).

70. W. A. Jones to the Secretary of the Interior, Washington, November 5, 1898, NARS, RG 48, Indian Division, LR.

71. P. McCormick to the Secretary of the Interior, Tacoma, March 9, 1894, NARS, RG 48, Indian Division, LR (Inspectors' Reports).

72. William A. Newell to H. M. Teller, Olympia, November 3, 1884; M. A. Thomas to the Secretary of the Interior, Nisqually and S'Kokomish Agency, January 26, 1887; Robert S. Gardner to Secretary of the Interior, Tacoma, November 22, 1887; Frank C. Armstrong to L. Q. C. Lamar, Nisqually and S'Kokomish Agency, July 13, 1887 (two reports); NARS, RG 48, Indian Division, LR (Inspectors' Reports).

73. J. D. C. Atkins to the Secretary of the Interior, Washington, September 22, 1887, NARS, RG 48, Indian Division, LR.

74. James H. Cisney to the Secretary of the Interior, Tacoma, December 21, 1889, NARS, RG 48, Indian Division, LR (Inspectors' Reports).

75. E. D. Bannister to the Secretary of the Interior, Seattle, February 20, 1886, NARS, RG 48, Indian Division, LR (Inspectors' Reports).

76. T. D. Marcum to the Secretary of the Interior, Tacoma, May 4, 1889, NARS, RG 48, Indian Division, LR (Inspectors' Reports).

77. Robert S. Gardner to the Secretary of the Interior, Tacoma, September 29, 1890, NARS, RG 48, Indian Division, LR (Inspectors' Reports).

78. Benjamin H. Miller to the Secretary of the Interior, Ashton, Maryland, February 29, 1892; P. McCormick to the Secretary of the Interior, Tacoma, March 11, 1894; NARS, RG 48, Indian Division, LR (Inspectors' Reports).

79. Affidavit of Frank A. Smally, September 20, 1893: Affidavit of H. W. Blandy, September 22, 1893; enclosed in P. McCormick to the Secretary of the Interior, Tacoma, March 11, 1894, NARS, RG, 48, Indian Division, LR (Inspectors' Reports).

80. P. McCormick to the Secretary of the Interior, Tacoma, January 7, 1896; McCormick to Secretary of the Interior, Shelton, Washington, March 5, 1895; NARS, RG 48, Indian Division, LR (Inspectors' Reports).

81. D. M. Browning to the Secretary of the Interior, Washington, February 12, 1896, NARS, RG 48, Indian Division, LR.

82. John Lam to the Secretary of the Interior, Tacoma, December 9, and 10, 1896; Seattle, December 13, and 21, 1896; Dungeness, Washington, December 17, 1896; NARS, RG 48, Indian Division, LR (Inspectors' Reports).

83. W. J. McConnell to the Secretary of the Interior, Tacoma, September 24, 28, and 30, 1897; W. J. McConnell to the Secretary of the Interior, Tacoma, September 24, 28, and 30 1897;

W. J. McConnell to the Secretary of the Interior, Tacoma, January 28, 1899; NARS, RG 48, Indian Division, LR (Inspectors' Reports). Congress created the Puyallup Land Commission in the Indian Appropriations Act, approved March 3, 1893, in U.S., *Statutes at Large*, XXVII, 633.

84. James McLaughlin to the Secretary of the Interior, St. Paul, Minnesota, April 7, 1905, NARS, RG 48, Indian Division, LR (Inspectors' Reports), reported the reluctant agreement of the Standing Rock Sioux to allotment under the terms of the Sioux Agreement, Act of March 2, 1889, in U.S., *Statutes at Large*, XXV, 888, Sections 8-9. McLaughlin enclosed a petition requesting allotment on which he had the Indians affix their thumb prints so they could not later deny they had signed.

85. M.R. Barr to H.M. Teller, Devil's Lake Indian Agency, Fort Totten, Dakota, July 5, 1884; E.D. Bannister to the Secretary of the Interior, Bismark, Dakota, November 18, 1887; NARS, RG 48, Indian Division, LR (Inspectors' Reports).

86. Edmond Mallet to the Secretary of the Interior. East Pierre, Dakota, December 29, 1888; NARS, RG 48, Indian Division, LR (Inspectors' Reports).

87. Arthur W. Tinker to the Secretary of the Interior, Standing Rock Agency, November 20, 1889; James. H. Cisney to the Secretary of the Interior, Rosebud Agency, South Dakota, September 22, 1890; NARS, RG 48, Indian Division, LR (Inspectors' Reports).

88. James H. Cisney to the Secretary of the Interior, Crow Creek Agency, South Dakota, March 3, 1892; John W. Cadman to the Secretary of the Interior, Standing Rock Agency, January 15, 1894; James McLaughlin to Secretary of the Interior, Fort Yates, North Dakota, January 7, 1896; NARS, RG 48, Indian Division, LR (Inspectors' Reports).

89. James H. Cisney to the Secretary of the Interior, Rosebud Agency, September 22, 1890; Benjamin H. Miller to the Secretary of the Interior, Ashton, Maryland, November 18, 1892; NARS, RG 48, Indian Division, LR (Inspectors' Reports).

90. Thomas P. Smith to the Secretary of the Interior, Standing Rock Agency, June 30, 1894, NARS, RG 48, Indian Division, LR (Inspectors' Reports).

91. George R. Pearsons to L.Q.C. Lamar, Devil's Lake, Dakota, September 17, 1886 (two reports), NARS, RG 48, Indian Division, LR (Inspectors' Reports).

92. Robert S. Gardner to the Secretary of the Interior, Standing Rock Agency, December 8 and 9, 1890, NARS, RG 48, Indian Division, LR (Inspectors' Reports). Gardner made his reports a few days before the attempted arrest and fatal shooting of the Hunkpapa chief and medicine man Sitting Bull. See Robert M. Utley, *The Last Days of the Sioux Nation* (New Haven, 1963), 147-160.

93. Arthur W. Tinker to the Secretary of the Interior, Cheyenne River Agency, South Dakota, September 30, 1899, NARS, RG 48, Indian Division, LR (Inspectors' Reports).

94. M.R. Barr to H.M. Teller, Devil's Lake Indian Agency, Fort Totten, July 5, 1884; Henry Ward to H.M. Teller, Standing Rock Agency, January 10, 1885; M.A. Thomas to the Secretary of the Interior, Standing Rock Agency, November 2, 1885; George R. Pearsons to L. Q. C. Lamar, Devil's Lake, September 17, 1886 (two reports); NARS, RG 48, Indian Division, LR (Inspector's Reports).

95. Thomas P. Smith to the Secretary of the Interior, Standing Rock Agency, June 28 and 30,

1894; John W. Cadman to the Secretary of the Interior, Standing Rock Agency, October 9 and 10, 1894; James McLaughlin to the Secretary of the Interior, Ft. Yates, North Dakota, December 31, 1895, and January 7, 1896; NARS RG 48, Indian Division, LR (Inspectors' Reports).

96. W. J. McConnell to the Secretary of the Interior, Tacoma, Washington, January 23, 1901, and enclosures: C. A. Snowden, Puyallup Land Commission, to McConnell, Tacoma, January 24, 1901; Frank Terry, Superintendent, Puyallup Consolidated Agency, to the Commissioner of Indian Affairs, Tacoma, May 3, 1900 (copy): Edwin Eells to McConnell, Tacoma, January 10, 1901; NARS, RG 48, Indian Division, LR (Inspectors' Reports).

97. James E. Jenkins to the Secretary of the Interior, In the Field, August 25, 1901; NARS, RG 48, Indian Division, LR (Inspectors' Reports).

98. S. M. Brosius to the Secretary of the Interior, Washington, October 10, 1901, NARS, RG 48, Indian Division, LR.

99. James E. Jenkins to the Secretary of the Interior, In the Field, November 3, 1901, NARS, RG 48, Indian Division, LR (Inspectors' Reports). Jenkins also investigated charges that the assistant matron at the Grand River Boarding School, Mrs. Nellie M. Brown, was "a common prostitute." Jenkins found these charges to be without foundation also.

100. C. F. Nesler to the Secretary of the Interior, Denver, Colorado, June 15, 1902; Nesler to Secretary of the Interior, Washington, July 5, 1902; NARS, RG 48, Indian Division, LR (Inspectors' Reports).

101. Levi Chubbuck to the Secretary of the Interior, Cheyenne [River] Agency, South Dakota, September, 10, 1902; Chubbuck to Secretary of the Interior, Billings, Montana, August 14 and 15, 1903, NARS RG 48, Indian Division, LR (Inspectors' Reports).

102. James McLaughlin to the Secretary of the Interior, St. Paul, Minnesota, April 6 and 7, 1905, NARS, RG 48, Indian Division, LR (Inspectors' Reports).

103. Levi Chubbuck to the Secretary of the Interior, Everett, Washington, September 27, 1906, NARS, RG 48, Indian Division, LR (Inspectors' Reports).

104. "Rosters of Field Officials, 1849-1911," NARS, RG 75 (Entry 976).

CHAPTER IX

1. Philip Selznick, *Leadership in Administration: A Sociological Interpretation* (New York, 1957), 66.

2. *Ibid.*, 91-100.

3. See Helen M. Bannan, "The Idea of Civilization and American Indian Policy Reformers in the 1880s," *Journal of American Culture*, I (Winter, 1978), 787-799.

4. See William T. Hagan, "Private Property: The Indian's Door to Civilization," *Ethnohistory*, III (Spring, 1956), 126-137.

5. The presumed educational value of citizenship was expressed well in a resolution passed by the Lake Mohonk Conference in 1886: "Quicker and surer progress will be secured in industry, education, and morality by giving citizenship first [to the Indians] than by making citizenship

conditional upon the attainment of any standard of education and conduct." "Proceedings of the Mohonk Lake Conference," October 13-15, 1886, in Board of Indian Commissioners, *Annual Report, 1886*, in U.S., House of Representatives, *Executive Documents*, 49th Congress, 2nd Session, No, 1, Part 5 (Serial 2467), 1003. For a useful discussion of reformers' attitudes toward the citizenship question, see Loring Benson Priest, *Uncle Sam's Stepchildren: The Reformation of United States Indian Policy* (New Brunswick, N.J., 1942), Chapter XVI.

6. See, for example, Commissioner of Indian Affairs, *Annual Report, 1878*, in U.S., House of Representatives, *Executive Documents*, 45th Congress, 3rd Session, No. 1, Part 5 (Serial 1850), 457-459.

7. See Paul Wallace Gates, "Indian Allotments Preceeding the Dawes Act," in *The Frontier Challenge: Responses to the Trans-Mississippi West*, edited by John G. Clark (Lawrence, Kans., 1971), 141-170, and Mary E. Young, *Redskins, Ruffleshirts and Rednecks: Indian Allotments in Alabama and Mississippi, 1830-1860* (Norman, Okla., 1961).

8. For a fuller discussion than is presented here, see Roy W. Meyer, *History of the Santee Sioux: United States Indian Policy Trial* (Lincoln, Nebr., 1967), chapters VI-VIII.

9. "Treaty with the Sioux—Brule, Oglala, Miniconjou, Yanktonai, Hunkpapa, Blackfeet, Cuthead, Two Kettle, Sans Arcs, and Santee—and Arapahoe, 1868," ratified February 16, 1869 (U.S., *Statutes at Large*, XV, 635), Article 6, in Charles J. Kappler, comp., *Indian Affairs: Laws and Treaties*, II (Washington, 1904), 1000.

10. Alice C. Fletcher, "Allotment of Land to Indians," *Proceedings of the National Conference of Charities and Corrections, 1887* (Boston, 1887), 172-183.

11. General Allotment Act, approved February 8, 1887, in U.S., *Statutes at Large*, XXIV, 388-391; D.S. Otis, *The Dawes Act and the Allotment of Indian Lands* (1934; rev. ed., Norman, Okla., 1973), 3-7.

12. Section 10, General Allotment Act, approved February 8, 1887, in U.S., *Statutes at Large*, XXIV, 391; D.S. Otis, in *The Dawes Act*, 22-28, suggested that this section may have increased the support of railroads for the act. During the late 1890s, Congress passed many acts granting rights-of-way to railroads. Further, "regarding the interest of railroads in allotment, one salient fact that must be borne in mind is that the allotment system would throw open large areas to white settlement, and in this period especially railroad leaders were lavishly expending money and effort in building up Western settlements to furnish railroad traffic." *Ibid.*, 25.

13. The number of allotment agents and surveyors employed by the Indian Office was 8 in 1889, 25 in 1891, 14 in 1893, and 15 in 1895 and 1897, according to the *Official Registers* for those years.

14. Farmers had "general supervision of that portion of the reservations remote from the Agencies," wrote Commissioner of Indian Affairs W.A. Jones to a correspondent. To an applicant for a position, he wrote, "A certain territory or number of Indians will be placed in your charge and you will report to the Agent having charge of the reservation. The duties are not hard but they require faithful and conscientious application, as of course very much of the progress the Indian makes depends on the Farmer in charge. They really act as a sub-agent to the regular Indian Agent." W.A. Jones to R.M. Bashford, Washington, July 19, 1901, and Jones to W.C. Hughes, Washington, November 1, 1901, NARS, RG 75, CIA, LS (Entry 165). See

also Institute for Government Research, *The Problem of Indian Administration* (Baltimore, 1928), 540-541.

15. Act of February 28, 1891, in U.S., *Statutes at Large*, XXVI, 794-796.

16. Act of May 8, 1906, in U.S., *Statutes at Large,* XXXIV, 182.

17. The Dawes Act, in contrast, was based on the assumption that the possession of citizenship itself had pedagogical value. A.C.L., "Preliminary Report on the Policy of the Burke Act as Compared with that of the Dawes Act, etc., Memorandum in Reply to Mr. Ernest Thompson Seton," April 25, 1912, NARS, RG 75, Comparison of Policies of the Burke Act and Dawes Act, Special Series A, 1859-1934 (Entry 126).

18. Indian Appropriations Act, approved March 3, 1875, in U.S., *Statutes at Large*, XVIII, 450.

19. "Tabular Statement of Disbursements made from the Appropriations for the Indian Department for the Fiscal Year Ending June 30, 1974 . . ." U. S., House of Representatives, *Executive Documents*, 43rd Congress, 2nd Session, No. 6 (Serial 1643). Since the title for each year's statement was the same, I report citation information in an abbreviated form below:

Fiscal Year	H. E. D. No.	Congress	Session	Serial
1873–74	6	43	2	1643
1874–75	6	44	1	1685
1875–76	6	44	2	1754
1876–77	6	45	2	1805
1877–78	6	45	3	1855
1878–79	6	46	2	1916
1879–80	6	46	3	1965
1880–81	6	47	1	2024
1881–82	6	47	2	2106
1882–83	6	48	1	2193
1883–84	6	48	2	2290
1884–85	6	49	1	2387
1885–86	6	49	2	2477
1886–87	8	50	1	2550
1887–88	8	50	2	2645
1888–89	8	51	1	2739
1889–90	8	51	2	2855
1890–91	8	52	1	2949
1891–92	239	52	2	3107
1892–93	36	53	2	3223
1893–94 *				
1894–95	36**	54	1	3414

*   Not in Serial Set
**   House, *Documents* (H. D.)   **

20. Priest, *Uncle Sam's Stepchildren*, 282.

21. Glenn Porter, *The Rise of Big Business, 1860-1910* (New York, 1973), 57-58.

22. G.F. Warren and F.A. Pearson, "Wholesale Prices in the United States for 135 Years, 1797 to

1932," in *Wholesale Prices for 213 Years, 1720 to 1932* (Ithaca, N.Y., 1932), 10-11; Porter, *The Rise of Big Business*, 58-59.

23. The table from which I constructed the index may be found in Warren and Pearson, "Wholesale Prices," 6-10. Warren and Pearson used variable weights to take into account the changing importance of the commodities used to make up their index. See *Ibid.*, 120-133. Warren and Pearson's series was based primarily on wholesale prices in New York City; however, the trends they report are broadly consistent with those reported by other investigators. See Simon Kuznets, *National Product Since 1869* (New York, 1946), 90-101, and Dorothy S. Brady, "Price Deflators for Final Product Estimates," in *Output, Employment, and Productivity in the United States after 1800* (New York, 1966), 91-115. Further, Warren and Pearson report index numbers for months, making it possible to construct a series of index numbers for fiscal, rather than calendar years.

24. U.S., *Register of Officers and Agents, Civil, Military, and Naval in the Service of the United States on the Thirtieth of September, 1865* (Washington, 1866); U.S., *Register of Officers and Agents. . . . 1867-1877* (Washington, 1868-1878); U.S., *Official Register of the United States, Containing a list of Officers and Employees in the Civil, Military, and Naval Service on the Thirtieth of June 1879* (Washington, 1879); U.S., *Official Register. . . . 1881-1897* (Washington, 1881-1897).

25. In 1878, Congress set the pay of privates in the Indian police at $5.00 per month; officers received $8.00 per month. Indian Appropriations Act, approved May 27, 1878, in U.S., *Statutes at Large*, XX, 86. The Indian Appropriations Act of June 29, 1888, increased the monthly pay of privates to $8.00 per month; officers received $10.00 per month. U. S., *Statutes at Large*, XXV, 233.

26. "Treaty with the Navaho, 1868," ratified July 25, 1868 (U. S., *Statutes at Large*, XV, 667), Article 6, in Kappler, *Indian Affairs*, II, 1017; Donald L. Parman, *The Navajos and the New Deal* (New Haven, 1976), 193.

27. Richard L. Guenther, "The Santee Normal Training School," *Nebraska History*, LI (Fall, 1970), 359-378.

28. As a result of the contracting provisions of the Peace Policy, the number of Catholic schools for Indians increased from eight in 1870 to thirty by 1878. Peter J. Rahill, *The Catholic Indian Missions and Grant's Peace Policy, 1870-1884* (Washington, 1953), 273-274.

29. Edward P. Smith to William Loughridge, House of Representatives, Washington, February 27, 1874, NARS, RG 75, LS, CIA (Entry 165).

30. Henry L. Dawes, "The Indian Territory," In Commissioner of Education, *Annual Report, 1899-1900*, in U. S., House of Representatives, *Documents*, 56th Congress, 2nd Session, No. 5, Vol. II (Serial 4115), 1339.

31. Commissioner of Indian Affairs, *Annual Report, 1877*, in U. S., House of Representatives, *Executive Documents*, 45th Congress, 2nd Session, No. 1, Part 5 (Serial 1800), 399-400.

32. *Ibid.*, 397-398.

33. Commissioner of Indian Affairs, *Annual Report, 1878*, in U.S., House of Representatives, *Executive Documents*, 45th Congress, 3rd Session, No. 1, Part 5 (Serial 1850), 458-459.

34. R. H. Pratt to Carl Schurz, Hampton, Virginia, February 17, 1879, Carl Schurz Papers, Library of Congress; Commissioner of Indian Affairs, *Annual Report, 1879*, in U. S., House of Respresentatives, *Executive Documents*, 46th Congress, 2nd Session, No. 1, Part 5 (Serial 1910), 73-74.

35. Commissioner of Indian Affairs, *Annual Report, 1880*, in House of Representatives, *Executive Documents*, 46th Congress, 3rd Session, No. 1, Part 5 (Serial 1959), 85.

36. "Journal of the Eleventh Annual Conference with Representatives of Missionary Boards," January 12, 1882, in Board of Indian Commissioners, *Annual Report, 1881*, in U.S., House of Representatives, *Executive Documents*, 47th Congress, 1st Session, No. 79 (Serial 2027), 77-90. The text of the resolution is on 84-85.

37. *Ibid.*, 90.

38. Indian Appropriations Act, approved May 17, 1882, in U.S., *Statutes at Large*, XX, 70.

39. "Report of the Inspector of Indian Schools," October 10, 1882, in Secretary of the Interior, *Annual Report, 1882*, in U. S., House of Representatives, *Executive Documents*, 47th Congress, 2nd Session, No. 1, Part 5, Vol. II (Serial 2100), 1011-1028. Hereafter cited as "Report of Inspector," 1882.

40. H. M. Teller to Inspector J. M. Haworth, Washington, June 25, 1882, NARS, RG 48, Indian Division, LS, Indian Inspectors, LB, 171.

41. "Report of Inspector," 1882; M. L. Joslyn, Acting Secretary of the Interior, to James M. Haworth, Washington, August 10, 1882; H. M. Teller to Haworth, Washington, October 21, 1882; and Teller to Haworth, Washington, December 30, 1882; all in NARS, RG 48, Indian Division, LS, Indian Inspectors, LB, 176, 204, 214-215.

42. "Report of Inspector," 1882, 1015.

43. Commissioner of Indian Affairs, *Annual Report, 1882*, in U. S., House of Representatives, *Executive Documents*, 47th Congress, 2nd Session, No. 1, Part 5, Vol. II (Serial 2100), 31. Emphasis in original.

44. *Ibid.*, 27.

45. Secretary of the Interior, *Annual Report, 1882*, in U. S., House of Representatives, *Executive Documents*, 47th Congress, 2nd Session, No. 1, Part 5 (Serial 2099), xiv. Peter J. Rahill interpreted this comment as a condemnation of the Peace Policy because of the literary emphasis of most contract school curricula. See his *Catholic Indian Missions*, 323.

46. "Education of Indian Children," February 21, 1882, U. S., Senate, *Executive Documents*, 47th Congress, 1st Session, No, 113 (Serial 1990); Commissioner of Indian Affairs, *Annual Report, 1882*, in U. S., House of Representatives, *Executive Documents*, 47th Congress, 2nd Session, No. 1, Part 5, Vol. II (Serial 2100), 32. Appropriations for education in fulfillment of treaty obligations actually declined between 1877 and 1881, from $78,422 to $57,450. See "Education of Indian Children," 3.

47. Commissioner of Indian Affairs, *Annual Report, 1882*, in U. S., House of Representatives,

Executive Documents, 47th Congress, 2nd Session, No. 1, Part 5, Vol. II (Serial 2100), 32-33.

48. Indian Appropriations Act, approved March 1, 1883, in U. S., *Statutes at Large*, XXII, 448-449.

49. Indian Appropriations Act, approved May 17, 1882, in *Ibid.*, 85-86.

50. Indian Appropriations Act, approved March 1, 1883, in *Ibid.*, 434.

51. Commissioner of Indian Affairs, *Annual Report, 1883*, in U. S., House of Representatives, *Executive Documents*, 48th Congress, 1st Session, No. 1, Part 5, Vol. II (Serial 2191), 27-29.

52. *Ibid.*, 31.

53. *Ibid.*, 5.

54. *Ibid.*, 30.

55. *Ibid.*, 32-33, 298-303. The contract schools enrolled 813 pupils; non-contract schools accounted for 260.

56. R. V. Belt, Acting Commissioner of Indian Affairs, to Daniel Dorchester, Washington, June 18, 1889; Belt to Rev. C. C. McCabe, Corresponding Secretary, Methodist Episcopal Church, Washington, July 5, 1889; both in NARS, RG 75, Chief Clerk, LS (Entry 181). See the Indian Appropriations Acts for 1882 and 1883, in U. S., *Statutes at Large*, XXII, 85-86, 448-449.

57. "Report of the Indian School Superintendent [John H. Oberly]," November 1, 1885, in Commissioner of Indian Affairs, *Annual Report, 1885*, in U. S., House of Representatives, *Executive Documents*, 49th Congress, 1st Session, No. 1, Part 5, Vol. II (Serial 2379), 75. Hereafter cited as "Report of Indian School Superintendent," 1885.

58. "Report of the Superintendent of Indian Schools [James M. Haworth]" September 25, 1883, in Secretary of the Interior, *Annual Report, 1883*, in U. S., House of Representatives, *Executive Documents*, 48th Congress, 1st Session, No. 1, Part 5, Vol. II (Serial 2191), 469-485.

59. "Journal of the Thirteenth Annual Conference with Representatives of Missionary Boards," January 18, 1884, in Board of Indian Commissioners, *Annual Report, 1883*, in *Ibid.*, 724-725.

60. "Journal of Fourteenth Annual Conference with Representatives of Missionary Boards," January 8, 1885, in Board of Indian Commissioners, *Annual Report, 1884*, in U. S., House of Representatives, *Executive Documents*, 48th Congress, 1st Session, No. 1, Part 5, Vol. II (Serial 2287), 732, 737-743.

61. J.D.C. Atkins, Commissioner of Indian Affairs, Order dated July 17, 1885, copy in NARS, RG 75, Chief Clerk, LS (Entry 181).

62. "Report of Indian School Superintendent," 1885, 75.

63. *Ibid.*, 121-122.

64. *Ibid.*, 126-127.

65. See Allan Nevins, *Grover Cleveland: A Study in Courage* (New York, 1932), 250-251.

66. Harry J. Sievers, *Benjamin Harrison: Hoosier President* (Indianapolis, 1968), 144.

67. "The Question of Commissioner Oberly's Retention," Indian Rights Association Pamphlet (Philadelphia, 1889).

68. See pp. 48-49. In 1886, Congress abolished the position of Chief Clerk of the Indian Office, replacing it with an Assistant Commissioner of Indian Affairs. Act of July 31, 1886, in U. S., *Statutes at Large*, XXIV, 200.

69. "Third Annual Meeting of the Lake Mohonk Conference," October 7-9, 1885, in Board of Indian Commissioners, *Annual Report, 1885*, in U. S., House of Representatives, *Executive Documents*, 49th Congress, 1st Session, No. 109 (Serial 2398), 96-103.

70. *Ibid.*, 99-100.

71. "Report of the Indian School Superintendent [John B. Riley]," November 1, 1886, in Secretary of the Interior, *Annual Report, 1886* in U. S., House of Representatives, *Executive Documents*, 49th Congress, 2nd Session, No, 1, Part 5, (Serial 2467), 135.

72. Quoted in L. Q. C. Lamar, Secretary of the Interior, to the President, August 8, 1887 (not sent), attached to J. D. C. Atkins to Lamar, July 6, 1887, NARS, RG 48, Indian Division, LR.

73. Atkins to Lamar, July 6, 1887, NARS, RG 48, Indian Division, LR.

74. R. V. Belt, Chief, Indian Division, Office of the Secretary of the Interior, memorandum, August 19, 1887, attached to Lamar to the President, Washington, August 8, 1887, NARS, RG 48, Indian Division, LR.

75. Lamar to the President, Washington, August 8, 1887, NARS, RG 48, Indian Division, LR.

76. James E. Rhoads, "Our Next Duty to the Indians," Indian Rights Association Pamphlet (Philadelphia, 1887).

77. J. B. Harrison, *The Latest Studies on Indian Reservations* (Philadelphia, 1887), 139-146.

78. *Ibid.*, 186.

79. *Ibid.*, 139-146.

80. John B. Riley to L. Q. C. Lamar, Plattsburgh, N.Y., October 31, 1887, NARS, RG 48, Indian Division, Memorandum and Information File of R. V. Belt.

81. Riley's last annual report as Superintendent of Indian Schools may be found in Secretary of the

Interior, *Annual Report, 1887*, in U. S., House of Representatives, *Executive Documents*, 50th Congress, 1st Session, No. 1, Part 5, Vol. II (Serial 2542), 757-791.

82. Indian Appropriations Act, approved June 29, 1888, Section 8, in U. S., *Statutes at Large*, XXV, 238.

83. Commissioner of Indian Affairs, *Annual Report, 1888*, in U. S., House of Representatives, *Executive Documents*, 50th Congress, 2nd Session, No. 1, Part 5, Vol. II (Serial 2637), xxi-xxiv.

84. Indian Appropriations Act, approved March 2, 1889, Section 10, in U. S., *Statutes at Large*, XXV, 103.

85. R. V. Belt, Acting Commissioner of Indian Affairs, to B. W. Perkins, House of Representatives, Washington, June 6, 1890; Belt to Dr. Daniel Dorchester, Washington, June 7, 1890; both in NARS, RG 75, Chief Clark, LS (Entry 181).

86. R. V. Belt to Daniel Dorchester, Washington, May 26, 1892, NARS, RG 75, Chief Clerk, LS (Entry 181).

87. Belt to Mrs. H. C. McCabe, Washington, June 25, 1889, NARS, RG 75, Chief Clerk, LS (Entry 181).

88. R. V. Belt to Rev. C. C. McCabe, Washington, July 5, 1889, NARS, RG 75, Chief Clerk, LS (Entry 181).

89. Harry J. Sievers, "The Catholic Indian School Issue and the Presidential Election of 1892," *The Catholic Historical Review*, XXXVIII (July, 1952), 129-155.

90. T. J. Morgan to Senator H. L. Dawes, Washington, January 6, 1890, NARS, RG 75, CIA, LS (Entry 165).

91. T. J. Morgan to the Secretary of the Interior, Washington, November 26, 1889; Morgan to Secretary of the Interior, Washington, January 7, 1890; NARS, RG 75, CIA, LS (Entry 165).

92. Morgan to the Secretary of the Interior, Washington, January 7, 1890, NARS, RG 75, CIA, LS (Entry 165).

93. R. V. Belt to Mrs. H. C. McCabe, Washington, August 15, 1889, NARS, RG 75, Chief Clerk, LS (Entry 181); T. J. Morgan to [E. W.] Halford, Washington, January 13, 1891, NARS, RG 75, CIA, LS (Entry 165).

94. Sievers, "The Catholic Indian School Issue," 140-141.

95. Thomas J. Morgan to E. W. Halford, Washington, July 20, 1891, NARS, RG 75, CIA, LS (Entry 165). See also Morgan to Halford, Washington, July 14, 1891; Morgan to the Secretary of the Interior, Washington, July 14, 1891; Morgan to J. Cardinal Gibbons, Archbishop of Baltimore, Washington, July 16, 1891; all in NARS, RG 75, CIA, LS (Entry 165).

96. Sievers, "The Catholic Indian School Issue," 150.

97. "Report of Special Agent in the Indian School Service [Merial A. Dorchester]," September 2, 1889, in Commissioner of Indian Affairs, *Annual Report, 1889*, in U. S., House of Representatives, *Executive Documents*, 51st Congress, 1st Session, No. 1, Part 5, Vol. II (Serial 2725), 342-346.

98. Mrs. Merial A. Dorchester, "Suggestions from the Field," in Commissioner of Indian Affairs, *Annual Report, 1891*, in U. S., House of Representatives, *Executive Documents*, 52nd Congress, 1st Session, No. 1, Part 5, Vol. II (Serial 2934), 542-548. Indian Appropriations Act, approved March 3, 1891, in U. S., *Statutes at Large*, XXVI, 1009. For an account of the activities of Indian Service field matrons in the 1920s, see Elinor D. Gregg, *The Indians and the Nurse* (Norman, Oklahoma, 1965), 19-25.

99. "Report of Supervisor of Education among the Sioux [Elaine Goodale]" September 27, 1890, in Commissioner of Indian Affairs, *Annual Report, 1890*, in U. S., House of Representatives, *Executive Documents*, 51st Congress, 2nd Session, No. 1, Part 5, Vol. II (Serial 2841), 276-279; T. J. Morgan to the Secretary of the Interior, Washington, July 11, 1890, and Morgan to Miss Elaine Goodale, Washington, July 1, 1890, NARS, RG 75, CIA, LS (Entry 165).

100. Commissioner of Indian Affairs, *Annual Report, 1889*, in U. S., House of Representatives, *Executive Documents*, 51st Congress, 1st Session, No. 1, Part 5, Vol. II (Serial 2725), 335-336. See also T. J. Morgan to the Secretary of the Interior, Washington, May 8, 1890, NARS, RG 75, CIA, LS (Entry 165).

101. T. J. Morgan to Professor W. Rich, Washington, May 21, 1890, NARS, RG 75, CIA, LS (Entry 165).

102. Indian Appropriations Act, approved August 19, 1890, in U. S., *Statutes at Large*, XXVI, 338.

103. T. J. Morgan to Daniel Dorchester, Washington, August 26, 1890, NARS, RG 75, CIA, LS (Entry 165).

104. See T. J. Morgan to R. V. Belt, Washington, July 1, 1891, NARS, RG 75, CIA, LS (Entry 165).

105. See T. J. Morgan to Rev. J. H. Meteer, Washington, August 12, 1890, NARS, RG 75, CIA, LS (Entry 165).

106. T. J. Morgan to E. E. Riopel, Washington, April 21, 1892, NARS, RG 75, CIA, LS (Entry 165).

107. "Reports of Supervisors of Education," in Commissioner of Indian Affairs, *Annual Report, 1892*, in U. S., House of Representatives, *Executive Documents*, 52nd Congress, 2nd Session, No. 1, Part 5, Vol. II (Serial 3088), 619-646. Morgan commented, "Under the system of supervision now in successful operation, the schools are receiving a kind and amount of oversight which have never been extended to them before, and by reason of this the quality of the work done in them has greatly improved." *Ibid.*, 59.

108. "Report of the Superintendent of Indian Schools [Daniel Dorchester]," August 16, 1892, in *Ibid.*, 526-599.

109. Commissioner of Indian Affairs, *Annual Report, 1891*, in U. S., House of Representatives,

Executive Documents, 52nd Congress, 1st Session, No. 1, Part 5, Vol. II (Serial 2934), 54; T. J. Morgan to T. B Reed, House of Representatives, Washington, February 23, 1892; Memorandum, "Work and Accomplishments in the First Three Years of the Harrison Administration," undated, In Morgan to H. C. Lodge, House of Representatives, Washington, February 25, 1892, both in NARS, RG 75, CIA, LS (Entry 165).

110. D. M. Browning to Frank W. Beane, Washington, July 1, 1893, NARS, RG 75, CIA, LS (Entry 165).

111. John H. Seger to C. C. Painter, Seger, Oklahoma Territory, May 29, 1894, copy enclosed in Charles C. Painter to the Secretary of the Interior, Washington, June 18, 1894; W. H. Hailmann to the Secretary of the Interior, May 23, 1894, NARS, RG 48, Indian Division, LR.

112. Herbert Welsh, "The Secretary of the Interior and the Indian Educational Problem—A Rift in the Cloud," Indian Rights Association Pamphlet, 2nd Series, No. 12 (Philadelphia, 1893).

113. W. N. Hailmann to the Secretary of the Interior, Washington, February 5, 1894; Hailmann to Secretary of the Interior, May 28, 1894; Hailmann to Secretary, November 20, 1894; all in NARS, RG 48, Indian Division, LR.

114. Herbert Welsh, "The Position of Superintendent of Indian Schools Threatened—A Serious Danger to be Averted," Indian Rights Association Pamphlet, 2nd Series, No. 14 (Philadelphia, April 12, 1894); "Indian School Welfare" and "Suspicious Economy" reprinted from the New York *Evening Post* and the New York *Times*, April 27, 1893 [sic—should be 1894] as Indian Rights Association Pamphlet No. 16, 2nd Series (Philadelphia, 1894).

115. W. C. Pollock, Chief, Indian Division, to Josephus Daniels, Chief Clerk, Department of the Interior, Washington, September 26, 1894; William H. Hailmann to Secretary of the Interior, Washington, October 8, 1894; both in NARS, RG 48, Indian Division, LR, Box 740.

116. See, for example, Indian Appropriations Act, approved March 1, 1899, in U. S., *Statutes at Large*, XXX, 924.

117. W. A. Jones to Miss Estelle Reel, Washington, November 21, 1900, NARS, RG 75, CIA, LS (Entry 165).

118. Selznick, *Leadership in Administration*, 61-64.

119. Alfred D. Chandler, Jr., *Strategy and Structure: Chapters in the History of the Industrial Enterprise* (Cambridge, 1962), 383.

120. In 1928, the authors of the Meriam Survey concluded that "The whole [Indian] problem must be regarded as fundamentally educational." While the survey staff believed that Indians who did not wish to assimilate should be helped "to live in the presence of [white] civilization in accordance with a minimum standard of health and decency," changes in the surroundings the reservation made maintenance of the old culture impossible. Institute for Government Research, *The Problem of Indian Administration* (Baltimore, 1928), 86-89.

CHAPTER X

1. See Helen M. Bannan, "The Idea of Civilization and American Indian Policy Reformers in the 1880s," *Journal of American Culture*, I (Winter, 1978), 787-799.

2. U. S., Bureau of the Census, *Historical Statistics of the United States, Colonial Times to 1970* (Washington, 1975), Series Y 308, II, 1102-1103.

3. *Ibid.*, Series Y 336, II, 1104.

4. Deflators for constant dollar values computed from G. F. Warren and F. A. Pearson, "Wholesale Prices in the United States for 135 Years, 1797 to 1932," in *Wholesale Prices for 213 Years, 1720-1932* (Ithaca, N.Y., 1932), 6-10. See Notes 22 and 23, Chapter IX. The Warren-Pearson wholesale price index for the fiscal year 1870-71 was 102 (1873-74 = 100).

5. *Historical Statistics of the United States*, Series Y 904, II, 1141-1142.

6. *Ibid.*, Series Y 308-311, II, 1102-1103.

7. Jonathan R. T. Hughes, *The Governmental Habit: Economic Controls from Colonial Times to the Present* (New York, 1977), 96-103.

8. Theodore Roosevelt to P. H. Grace, October 19, 1908, quoted in Samuel P. Hays, *Conservation and the Gospel of Efficiency: The Progressive Conservation Movement, 1890-1920* (Cambridge, 1959), 267-268.

9. Wright, appointed as the first Commissioner of Labor in 1885, served until 1905. Wright had served as Chief of the Massachusetts Bureau of Statistics and Labor from 1873 until Cleveland appointed him to the federal post. Sixteen states had Bureaus of Labor Statistics in 1885; by 1903, such bureaus existed in thirty-four states. G. W. W. Hanger, "Bureaus of Statistics of Labor in the United States," *Bulletin of the Bureau of Labor*, No. 54 (September, 1904), 993. For an account of Wright's career and the state and federal bureaus, see James Leiby, *Caroll Wright and Labor Reform: The Origin of Labor Statistics* (Cambridge, 1960).

10. Carl Grafton, "The Creation of Federal Agencies," *Administration and Society*, VII (November, 1975), 359.

11. *Ibid.*, 332-339.

12. *Ibid.*, 339.

13. *Ibid.*, 341.

14. Herbert Kaufman, *Are Government Organizations Immortal?* (Washington, 1976), 66.

15. *Ibid.*, 48-49.

16. Nelson W. Polsby, "The Institutionalization of the U. S. House of Representatives," *American Political Science Review*, LXII (March, 1968), 164-165.

17. Ari Hoogenboom, "An Analysis of Civil Service Reformers," *The Historian*, XXIII (November, 1960), 78.

18. Philip M. Sleznick, *Leadership in Administration: A Sociological Interpretation* (New York, 1957), 56-61.

19. *Ibid.*, 62-64.

20. Loring Benson Priest, *Uncle Sam's Stepchildren: The Reformation of United States Indian Policy, 1865-1887* (New Brunswick, N. J., 1942), 22.

21. Alan L. Sorkin, *American Indians and Federal Aid* (Washington, 1971), 1-20.

22. Helen W. Johnson, "American Indians in Rural Poverty," in U. S., Congress, Joint Economic Committee, *Toward Economic Development for Native American Communities* (1969; reprint edition, New York, 1970), 19; the Meriam Report concluded, "An overwhelming majority of the Indians are poor, even extremely poor, and they are not adjusted to the economic and social system of the dominant white civilization." Institute for Government Research, *The Problem of Indian Administration* (Baltimore, 1928), 3.

23. Albert Jenny II, "The American Indian: Needs and Problems," in *Toward Economic Development for Native American Communites,* 52.

24. William T. Hagan, *American Indians* (Chicago, 1961), 147-150.

25. *The Problem of Indian Administration*, 140-141.

26. Francis E. Leupp, *In Red Man's Land: A Study of the American Indian* (New York, 1914),45.

27. *Ibid.*, 43-46; Commissioner of Indian Affairs, *Annual Report, 1911-12* (Washington, 1912), 15-16.

28. Leupp, *In Red Man's Land*, 46.

29. Warren K. Moorehead, *The American Indian in the United States, Period 1850-1914* (Andover, Mass., 1914), 66-98.

30. *Ibid.*, 25.

31. Commissioner of Indian Affairs, *Annual Report, 1911-12* (Washington, 1912), 17.

32. *Ibid.*, 71.

33. *Ibid.*, 17-19.

34. In 1921, the Board of Indian Commissioners called for improvements in the Indian Service personnel classification system. Board of Indian Commissioners, *Annual Report, 1920-21* (Washington, 1921), 13-14. Five years later, hailing an administrative reorganization which promised to tighten Washington office supervision of the field units, the commissioners observed, "For some time it has been apparent to close observers that there are too many individualistic tendencies in the Indian field service." Board of Indian Commissioners, *Annual Report, 1925-26* (Washington, 1926), 2. In the same year the commissioners urged the Congress to place the Commissioner of Indian Affairs within the classified civil service. *Ibid.*, 4-5.

35. Paul Stuart, "United States Indian Policy: From the Dawes Act to the American Indian Policy Review Commission," *Social Service Review*, LI (September, 1977), 451-463. For an account of an Indian leader who opposed the Indian New Deal see Donald Parman, "J. C. Morgan: Navajo Apostle of Assimilation," *Prologue: The Journal of the National Archives*, IV (Summer, 1972), 83-98. Kenneth R. Philp discussed Indian opposition to the Indian New Deal in the context of the commitment to assimilation in "John Collier and the Controversy over the Wheeler-Howard Bill," in *Indian-White Relations: A Persistent Paradox*, edited by Jane F. Smith and Robert M. Kvasnicka (Washington, 1976), 171-200. See also Mary E. Young's valuable "Commentary" on Philp's paper in the same volume, 212-214, and Philp's assessment of Commissioner Collier's "Failure to Create a Red Atlantis," in *John Collier's Crusade for Indian Reform, 1920-1954* (Tucson, Ariz., 1977), 135-160.

36. See p. 11.

37. Henry E. Fritz, *The Movement for Indian Assimilation, 1860-1890* (Philadelphia, 1963), 221.

38. U. S., Congress, *American Indian Policy Review Commission: Final Report* [Committee Print] (Washington, 1977), I, 286-288.

BIBLIOGRAPHIC ESSAY

The student of Indian administration is confronted by an imposing and seemingly impenetrable mass of documents, government documents, monographs, and articles. This essay can only name the more important sources for a study of the Indian Office. Fortunately, the student can turn to Francis Paul Prucha's monumental *Bibliographical Guide to the History of Indian-White Relations in the United States* (1977), which is an indispensable reference tool. Prucha's critical bibliography on *United States Indian Policy* (1977), in the Newberry Library Center for the History of the American Indian Bibliographical Series, provides a briefer, more focused introduction. Recent writings on the history of Indian-white relations are summarized in Prucha's essay, "Books on American Indian Policy: A Half-Decade of Important Work, 1970-1975," *Journal of American History*, LXIII (December, 1976), and William T. Hagan, "On Writing the History of the American Indian," *Journal of Interdisciplinary History*, II (Summer, 1971). In June, 1972, the National Archives and Records Service sponsored a Conference on Research in the History of Indian-White Relations. The papers and proceedings of that conference, published as *Indian-White Relations: A Persistent Paradox*, edited by Jane F. Smith and Robert M. Kvasnicka (1976), provide a survey of the major resources for the study of Indian-government relations as well as reports on much recent research in the field.

The basic source for studies of organizational development, when the organization itself cannot be observed, is the organization's internal records, supplemented by the public documents produced by the organization. The internal records of the Indian Office are held by the National Archives and Records Service; the National Archives also has an excellent collection of printed Indian Office documents in its Printed Archives Branch. Indian Office records in the National Archives are collected in Record Group 75, Records of the Bureau of Indian Affairs. *The Preliminary Inventory of the Records of the Bureau of Indian Affairs (Record Group 75)* (2 vols., 1965), compiled by Edward E. Hill, is an admirable guide to this collection.

The letters sent by the Commissioner of Indian Affairs, 1871-1901 (Entry 165) and by the Chief Clerk and Assistant Commissioner, 1871-1893 (Entry 181) provide an inside look at the Indian Office's operation, as do the "Report on Methods," 1877 (Entry 169) and some of the items in Special Series A, 1859-1934 (Entry 126). The Inspectors' Reports, 1873-1880 (Entry 951) have been removed from Record Group 75 and consolidated with the Inspectors' Reports, 1880-1907, in Record Group 48, Records of the Secretary of the Interior. The pre-1900 reports are soon to be published as a National Archives Microfilm Publication. Other inspection reports and investigations, by personnel other than inspectors, may be found in the Special Files of the Office of Indian Affairs, 1807-1904 (Entry 98), National Archives Microfilm Publication 575.

Record Group 48, Records of the Office of the Secretary of the Interior, includes, in addition to the Inspectors' Reports, materials on appointments and other aspects of administration. An inventory is available at the National Archives building. The records of the Boards of Inquiry, convened during the early years of Carl Schurz's administration, are particularly interesting. Schurz's papers, in the Library of Congress, add useful detail. Much of his correspondence is also available in *Speeches, Correspondence and Political Papers of Carl Schurz* (6 vols., 1913), edited by Frederic Bancroft. The correspondence and minutes of meetings of the Civil Service Commission, in Record Group 146, Records of the U. S. Civil Service Commission, are useful for understanding the operation of the civil service system, which became increasingly important to the Indian Office in the years after 1891.

The publications of the Indian Office and of the Department of the Interior provide much useful information, although these sources must be used with care, since they reveal what administrators wanted to make public. Many of the documents issued by the executive department appear in the Congressional Serial Set; the *Checklist of United States Public Documents, 1789-1909* (3rd ed., 1911), issued by the Superintendent of Documents, provides a convenient means of checking the location of departmental publications in the Serial Set. I found the *CIS U.S. Serial Set Index*

(12 parts; 1975-79) to be more useful than Poore's *Descriptive Catalogue of the Government Publications of the United States, September 5, 1774-March 4, 1881* (1885) or Ames' *Comprehensive Index to the Publications of the United States Government* 1881-1893 (2 vols., 1905). The *Guide to American Indian Documents in the Congressional Serial Set: 1817-1899* (1977), compiled by Steven L. Johnson, is also useful.

The *Executive Documents* of the House of Representatives include the *Annual Reports* of the Civil Service Commission, the Secretary of the Interior, the Commissioner of Indian Affairs, and, for most years, the Board of Indian Commissioners. The "Tabular Statements of Disbursements" made by the Indian Office in the fiscal years 1873-74 through 1892-93 and in fiscal year 1894-95, along with the "Report to the President by the Indian Peace Commission, January 7, 1868," and a number of other documents are also to be found in the House *Executive Documents*. Francis Paul Prucha provides a convenient guide to the location of the *Annual Reports* of the Secretary of the Interior and the Commissioner of Indian Affairs in his *American Indian Policy in Crisis* (1976), pp. 405-410. The location of the other documents may be determined by consulting the *Checklist*.

The other series in the Serial Set provides occasional documents of interest, such as the 1867 report of the Doolittle Commission, published as "Condition of the Indian Tribes," in the Senate *Reports*, and the 1879 "Report of the Joint Transfer Committee," in the Senate *Miscellaneous Documents*. The location of these documents may also be determined by referring to the *Checklist*, the *CIS U.S. Serial Set Index*, or the *Guide to American Indian Materials in the Congressional Serial Set*.

Many of the departmental publications do not appear in the Serial Set, in particular the compilations of regulations issued by the Indian Office and the reports resulting from several special investigations. The *Report of Board of Inquiry Convened . . . to Investigate Certain Charges Against S.A. Galpin* (1878) covers a broad range of administrative issues; Galpin's *Report upon the Condition and Management of Certain Indian Agencies in the Indian Territory* (1877) defends his administration. These publications are listed, under the appropriate issuing agency, in the *Checklist*, which provides the Superintendent of Documents catalog number for each publication.

The *Statutes at Large* of the United States contain the laws which circumscribed the Indian Office's activity. Also in the *Statutes* are the treaties with Indian tribes ratified by the Senate before 1871 and the agreements with tribes approved by the Congress after that date. Charles J. Kappler's *Indian Affairs: Laws and Treaties* (5 vols., 1904-1947) is a convenient compilation of most of this material.

The Indian Rights Association carried out an ambitious publication program during the 1880s and '90s; the association's pamphlets provide an outside evaluation of developments in Indian administration. The publications, all of which are included in the microfilm publication, *Papers of the Indian Rights Association, 1882-1968* (1973), focus on allotment, education, and civil service reform. Administrators discuss their policies, and defend their administrations, in Francis A. Walker, *The Indian Question* (1874); Carl Schurz, "Present Aspects of the Indian Problem," *North American Review*, CXXXIII (July, 1881); S.A. Galpin, "Some Administrative Difficulties of the Indian Problem," *New Englander and Yale Review*, XLVI (April, 1887); and two books by Francis E. Leupp, *The Indian and His Problem* (1910) and *In Red Man's Land* (1914).

The literature on formal organizations is extensive; Charles Perrow, *Complex Organizations* (1972) provides a useful introduction. Max Weber is still worth reading; in addition to the two collections of his writings, edited by H. H. Gerth and C. Wright Mills (1946) and Talcott Parsons (1947), an edition of his *Economy and Society* is available in English, edited by Guenther Roth and Claus Wittich (3 vols., 1968). Philip Selznick's ideas, on which I rely for the framework of this study, are well expressed in his books, *TVA and the Grass Roots* (1949) and *Leadership and Administration* (1957), and in two articles, "An Approach to a Theory of Bureaucracy," *American Sociological Review*, VIII (February, 1943), and "Foundations of the Theory of Organization," in the same journal, XIII (February, 1948). James D. Thompson and William J. McEwan explicate Selznick's ideas regarding the relationship between organizations and their environments in "Organizational Goals and Environment," *American Sociological Review*, XXIII (February, 1958).

Selznick's student, Charles Perrow, provides an excellent institutional history of a general hospital in "Goals and Power Structures: A Historical Case Study," in *The Hospital in Modern Society* (1963), edited by Eliot Freidson. The essays by Nelson Polsby (1968) and Allan G. Bogue, Jerome M. Clubb, Carroll R. McKibbin, and Santa A. Traugott (1976) on the House of Representatives are analytical. Alfred D. Chandler's *Strategy and Structure* (1962) is useful for developments in big business.

Robert H. Wiebe, *The Search for Order, 1877-1920* (1967), is an excellent synthesis, on which I rely extensively. Developments in federal administration between 1869 and 1901 are reviewed in Leonard D. White, *The Republican Era* (1963). The civil service reform movement before 1883 is discussed by Ari Hoogenboom in *Outlawing the Spoils* (1961); he covers developments after 1883 in "The Pendleton Act and the Civil Service," *American Historical Review*, LXIV (January, 1957). Harry J. Carman and Reinhard J. Luthin discuss presidential appointments before the era of the civil service reform movement in *Lincoln and the Patronage* (1943). Eric McKitrick, *Andrew Johnson and Reconstruction* (1960), is useful for developments in the Johnson administration.

Robert F. Berkhofer, Jr., in "Space, Time, Culture and the New Frontier," *Agricultural History*, XXXVIII (January, 1964), presents some provocative ideas on the role of the frontier in the nineteenth century. Jack Ericson Eblen's discussion of the territorial system in *The First and Second United States Empires* (1968) is excellent. Earl Pomeroy's *The Territories and the United States* (1947) is still worth reading. Robert M. Utley, in *Frontiersmen in Blue* (1967) and *Frontier Regulars* (1973), covers military-Indian relations.

Utley's books provide useful insights into the military evaluation of late nineteenth century Indian policy and administration. His essay on "The Frontier Army: John Ford or Arthur Penn?" in *Indian-White Relations* (1976), touches on what the probable results of a transfer of the Indian Office to the Department of War would have been. Henry G. Waltmann's 1962 dissertation on "The Interior Department, War Department, and Indian Policy, 1865-1887," provides useful detail. Richard M. Ellis focuses on one military leader, in *General Pope and U.S. Indian Policy* (1970).

S. Lyman Tyler's *A History of Indian Policy* (1973) is the only one-volume account, although William T. Hagan's *American Indians* (1961) is useful, and Laurence F. Schmeckebier's discussion in *The Office of Indian Affairs* (1927) is still valuable. Several excellent monographs on United States Indian policy in the late nineteenth century are available. The best, and most recent, of these is Francis Paul Prucha, *American Indian Policy in Crisis* (1976), but Henry E. Fritz, *The Movement for Indian Assimilation* (1963), and Loring Benson Priest, *Uncle Sam's Stepchildren* (1942), remain valuable. Priest discusses recent writings on post-Civil War Indian policy (but not Prucha) in a "Commentary" in *Indian-White Relations* (1976). Robert A. Trennert, Jr., discusses Indian policy at midcentury, in *Alternative to Extinction* (1975). Edmund Jefferson Danziger, Jr., discusses Indian administration during the Civil War in *Indians and Bureaucrats* (1974).

Robert Winston Mardock emphasizes the role of the reformers in his study of *The Reformers and the American Indian* (1971). He provides a great deal of detail on the Ponca controversy during the Hayes administration, which resulted in a break between the reformers and Interior Secretary Schurz. In "The Board of Indian Commissioners and Ethnocentric Reform, 1878-1893," included in *Indian-White Relations* (1976), Henry Fritz discusses the functions of the Board after the Grant administration. In *The Lake Mohonk Conference of Friends of the Indian* (1975), Larry E. Burgess discusses the significance of that semi-official annual gathering of reformers, Indian administrators, and Congressmen.

Many specialized studies illuminate our understanding of specific aspects of late nineteenth century Indian policy. Kenneth E. Davison covers Indian Affairs in *The Presidency of Rutherford B. Hayes* (1972). While his assessment of Secretary Schurz's accomplishments emphasizes programatic innovations rather than administrative accomplishments, he provides a useful review. The most important programatic innovations were allotment, Indian police, and the off-reservation Indian boarding school. On allotment, D. S. Otis' *The Dawes Act and the Allotment of Indian Lands* (1934; revised edition, 1974) is basic; Wilcomb E. Washburn, in *The Assault on Indian Tribalism* (1975), reprints the basic documents with a valuable introductory essay. William T. Hagan's *Indian Police and Judges* (1966) is the only book-length treatment of an important subject. The development of the off-reservation boarding school owed much to Richard Henry Pratt; *Battlefield and Classroom*, his autobiography, was published in 1964 in an edition edited by Robert M. Utley. It supplants Elaine Goodale Eastman's *Pratt: The Red Man's Moses* (1935). Margaret Szasz discusses the boarding schools in *Education and the American Indian* (1974). Hazel W. Herzberg assesses the importance of the boarding schools for developing twentieth-century Indian leadership in *The Search for an American Indian Identity* (1971). Helen M. Bannan shows how these innovations came together to form a coherent Indian policy in "The Idea of Civilization and American Indian Policy Reformers in the 1880s,'' *Journal of American Culture*, I (Winter, 1978). Her essay should be read along with Hagan's "The Reservation Policy: Too Little and Too Late," in *Indian-White Relations* (1976), which emphasizes the failure to implement the policy and the consequences for the Indians.

Tribal histories provide evidence for the effects of federal policy on American Indian groups. Robert F. Berkhofer, Jr., provides a model for examining the effects of Indian-White contact on tribes in *Salvation and the Savage* (1965). Berkhofer emphasized the disintegrative potential of white contact on Indian communities; the pre-Civil War communities he studied often divided into factions advocating and rejecting cooperation with whites after they had been contacted by Christian missionaries. While none of the tribal histories of the post-Civil War period, with the possible exception of Deward Walker's, have adopted Berkhofer's framework, it remains an interesting and powerful hypothesis.

Walker's *Conflict and Schism in Nez Perce Acculturation* (1968) emphasized religion. The studies of William T. Hagan, *United States—Commanche Relations* (1976), and Donald J. Berthrong, *The Cheyenne and Arapahoe Ordeal* (1976), emphasize the effect of the civilization policy on land and its uses, as well as the intrusion of Whites on the reservations. Roy W. Meyer's *History of the Santee Sioux* (1967) emphasizes United States Indian policy and covers the late nineteenth century well. John Bret Harte's 1972 dissertation, "The San Carlos Indian Reservation, 1872-1887," is an administrative history.

No collective biography has replaced Flora Warren Seymour's anecdotal *Indian Agents of the Old Frontier* (1941). Such a work is needed, since the Indian agents occupied a strategic position in the Indian Office structure. Francis Paul Prucha suggested the potential of organizational theory for histories of Indian-White relations in "New Approaches to the Study of the Administration of Indian Policy," *Prologue*, III (Spring, 1971). H. Craig Miner, in "A Corps of Clerks," *Chronicles of Oklahoma*, LIII (Fall, 1975), describes the prominence of administrators in the life of late nineteenth century Indian Territory. In *The Corporation and the Indian* (1976), he discusses the intrusion of businesses on Indian sovereignty in the territory during the late nineteenth century.

I try to summarize twentieth century developments in "United States Indian Policy: From the Dawes Act to the American Indian Policy Review Commission," *Social Service Review*, LI (September, 1977). Two basic sources for Indian policy and administration in the twentieth century are the report of the Meriam Survey, published in 1928 by The Institute for Government Research as *The Problem of Indian Administration*, and the various reports of the American Indian Policy Review Commission, summarized in its *Final Report* (1977). Kenneth R. Philp, in *John Collier's Crusade for Indian Reform, 1920-1954* (1977), provides an account of Franklin D. Roosevelt's Commissioner of Indian Affairs. Lawrence C. Kelly's long-awaited study of Collier is soon to be published by the University of New Mexico Press. Kelly, in *The Navajo Indians and Federal Indian Policy, 1900-1935* (1968), and Donald L. Parman, in *The Navajos and the New Deal* (1976), cover developments on the largest reservation in the United States to World War II.

BIBLIOGRAPHY

I. PRIMARY SOURCES

A. MANUSCRIPTS

1. **Library of Congress, Washington, D.C.**

   Carl Schurz Papers
      Correspondence
      Scrapbooks

2. **National Archives and Records Service, Washington, D.C.**

   Record Group 48, Records of the Office of the Secretary of the Interior

      Appointments Division, Letters Sent and Letters Received

      Indian Division, Letters Sent and Letters Received

      Memorandum and Information File of R. V. Belt

      Special Records Letterbooks

   Record Group 75, Records of the Bureau of Indian Affairs

      Office of Indian Affairs, Letters Received, 1824-1880 (Entry 79, NARS Microfilm Publication 234)

      Office of Indian Affairs, Letters Sent, 1824-1886 (Entry 84)

      Office of Indian Affairs, Letters Received, 1881-1907 (Entry 91)

      Special Files of the Office of Indian Affairs, 1807-1904 (Entry 98, NARS Microfilm Publication 575)

      Special Series A, 1859-1934 (Entry 126)

      Commissioner of Indian Affairs, Letters Sent (Entry 165)

      Report on Methods, 1877 (Entry 169)

      Chief Clerk and Assistant Commissioner, Letters Sent (Entry 181)

      Abstracts of Inspectors' Reports, 1873-1880 (Entry 950)

      Inspectors' Reports, 1873-1880 (Entry 951)

      Rosters of Field Officials, 1849-1911 (Entry 976)

      Rosters of Agency Employees, 1853-1909 (Entry 978)

School Personnel Rating Books, 1889-1895 (Entry 990)

Index for School Employee Efficiency Ratings, 1895-1906 (Entry 991)

School Employee Efficiency Ratings, 1895-1906 (Entry 992)

Record Group 146, Records of the U.S. Civil Service Commission

Letters Sent

Letters Received

B. U.S. GOVERNMENT PUBLICATIONS

Note: Unless otherwise indicated, all government publications were published by the Government Printing Office.

1. Congressional Documents

a. *Serial Set*

House of Representatives, *Executive Documents*

"Indian Affairs in the Territories of Oregon and Washington," November 17, 1857, 35th Congress, 1st Session, No. 39 (Serial 955).

"Report to the President by the Indian Peace Commission," January 7, 1868, 40th Congress, 2nd Session, No. 97 (Serial 1337).

"Subsistence of Indian Tribes," May 26, 1868, 40th Congress, 2nd Session, No. 239 (Serial 1341).

"Indians in the Central Superintendency," December 18, 1873, 43rd Congress, 1st Session, No. 24 (Serial 1606).

"Tabular Statement of Disbursements made from the Appropriations for the Indian Department for the Fiscal Year Ending July 30, 1874 . . ." 43rd Congress, 2nd Session, No. 6 (Serial 1341).

————, 1875, 44th Congress, 1st Session, No. 6 (Serial 1685).

————, 1876, 44th Congress, 2nd Session, No. 6 (Serial 1754).

————, 1877, 45th Congress, 2nd Session, No. 6 (Serial 1805).

————, 1878, 45th Congress, 2nd Session, No. 6 (Serial 1855).

————, 1879, 46th Congress, 2nd Session, No. 6 (Serial 1916).

————, 1880, 46th Congress, 3rd Session, No. 6 (Serial 1965).

————, 1881, 47th Congress, 1st Session, No. 6 (Serial 2024).

————, 1882, 47th Congress, 2nd Session, No. 6 (Serial 2106).

————, 1883, 48th Congress, 1st Session, No. 6 (Serial 2193).

————, 1884, 48th Congress, 2nd Session, No. 6 (Serial 2290).

————, 1885, 49th Congress, 1st Session, No. 6 (Serial 2387).

————, 1886, 49th Congress, 2nd Session, No. 6 (Serial 2477).

————, 1887, 50th Congress, 1st Session, No. 8 (Serial 2550).

————, 1888, 50th Congress, 2nd Session, No. 8 (Serial 2645).

————, 1889, 51st Congress, 1st Session, No. 8 (Serial 2739).

————, 1890, 51st Congress, 2nd Session, No. 8 (Serial 2855).

————, 1891, 52nd Congress, 1st Session, No. 8 (Serial 2949).

————, 1892, 52nd Congress, 2nd Session, No. 239 (Serial 3107).

————, 1893, 53rd Congress, 2nd Session, No. 36 (Serial 3223).

————, 1895, 54th Congress, 1st Session, No. 36 (Serial 3414).

House of Representatives, *Reports*

"Affairs in the Indian Department," February 21, 1874, 41st Congress, 3rd Session, No. 39 (Serial 1464).

Senate, *Executive Documents*

"Indian Hostilities," July 13, 1867, 40th Congress, 1st Session, No. 13 (Serial 1308).

"Medical Inspector for the Indian Service," January 18, 1882, 47th Congress, 1st Session, No. 59 (Serial 1987).

"Education of Indian Children," February 21, 1882, 47th Congress, 1st Session, No. 113 (Serial 1990).

Indian Education and Civilization, by Alice C. Fletcher, 1885, 48th Congress, 2nd Session, No. 95 (Serial 2264).

Senate, *Miscellaneous Documents*

"Report of the Joint Transfer Committee," 1879, 45th Congress, 3rd Session, No. 53 (Serial 1835).

Senate, *Reports*

"Condition of the Indian Tribes, Report of the Joint Special Committee Appointed Under Joint Resolution of March 3, 1865," January 26, 1867, 39th Congress, 2nd Session, No. 156 (Serial 1279).

b.   *Other Congressional Publications*

American Indian Policy Review Commission, *Final Report* [Committee Print] (Washington, 1977).

Biographical Directory of the American Congress, 1774-1971 (Washington, 1971).

Comptroller General, *Report to the Congress: Federal Management Weaknesses Cry Out for Alternatives to Deliver Programs and Services to Indians to Improve Their Quality of Life* (Washington: General Accounting Office, 1978).

Congressional Globe, 41st Congress, 1869-1871.

Joint Economic Committee, *Toward Economic Development for Native American Communities* (Washington, 1969; reprint edition, New York: Arno Press, 1970).

Kappler, Charles J., comp., *Indian Affairs: Laws and Treaties* (5 Vols., Washington, 1904-1941).

U.S., *Statutes at Large*, IV, IX-XXXIV.

Warren King and Associates, Inc., *Bureau of Indian Affairs Management Study: Report on BIA Management Practices to the American Indian Policy Review Commission* [Committee Print] (Washington, 1976).

2.   Departmental (Executive Branch) Publications

Note: Many departmental publications are included in the Congressional Serial Set. Cross-listings are provided in the *Checklist of United States Public Documents, 1789-1909* (Washington, 1911).

a.   *Civil Service Commission*

Annual Reports, 1883 [January 16, 1883-January 16, 1884], 1890-1891, 1891-1892, 1892-1893, 1893-1894, 1894-1895, 1895-1896.

b.   *Department of Commerce*

Bureau of the Census, *Historical Statistics of the United States, Colonial Times to 1970* (2 vols., Washington, 1975).

c.   *Department of the Interior*

Secretary of the Interior, *Annual Reports*, 1865-1900.

General publications, Department of the Interior:

History and Business Methods of the Department of the Interior, Its Bureaus and Offices, by Emmett Womack (Washington, 1897).

Register of Officers and Agents, Civil, Military, and Naval, in the Service of the United States on the Thirtieth of September, 1865 (Washington, 1866).

——, 1867 (Washington, 1868).

——, 1869 (Washington, 1870).

——, 1871 (Washington, 1872).

——, 1873 (Washington, 1874).

————, 1875 (Washington, 1876).

————, 1877 (Washington, 1878).

Official Register of the United States, Containing a list of Officers and Employes in the Civil, Military, and Naval Service on the Thirtieth of June, 1879 (Washington, 1879).

————, 1881 (Washington, 1881).

————, 1883 (Washington, 1883).

————, 1885 (Washington, 1885).

————, 1887 (Washington, 1887).

————, 1889 (Washington, 1889).

————, 1891 (Washington, 1891).

————, 1893 (Washington, 1893).

————, 1895 (Washington, 1895).

————, 1897 (Washington, 1897).

Board of Indian Commissioners, *Annual Reports*, 1869-1886, 1920-21, 1925-26.

Commissioner of Education, *Annual Report*, 1899-1900.

Commissioner of Indian Affairs, *Annual Reports*, 1856, 1865-1900, 1911-12.

General publications, Indian Office:

Handbook of Federal Indian Law, by Felix Cohen (Washington, 1942).

Report of Board of Inquiry convened by Authority of the Secretary of the Interior of June 7, 1877, to Investigate Certain Charges Against S. A. Galpin, Chief Clerk of the Indian Bureau, and Concerning Irregularities in Said Bureau (Washington, 1878).

Report of Special Commission to Investigate Affairs of Red Cloud Indian Agency (Washington, 1875).

Report upon the Condition and Management of Certain Indian Agencies in the Indian Agencies in the Indian Territory, now under the Supervision of the Orthodox Friends, by S. A. Galpin (Washington, 1877).

Compilations of Laws, Instructions, and Regulations:

Instructions to Indian Agents (Washington, 1877).

————(Washington, 1880).

Instructions to Superintendents and Indian Agents (Washington, 1876).

————(Washington, 1877).

Laws and Instructions Relating to the Duties of Inspectors of the United States Indian Service (Washington, 1883).

————(Washington, 1885).

Laws and Regulations Relative to Trade with Indian Tribes (Washington, 1879).

————(Washington, 1904).

Regulations of the Indian Department (Washington, 1884).

Regulations of the Indian Office (Washington, 1894).

————(Washington, 1904).

Rules Governing the Court of Indian Offenses (Washington, 1883).

Rules for Indian Schools (Washington, 1890).

————(Washington, 1892).

Rules for Indian School Service (Washington, 1894).

————(Washington, 1898).

————(Washington, 1900).

————(Washington, 1904).

d.   *Department of War*

Secretary of War, *Annual Report*, 1868.

C.   OTHER PRINTED PRIMARY SOURCES

1.   Indian Rights Association Publications

Note: All publications of the Indian Rights Association are included in the microfilm publication, *Papers of the Indian Rights Association, 1882-1968* (Glen Rock, N.J.: Microfilming Corporation of America, 1973).

"Extract. Report of the Special Committee of the National Civil Service Reform League upon the Present Condition of the Reform Movement and the Relations to it of the National, State, and Municipal Administrations" (Philadelphia, 1887).

"The Condition of the Navajo Indians as an Argument for Making the Indian Service Non-partisan" (Philadelphia, 1895).

"A Good Field for Reform" reprinted from *The Nation*, March 15, 1888 (Philadelphia, 1888).

Harrison, J.B., *The Latest Studies on Indian Reservations* (Philadelphia, 1887).

"Indian School Welfare" and "Suspicious Economy," reprinted from the New York *Evening Post* and the New York *Times*, April 27, 1893 [sic] (Philadelphia, 1894).

Leupp, Francis E., "Civil Service Reform Essential to a Successful Indian Administration" (Philadelphia, 1893).

———[F.E.L.], "Ring Rule," reprinted from *City and State*, February 13, 1896 (Philadelphia, 1897).

"The Question of Commissioner Oberly's Retention" (Philadelphia, 1889).

"Reform in the Indian Service" (Philadelphia, 1887).

"Report of Hon. Theodore Roosevelt made to the United States Civil Service Commission upon a Visit to Certain Indian Reservations and Indian Schools in South Dakota, Nebraska, and Kansas" (Philadelphia, 1893).

2. Other Books, Articles, and Pamphlets

Cleveland, Grover, "The Independence of the Executive," in *Presidential Problems* (New York: The Century Company, 1904).

Dawes, Henry L., "The Indian Territory," in Commissioner of Education, *Annual Report, 1899-1900* (Washington: Government Printing Office, 1901), II, 1337-1341.

Fletcher, Alice C., "Allotment of Land to Indians," *Proceedings of the National Conference of Charities and Correction, 1887* (Boston: George H. Ellis, 1887), 172-180.

Galpin, S.A., "Some Administrative Difficulties of the Indian Problem," *New Englander and Yale Review*, XLVI (April, 1887), 305-318.

"The Indian Ring," *Harper's Weekly*, XXII (February 2, 1878), 86.

Leupp, Francis E., *In Red Man's Land: A Study of the American Indian* (New York: Fleming H. Revell Company, 1914).

———, *The Indian and his Problem* (New York: Charles Scribner's Sons, 1910).

Minutes of Associated Executive Committee of Friends on Indian Affairs, Philadelphia, Pennsylvania, 4th Month, 1874 (Richmond, Ind., 1874).

Moorehead, Warren K., *The American Indian in the United States, Period 1850-1914* (Andover, Mass.: The Andover Press, 1914).

Parker, E.S., *Report . . . to the Hon. Secretary of the Interior, on the Communication of William Welsh, Esq., Relative to the Management of Indian Affairs* (Washington: Joseph L. Pearson, 1870).

Poole, D.W., *Among the Sioux of Dakota: Eighteen Months Experience as an Indian Agent* (New York: D. Van Nostrand, 1881).

Pratt, Richard Henry, "The Advantages of Mingling Indians with Whites," *Proceedings of the National Conference of Charities and Corrections, 1892* (Boston: George H. Ellis, 1892), 45-59.

———, *Battlefield and Classroom: Four Decades with the American Indian, 1867-1904*, edited by Robert M. Utley (New Haven, Conn.: Yale University Press, 1964).

Schurz, Carl, "Present Aspects of the Indian Problem," *North American Review*, CXXXIII (July, 1881), 1-24.

————, *Speeches, Correspondence, and Political Papers of Carl Schurz*, edited by Frederic Bancroft (6 vols.; New York: G.P. Putnam's Sons, 1913).

Sherman, William T., *Memoirs of General W.T. Sherman* (4th edition, 2 vols.; New York: Charles L. Webster and Company, 1891).

Thayer, James B., "A People without Law," *Atlantic Monthly*, LXVIII (October, 1891), 540-554.

Walker, Francis A., *The Indian Question* (Boston: James R. Osgood and Company, 1874).

II. SECONDARY SOURCES

A.   BIBLIOGRAPHIES, GUIDES, AND INDEXES

Ames, John G., *Comprehensive Index to the Publications of the United States Government, 1881-1893* (2 vols.; Washington: Government Printing Office, 1905).

Congressional Information Service, *CIS U.S. Serial Set Index* (12 Parts; Washington: Congressional Information Service, 1975-79).

Hill, Edward E., *The Office of Indian Affairs 1824-1880: Historical Sketches* (New York: Clearwater Publishing Company, 1974).

————, comp., *Preliminary Inventory of the Records of the Bureau of Indian Affairs (Record Group 75)* (2 vols.; Washington: National Archives, 1965).

Johnson, Steven L., comp., *Guide to American Indian Documents in the Congressional Serial Set: 1817-1899* (New York: Clearwater Publishing Company, 1977).

National Archives and Records Service, *The American Indian: Select Catalog of National Archives Microfilm Publications* (Washington: National Archives and Records Service, 1972).

————, *Catalog of National Archives Microfilm Publications* (Washington: National Archives and Records Service, 1974).

————, *Guide to the National Archives of the United States* (Washington: National Archives and Records Service, 1974).

Poore, Benjamin Perley, *A Descriptive Catalogue of the Government Publications of the United States, September 5, 1774-March 4, 1881* (Washington: Government Printing Office, 1885).

Prucha, Francis Paul, *A Bibliographical Guide to the History of Indian-White Relations in the United States* (Chicago, University of Chicago Press, 1977).

————, *A Guide to the Military Posts of the United States, 1789-1895* (Madison: State Historical Society of Wisconsin, 1964).

Schmeckebier, Laurence F., and Roy B. Eastin, *Government Publications and Their Use* (2nd edition; Washington: Brookings Institution, 1969).

U.S., Superintendent of Documents, *Checklist of United States Public Documents, 1789-1909* (3rd edition; Washington: Government Printing Office, 1911).

B.   DISSERTATIONS

Bret Harte, John, "The San Carlos Indian Reservation, 1872-1886: An Administrative History," Ph.D. dissertation, University of Arizona, 1972.

Waltmann, Henry G., "The Interior Department, War Department, and Indian Policy, 1865-1887," Ph.D. dissertation, University of Nebraska, 1962.

C.   BOOKS

Baird, W. David, *The Quapaw People* (Phoenix, Ariz.: Indian Tribal Series, 1975).

Beaver, R. Pierce, *Church, State, and the American Indians: Two and a Half Centuries of Partnership in Missions Between Protestant Churches and Government* (St. Louis: Concordia Publishing House, 1966).

Benson, Lee, *The Concept of Jacksonian Democracy: New York as a Test Case* (Princeton, N.J.: Princeton University Press, 1961).

Berkhofer, Robert F., Jr., *Salvation and the Savage: An Analysis of Protestant Missions and American Indian Response, 1787-1862* (Lexington: University of Kentucky Press, 1965).

Berthrong, Donald J., *The Cheyenne and Arapahoe Ordeal: Reservation and Agency Life in the Indian Territory* (Norman: University of Oklahoma Press, 1976).

Brophy, William A., and Sophie D. Aberle, *The Indian: America's Unfinished Business* (Norman: University of Oklahoma Press, 1966).

Burgess, Larry E., *The Lake Mohonk Conference of Friends of the Indian: Guide to the Annual Reports* (New York: Clearwater Publishing Company, 1975).

Cahn, Edgar S., *Our Brother's Keeper: The Indian in White America* (New York: World Publishing Company, 1969).

Carman, Harry J., and Reinhard J. Luthin, *Lincoln and the Patronage* (New York: Columbia University Press, 1943).

Chandler, Alfred D., Jr., *Strategy and Structure: Chapters in the History of the Industrial Enterprise* (Cambridge, Mass.: M.I.T. Press, 1962).

Clark, Dan Elbert, *Samuel Jordan Kirkwood* (Iowa City: State Historical Society of Iowa, 1917).

Clark, John G., ed., *The Frontier Challenge: Responses to the Trans-Mississippi West* (Lawrence: University Press of Kansas, 1971).

Dangerfield, George, *The Era of Good Feelings* (New York: Harcourt, Brace, and Company, 1952).

Danziger, Edmund Jefferson, Jr., *Indians & Bureaucrats: Administering the Reservation Policy During the Civil War* (Urbana: University of Illinois Press, 1974).

Davison, Kenneth E., *The Presidency of Rutherford B. Hayes* (Westport, Conn.: Greenwood Press, 1972).

Deloria, Vine, Jr., *Custer Died for Your Sins: An Indian Manifesto* (New York: Macmillan Company, 1969).

Dodge, D. Stuart, *Memorials of William E. Dodge* (New York: A.D.F. Randolph and Company, 1887).

Eastman, Elaine Goodale, *Pratt: The Red Man's Moses* (Norman: University of Oklahoma Press, 1935).

Eblen, Jack Ericson, *The First and Second United States Empires: Governors and Territorial Government.* (Pittsburgh: University of Pittsburgh Press, 1968).

Ellis, David M., ed., *The Frontier in American Development: Essays in Honor of Paul Wallace Gates* (Ithaca, N.Y.: Cornell University Press, 1969).

Ellis, Elmer, *Henry Moore Teller: Defender of the West* (Caldwell, Idaho: The Caxton Printers, 1941).

Ellis, Richard M., *General Pope and U.S. Indian Policy* (Albuquerque: University of New Mexico Press, 1970).

Freidson, Eliot, ed., *The Hospital in Modern Society* (New York: The Free Press, 1963).

————, ed., *The Professions and their Prospects* (Beverly Hills, Calif.: Sage Publications, 1973).

Fritz, Henry E., *The Movement for Indian Assimilation, 1860-1890* (Philadelphia: University of Pennsylvania Press, 1963).

Fuess, Claude Moore, *Carl Schurz, Reformer* (New York: Dodd, Mead, and Company, 1932).

Gregg, Elinor D., *The Indians and the Nurse* (Norman: University of Oklahoma Press, 1965).

Hagan, William T., *American Indians* (Chicago: University of Chicago Press, 1961).

————, *Indian Police and Judges: Experiments in Acculturation and Control* (New Haven, Conn.: Yale University Press, 1966).

————, *United States-Commanche Relations: The Reservation Years* (New Haven, Conn.: Yale University Press, 1976).

Hays, Samuel P., *Conservation and the Gospel of Efficiency: the Progressive Conservation Movement, 1890-1920* (Cambridge, Mass.: Harvard University Press, 1959).

————, *The Response to Industrialism, 1885-1914* (Chicago: University of Chicago Press, 1956).

Helm, June, ed., *Pioneers of American Anthropology: The Uses of Biography* (Seattle: University of Washington Press, 1966).

Hollingsworth, J. Rogers, ed., *Nation and State Building in America: Comparative Historical Perspectives* (Boston: Little, Brown, and Company, 1971).

Hoogenboom, Ari, *Outlawing the Spoils: A History of the Civil Service Reform Movement, 1865-1883* (Urbana: University of Illinois Press, 1961).

Hughes, Jonathan R.T., *The Governmental Habit: Economic Controls from Colonial Times to the Present* (New York: Basic Books, 1977).

Huntington, Samuel, P., *Political Order in Changing Societies* (New Haven, Conn.: Yale University Press, 1968).

Institute for Government Research, *The Problem of Indian Administration* (Baltimore: Johns Hopkins Press, 1928).

Kaufman, Herbert, *Are Government Organizations Immortal?* (Washington: Brookings Institution, 1976).

Kelly, Lawrence C., *The Navajo Indians and Federal Indian Policy, 1900-1935* (Tucson: University of Arizona Press, 1968).

Kuznets, Simon, *National Product Since 1869* (New York: National Bureau of Economic Research, 1946).

Leiby, James, *Carroll Wright and Labor Reform: The Origin of Labor Statistics* (Cambridge, Mass.: Harvard University Press, 1960).

Mardock, Robert Winston, *The Reformers and the American Indian* (Columbia: University of Missouri Press, 1971).

McKitrick, Eric, *Andrew Johnson and Reconstruction* (Chicago: University of Chicago Press, 1960).

Meyer, Roy W., *History of the Santee Sioux: United States Indian Policy on Trial* (Lincoln: University of Nebraska Press, 1967).

Michels, Robert, *Political Parties: A Sociological Study of the Oligarchic Tendencies of Modern Democracy* (Glencoe, Ill.: Free Press, 1949).

Miner, H. Craig, *The Corporation and the Indian: Tribal Sovereignty and Industrial Civilization in Indian Territory, 1865-1907* (Columbia: University of Missouri Press, 1976).

Moore, Barrington, Jr., *Social Origins of Dictatorship and Democracy: Lord and Peasant in the Making of the Modern World* (Boston: Beacon Press, 1966).

National Bureau of Economic Research, *Output, Employment, and Productivity in the United States after 1800* (New York: Columbia University Press, 1966).

Nevins, Allan, *Grover Cleveland: A Study in Courage* (New York: Dodd, Mead, and Company, 1932).

Otis, D.S., *The Dawes Act and the Allotment of Indian Lands*, edited by Francis Paul Prucha (1934; revised edition, Norman: University of Oklahoma Press, 1974).

Parman, Donald L., *The Navajos and the New Deal* (New Haven: Yale University Press, 1976).

Perrow, Charles, *Complex Organizations: A Critical Essay* (Glenview, Ill.: Scott, Foresman, and Company, 1972).

Philip, Kenneth R., *John Collier's Crusade for Indian Reform, 1920-1954* (Tucson: University of Arizona Press, 1977).

Pomeroy, Earl S., *The Territories and the United States, 1861-1890: Studies in Colonial Administration* (Philadelphia: University of Pennsylvania Press, 1947).

Porter, Glenn, *The Rise of Big Business, 1860-1910* (New York: Thomas Y. Crowell Company, 1973).

Price, James L., *Organizational Effectiveness: An Inventory of Propositions* (Homewood, Ill.: Richard D. Irwin, 1968).

Priest, Loring Benson, *Uncle Sam's Stepchildren: The Reformation of United States Indian Policy, 1865-1887* (New Brunswick, N.J.: Rutgers University Press, 1942).

Prucha, Francis Paul, *American Indian Policy in Crisis: Christian Reformers and the Indian, 1865-1900* (Norman: University of Oklahoma Press, 1976).

———, ed., *Americanizing the American Indian: Writings by "Friends of the Indian," 1880-1900* (Cambridge, Mass.: Harvard University Press, 1973).

Rahill, Peter J., *The Catholic Indian Missions and Grant's Peace Policy, 1870-1884* (Washington: Catholic University of America Press, 1953).

Schmeckebier, Laurence F., *The Office of Indian Affairs: Its History, Activities, and Organization* (Baltimore: Johns Hopkins Press, 1927).

Selznick, Philip, *Leadership in Administration: A Sociological Interpretation* (New York: Harper and Row, 1957).

———, *TVA and the Grass Roots: A Study in the Sociology of Formal Organization* (Berkley: University of California Press, 1949).

Seymour, Flora Warren, *Indian Agents of the Old Frontier* (New York: D. Appleton-Century Company, 1941).

Sievers, Harry J., *Benjamin Harrison: Hoosier President* (Indianapolis: Bobbs-Merrill Company, 1968).

Slattery, Charles Lewis, *Felix Reville Brunot* (New York: Longmans, Green and Company, 1901).

Smith, Jane F. and Robert M. Kvasnicka, eds., *Indian-White Relations: A Persistent Paradox* (Washington: Howard University Press, 1976).

Smith, Marian W., *The Puyallup-Nisqually* (New York: Columbia University Press, 1940).

Sorkin, Alan L., *American Indians and Federal Aid* (Washington: Brookings Institution, 1971).

Sosin, Jack M., *Whitehall and the Wilderness: The Middle West in British Colonial Policy, 1760-1775* (Lincoln: University of Nebraska Press, 1961).

Szasz, Margaret G., *Education and the American Indian: The Road to Self-Determination, 1928-1973* (Albuquerque: University of New Mexico Press, 1974).

Tannenbaum, Arnold S., *Control in Organizations* (New York: McGraw-Hill, 1968).

Trennert, Robert A., Jr., *Alternative to Extinction: Federal Indian Policy and the Beginnings of the Reservation System, 1846-51* (Philadelphia: Temple University Press, 1975).

Tribal History Program, *History of the Flandreau Santee Sioux Tribe* (Flandreau, S.D.: Flandreau Santee Sioux Tribe, 1971).

Tyler, S. Lyman, *A History of Indian Policy* (Washington: Government Printing Office, 1973).

Utley, Robert., *Frontier Regulars: The United States Army and the Indian, 1866-1891* (New York: Macmillan Company, 1973).

——, *Frontiersmen in Blue: The United States Army and the Indian, 1848-1865* (New York: Macmillan Company, 1967).

——, *The Last Days of the Sioux Nation* (New Haven, Conn: Yale University Press, 1963).

Walter, Deward E., Jr., *Conflict and Schism in Nez Perce Acculturation: A Study of Religion and Politics* (Pullman: Washington State University Press, 1968).

Warren, G.F. and F.A. Pearson, *Wholesale Prices for 213 Years, 1720 to 1932* (Ithaca, N.Y.: Agricultural Experiment Station, Cornell University, 1932).

Washburn. Wilcomb E., ed., *The Assault on Indian Tribalism: The General Allotment Law (Dawes Act) of 1887* (Philadelphia: J.B. Lippincott Company, 1975).

Warner, W. Lloyd, *et al.*, *The Emergent American Society: Large Scale Organizations.* (New Haven, Conn.: Yale University Press, 1967).

Weber, Max, *Economy and Society: An Outline of Interpretive Sociology*, edited by Guenther Roth and Claus Wittich (3 vols.; New York: Bedminister Press, 1968).

——, *From Max Weber: Essays in Sociology*, edited by H.H. Gerth and C. Wright Mills (New York: Oxford University Press, 1946).

——, *The Theory of Social and Economic Organization*, edited by Talcott Parsons (New York: Oxford University Press, 1947).

White, Leonard D., *The Republican Era: 1869-1901, A Study in Administrative History* (New York: Macmillan Company 1958).

Wiebe, Robert H., *The Search for Order, 1877-1920* (New York: Hill and Wang, 1967).

Young, Mary E., *Redskins, Ruffleshirts, and Rednecks: Indian Allotments in Alabama and Mississippi, 1830-1860* (Norman: University of Oklahoma Press, 1961).

D.   ARTICLES

Aldrich, Howard, "Organizational Boundaries and Inter-organizational conflict," *Human Relations*, XXIV (August 1971), 279-293.

Bannan, Helen M., "The Idea of Civilization and American Indian Policy Reformers in the 1880s," *Journal of American Culture*, I (Winter, 1978), 787-799.

Berkhofer, Robert F., Jr., "Commentary," in Jane F. Smith and Robert M. Kvasnicka, eds., *Indian-White Relations: A Persistent Paradox* (Washington: Howard University Press, 1976), 79-86.

———, "Space, Time, Culture and the New Frontier," *Agricultural History*, XXXVIII (January, 1964), 21-30.

Berthrong, Donald J., "Cattlemen on the Cheyenne-Arapahoe Reservation, 1883-1885," *Arizona and the West*, XIII (Spring, 1971), 5-32.

———, "Federal Indian Policy and the Southern Cheyennes and Arapahoes, 1887-1907," *Ethnohistory*, III (Spring, 1956), 138-153.

Bogue, Allan G., Jerome M. Clubb, Carroll R. McKibbin, and Santa A. Traugott, "Members of the House of Representatives and the Process of Modernization, 1789-1960," *Journal of American History*, LXII (September, 1976), 275-302.

Brady, Dorothy S., "Price Deflaters for Final Product Estimates," in National Bureau of Economic Research, *Output, Employment, and Productivity in the United States* (New York, Columbia University Press, 1966), 91-115.

Chaput, Donald, "Generals, Indian Agents, Politicians: The Doolittle Survey of 1865," *Western Historical Quarterly*, III (July, 1972), 269-282.

Danzinger, Edmund J., Jr., "The Indian Office During the Civil War: Impotence in Indian Affairs," *South Dakota History*, V (Winter, 1974), 52-72.

Davison, Kenneth E., "President Hayes and the Reform of American Indian Policy," *Ohio History*, LXXXII (Summer-Autumn, 1973), 205-214.

D'Elia, Donald J., "The Argument over Civilian or Military Control," *The Historian*, XXIV (January, 1962), 207-225.

Edwards, Martha L., "A Problem of Church and State in the 1870s," *Mississippi Valley Historical Review*, XI (June, 1924), 27-53.

Friedson, Eliot, "Professions and the Occupational Principle," in Eliot Friedson, ed., *The Professions and Their Prospects* (Beverly Hills, Calif.: Sage Publications, 1973), 19-38.

Fritz, Henry E., "The Board of Indian Commissioners and Ethnocentric Reform, 1878-1893," in Jane F. Smith and Robert M. Kvasnicka, eds., *Indian-White Relations: A Persistent Paradox* (Washington: Howard University Press, 1976), 57-78.

Gates, Paul W., "Indian Allotments Preceeding the Dawes Act," in John G. Clark, ed., *The Frontier Challenge: Responses to the Trans-Mississippi West* (Lawrence: University Press of Kansas, 1971), 141-170.

Grafton, Carl, "The Creation of Federal Agencies," *Administration and Society*, VII (November, 1975), 328-365.

Guenther, Richard L., "The Santee Normal Training School," *Nebraska History*, LI (Fall 1970), 359-378.

Hagan, William T., "Kiowas, Commanches, and Cattlemen, 1867-1906: A Case Study of the Failure of U.S. Reservation Policy," *Pacific Historical Review*, XL (August, 1971), 333-355.

———, "On Writing the History of the American Indian," *Journal of Interdisciplinary History*, II (Summer, 1971) 149-154.

————, "Private Property: The Indian's Door to Civilization," *Ethnohistory*, III (Spring, 1956), 126-137.

————, "The Reservation Policy: Too Little and Too Late," in Jane F. Smith and Robert M. Kvasnicka, eds., *Indian-White Relations: A Persistent Paradox* (Washington: Howard University Press, 1976), 157-169.

Hage, Jerald, Michael Aiken, and Cora Bagley Marrett, "Organization Structure and Communications," *American Sociological Review*, XXXVI (October, 1971), 860-871.

Hanger, G.W.W., "Bureaus of Statistics of Labor in the United States," *Bulletin of the Bureau of Labor*, Number 54 (September, 1904), 991-1021.

Hollingsworth, J. Rogers, "An Approach to the Study of Comparative Historical Politics," in J. Rogers Hollingsworth, ed., *Nation and State Building in America: Comparative Historical Perspectives* (Boston: Little, Brown, and Company, 1971), 251-277.

Hoogenboom, Ari, "An Analysis of Civil Service Reformers," *The Historian*, XXIII (November, 1960), 54-78.

————, "The Pendleton Act and the Civil Service," *American Historical Review*, LXIV (January, 1957), 301-318.

Jackson, W. Turrentine, "Indian Affairs and Politics in Idaho Territory, 1863-1870," *Pacific Historical Review*, XIV (September, 1945), 311-325.

Jenny, Albert, II, "The American Indian: Needs and Problems," in U.S., Congress, Joint Economic Committee, *Toward Economic Development for Native American Communities* (Washington, 1969; reprint edition, New York: Arno Press, 1970), 46-60.

Johnson, Helen W., "American Indians in Rural Poverty," in U.S., Congress, Joint Economic Committee, *Toward Economic Development for Native American Communities* (Washington, 1969; reprint edition, New York: Arno Press, 1970), 19-45.

Kelsey, Harry, "The Doolittle Report: Its Preparation and Shortcomings," *Arizona and the West*, XVII (Summer, 1975), 107-120

Lurie, Nancy Oestreich, "Women in Early American Anthropology," in June Helm, ed., *Pioneers of American Anthropology: The Uses of Biography* (Seattle: University of Washington Press, 1966), 43-54.

Masterson, James R., "Research Suggestions: The Records of the Washington Superintendency of Indian Affairs," *Pacific Northwest Quarterly*, XXXVII (January, 1946), 31-57.

Mechanic, David, "Sources of Power of Lower Participants in Complex Organizations," *Administrative Science Quarterly*, XII (December, 1962), 349-362.

Merton, Robert K., "Bureaucratic Structure and Personality," *Social Forces*, XVIII (May, 1940), 560-568.

Miner, H. Craig, " 'A Corps of Clerks:' The Bureaucracy of Industrialization in Indian Territory, 1866-1907," *Chronicles of Oklahoma*, LIII (Fall, 1975), 322-331.

Morgan, Dale L., "The Administration of Indian Affairs in Utah, 1851-1858," *Pacific Historical Review*, XVII (November, 1948), 383-409.

Neil, William M., "The Territorial Governor as Indian Superintendent in the Trans-Mississippi West," *Mississippi Valley Historical Review*, XLII (September, 1956), 213-237.

Parman, Donald L., "J.C. Morgan: Navajo Apostle of Assimilation," *Prologue: The Journal of the National Archives*, IV (Summer, 1972), 83-98.

Parsons, Talcott, "The Professions and Social Structure," *Social Forces*, XVII (May, 1939), 457-467.

Perrow, Charles, "The Analysis of Goals in Complex Organizations," *American Sociological Review*, XXVI (December, 1961), 854-866.

———, "Goals and Power Structures: A Historical Case Study," in Eliot Friedson, ed., *The Hospital in Modern Society* (New York: The Free Press, 1963), 112-146.

Pfautz, Harold W., "The Sociology of Secularization: Religious Groups," *American Journal of Sociology*, LXI (September, 1955), 121-128.

Philip, Kenneth, R., "John Collier and the Controversy Over the Wheeler-Howard Bill," in Jane F. Smith and Robert M. Kvasnicka, eds., *Indian-White Relations: A Persistent Paradox* (Washington: Howard University Press, 1976), 171-200.

Polsby, Nelson W., "The Institutionalization of the U.S. House of Representatives," *American Political Science Review*, LXII (March, 1968), 144-168.

Priest, Loring B., "Commentary," in Jane F. Smith and Robert M. Kvasnicka, eds. *Indian-White Relations: A Persistent Paradox* (Washington: Howard University Press, 1976), 87-95.

Prucha, Francis Paul, "Books on American Indian Policy: A Half-Decade of Important Work, 1970-1975," *Journal of American History*, LXIII (December, 1976), 658-669.

———, "New Approaches to the Study of the Administration of Indian Policy," *Prologue: The Journal of the National Archives*, III (Spring, 1971), 15-19.

Selznick, Philip, "An Approach to a Theory of Bureaucracy," *American Sociological Review*, VIII (February, 1943), 47-54.

———, "Foundations of the Theory of Organization," *American Sociological Review*, XIII (February, 1948), 25-35.

Sievers, Harry J., "The Catholic Indian School Issue and the Presidential Election of 1892," *Catholic Historical Review*, XXXVIII (July, 1952), 129-155.

Stern, Theodore, and James P. Boggs, "White and Indian Farmers on the Umatilla Indian Reservation," *Northwest Anthropological Research Notes*, V (Spring, 1971), 37-76.

Stuart, Paul, "United States Indian Policy: From the Dawes Act to the American Indian Policy Review Commission," *Social Service Review*, LI (September, 1977), 451-463.

Thompson, James D., and William J. McEwan, "Organizational Goals and Environment: Goal-Setting as an Interaction Process," *American Sociological Review*, XXIII (February, 1958), 23-31.

Utley, Robert M., "The Frontier Army: John Ford or Arthur Penn?" in Jane F. Smith and

Robert M. Kvasnicka, eds., *Indian-White Relations: A Persistent Paradox* (Washington: Howard University Press, 1976), 133-145.

Waltmann, Henry G., "Circumstantial Reformer: President Grant and the Indian Problem," *Arizona and the West*, XIII (Winter, 1971), 323-342.

Warren, G.F. and F.A. Pearson, "Wholesale Prices in the United States for 135 years, 1797 to 1932," in *Wholesale Prices for 213 Years, 1720 to 1932* (Ithaca, N.Y.: Agricultural Experiment Station, Cornell University, 1932), 5-200.

Whitner, Robert L., "Grant's Indian Peace Policy on the Yakima Reservation, 1870-1882," *Pacific Northwest Quarterly*, L (October, 1959), 135-142.

Young, Mary E., "Commentary," in Jane F. Smith and Robert M. Kvasnicka, Eds., *Indian-White Relations: A Persistent Paradox* (Washington: Howard University Press, 1976), 212-214.

————, "Congress Looks West: Liberal Ideology and Public Land Policy in the Nineteenth Century," in David M. Ellis, ed., *The Frontier in American Development: Essays in Honor of Paul Wallace Gates* (Ithaca, N.Y.: Cornell University Press, 1969), 74-112.

INDEX